GOOD PRACTICE DETAILS

A Designers' Manual of over 140 Standard Details

Butterworth Architecture
London Boston Singapore Sydney Toronto Wellington

Butterworth Architecture
is an imprint of Butterworth Scientific

 PART OF REED INTERNATIONAL P.L.C.

First published in Great Britain by
The Architectural Press Ltd: London 1979

Reprinted 1981, 1987
Reprinted by Butterworth Architecture 1989

ISBN: 0 85139 242 3 (paper)

Composition by Genesis Typesetting, Borough Green, Sevenoaks, Kent
Printed and bound by Hartnolls Ltd, Bodmin, Cornwall

Contents

Foreword

by Gordon Wigglesworth
Housing Architect
GLC Department of
Architecture and
Civic Design

The British climate is hard on buildings. Shedding water efficiently and the need to allow for the movement that inevitably takes place with alternate wetting and drying are vitally important in even the simplest buildings. The GLC as a landlord of a large stock of buildings as well as a developer has a vested interest in making sure that the buildings it commissions give little trouble in use.

The GLC Department of Architecture and Civic Design has put together a range of details for the external envelope of housing selected from those known to be reliable in practice. They have been subjected to wide and deep constructive criticism by architects, quantity surveyors, structural engineers, housing management and maintenance staff, and Clerks of Works. We have called them "Good Practice Details" and we believe they represent just that—details which in practice have been shown to work well, and which conform with the latest codes and standards.

Background and Objectives

For many years the Department of Architecture and Civic Design of the Greater London Council has produced Standard Drawings of common recurring details such as refuse chutes, man-holes, hard paving details, etc, in order to save architects the tedious task of re-drawing such details for individual projects. Because of the complexities of the housing programme in the late sixties and early seventies it was not considered practical to produce standard drawings of the external fabric of buildings. However, the current policy of building low rise houses with gardens and the production of the Preferred Dwelling Plan range provided an opportunity to re-examine the situation.

It was decided therefore to produce a series of drawings related to the external fabric of simple building types which would show good building practice. These drawings could be used either 'cold' by architects in the Department, or could be used as guidance where the drawings did not exactly reflect the designer's intentions. The Technical Policy Division of the Department also provides an advisory service to architects on constructional detailing. The details illustrated have been produced by various methods, the most important of which is the retrieval of details found to have been successful in practice. All the drawings have been examined by a team comprising Clerk of Works, Quantity Surveyor, Maintenance Adviser, Structural Engineer, Client Adviser and Job Architects, and the economics of construction as well as practicability have been taken into account.

The title Good Practice Details is somewhat anomalous in that certain details, for example, flush brick cills, would not normally be recommended. It was felt, however, that if architects found the need to use such an aesthetic, then details should be produced to minimize any future problems and Notes for Guidance are produced giving architects the reasons why certain constructional solutions are recommended. One of the most interesting factors which has been noticed during the twelve months that Good Practice Details have been developed is the frequency with which these details have to be changed after completion due to changes in either materials, regulations, standards or client requirements. Typical examples of this are the change from asbestos-based materials to asbestos-free materials; the debate as to whether a 10mm gap or a 20mm gap should be provided for venting simple roofs; and the change in U values etc. For these and other reasons many of the drawings now reproduced may well have been amended since they went to print; the GLC therefore takes no responsibility in the event of the use of these drawings by others. Nevertheless, it is felt that the details will be useful to all architects as a guide to the standard obtaining at this time in Greater London Council building projects.

External Envelope

Foundations

The examples shown are typical for simple foundations. The Council's Structural Engineer would normally be consulted for all foundations carried out within the GLC.

Suspended Floor

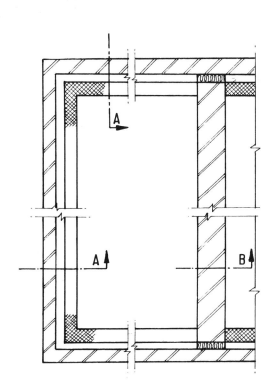

KEY PLAN

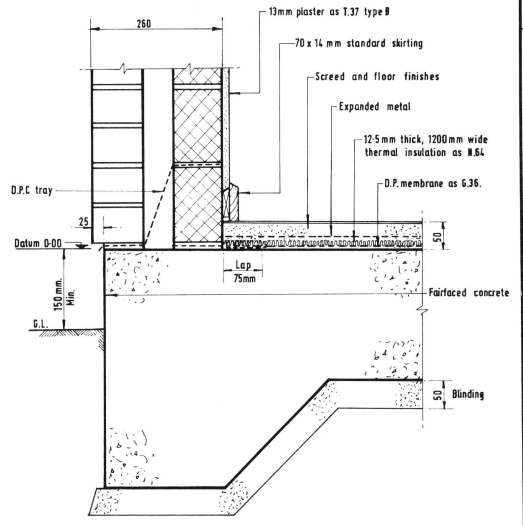

SECTION – 'A'

13mm plaster as T.37 type B

70 x 14 mm standard skirting

Screed and floor finishes

Expanded metal

12·5 mm thick, 1200 mm wide thermal insulation as N.64

D.P. membrane as G.36.

D.P.C tray

Datum 0·00

Lap 75mm

Fairfaced concrete

G.L.

Blinding

NOTE:

For reinforcement sizes and ground treatment see structural engineers drawing.

GLC ILEA

Department of Architecture and Civic Design
County Hall SE1 7PB
Architect F B Pooley CBE

References following notes are clause numbers from G.L.C. preambles to bills of quantities

For external door and threshold see drg. G.P. D.5528.

For external door to mobility dwelling see drg. G.P. D.5529.

For SECTION 'B' see drg. G.P. D.5515.

Departmental Standard Drawing

title
RAFT GROUND FLOOR SLAB. — TYPE 1 — SECTION-'A'

scale
1 : 5

GP   drawing no   rev
      D.5514

bldg type | space use | element | feature | material | key
19

67€010 - 0€

12027£

13

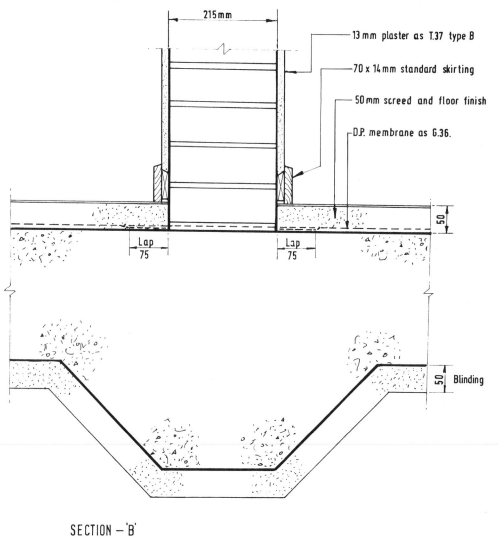

KEY PLAN

215mm

13 mm plaster as T.37 type B

70 x 14mm standard skirting

50mm screed and floor finish

D.P. membrane as G.36.

Lap 75

Lap 75

50

50 Blinding

SECTION – 'B'

NOTE:
For reinforcement sizes and ground treatment
see structural engineers drawing.

GLC ILEA

Department of Architecture
and Civic Design
County Hall SE1 7PB
Architect F B Pooley C B E

References following
notes are clause
numbers from G.L.C.
preambles to bills of
quantities

For SECTION 'A' see drawing
GP. D.5514 and GP. D.5516.

00 – 010379

120279

bldgtype

spaceuse

element

19

feature

material

key

Departmental
Standard
Drawing

title
RAFT GROUND FLOOR
SLAB – TYPES 1 & 2.
SECTION – 'B'

scale
1 : 5

GP

drawing no
D.5515

rev

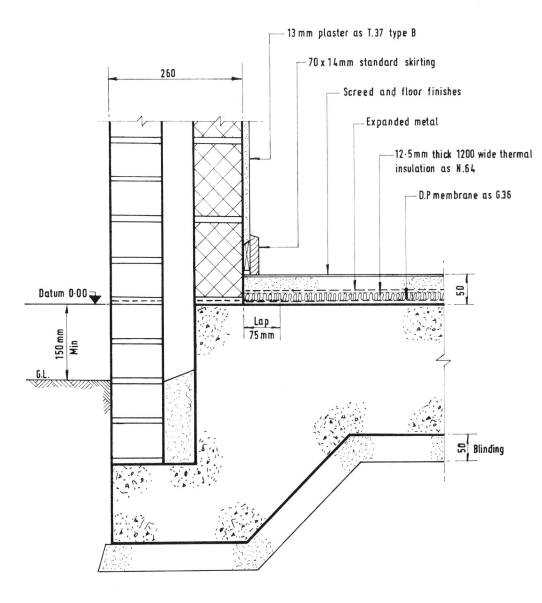

KEY PLAN

SECTION – 'A'

260

13 mm plaster as T.37 type B

70 x 14mm standard skirting

Screed and floor finishes

Expanded metal

12·5mm thick 1200 wide thermal insulation as N.64

D.P membrane as G.36

Datum 0·00

150 mm Min

G.L.

Lap 75mm

50

50 Blinding

NOTE:

For reinforcement sizes and ground treatment see structural engineers drawing.

GLC ILEA

Department of Architecture and Civic Design
County Hall SE1 7PB
Architect F B Pooley C B E

References following notes are clause numbers from G.L.C. preambles to bills of quantities

For external doors and threshold see drg. G.P.D.5530.

For external door to mobility dwelling see drg. GP.D.5531.

For SECTION 'B' see drg. GP.D.5515.

Departmental Standard Drawing

title

RAFT GROUND FLOOR SLAB TYPE. 2. SECTION – 'A'

scale

1 : 5.

GP	drawing no	rev
	D.5516	

bldgtype | spaceuse | element 19 | feature | material | key

963076 - 010379

070279

15

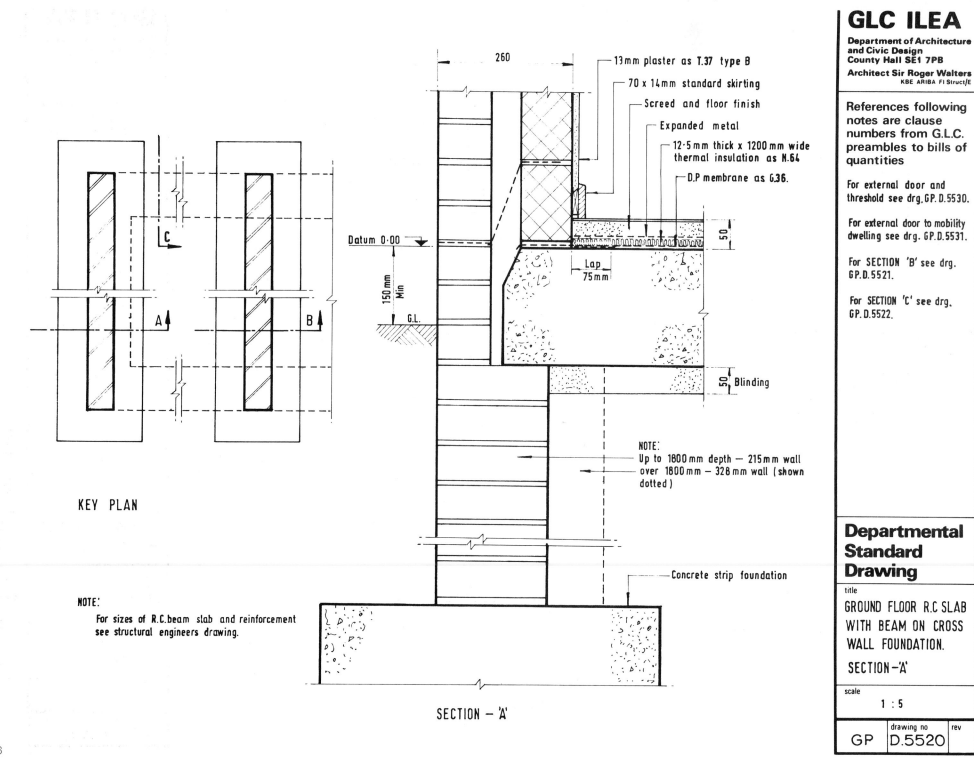

KEY PLAN

260

13mm plaster as T.37 type B
70 x 14mm standard skirting
Screed and floor finish
Expanded metal
12·5mm thick x 1200mm wide thermal insulation as N.64
D.P membrane as G.36.

Datum 0·00

150 mm Min

G.L.

Lap 75mm

50

50 Blinding

NOTE:
Up to 1800mm depth — 215mm wall over 1800mm — 328mm wall (shown dotted)

Concrete strip foundation

NOTE:
For sizes of R.C.beam slab and reinforcement see structural engineers drawing.

SECTION — 'A'

GLC ILEA

Department of Architecture and Civic Design
County Hall SE1 7PB

Architect Sir Roger Walters
KBE ARIBA FI Struct/E

References following notes are clause numbers from G.L.C. preambles to bills of quantities

For external door and threshold see drg. GP. D.5530.

For external door to mobility dwelling see drg. GP. D.5531.

For SECTION 'B' see drg. GP. D.5521.

For SECTION 'C' see drg. GP. D.5522.

010379

080279 — 00

080080

bldg type | space use | element | feature | material | key

19

Departmental Standard Drawing

title

GROUND FLOOR R.C SLAB WITH BEAM ON CROSS WALL FOUNDATION.

SECTION—'A'

scale

1 : 5

drawing no	rev
GP	D.5520	

16

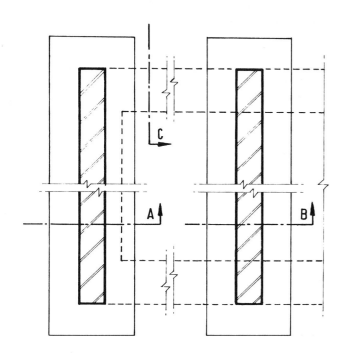

KEY PLAN

NOTE: For sizes of foundations, beams and reinforcement see structural engineers drawing.

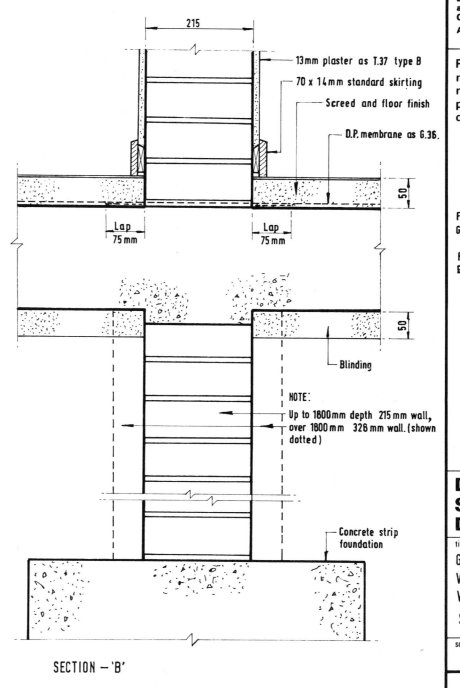

215

- 13mm plaster as T.37 type B
- 70 x 14mm standard skirting
- Screed and floor finish
- D.P. membrane as G.36.

Lap 75 mm

Lap 75 mm

50

50

- Blinding

NOTE:
Up to 1800mm depth 215 mm wall, over 1800 mm 328 mm wall.(shown dotted)

- Concrete strip foundation

SECTION – 'B'

GLC ILEA

Department of Architecture and Civic Design
County Hall SE1 7PB
Architect F B Pooley C B E

References following notes are clause numbers from G.L.C. preambles to bills of quantities

For SECTION 'A' see drg. GP.D.5520.

For SECTION 'C' see drg. GP. D.5522.

63E310 - 010379

130279

Departmental Standard Drawing

bldgtype | space use | element | feature | material | key

19

title
GROUND FLOOR R.C SLAB WITH BEAM ON CROSS WALL FOUNDATION.
SECTION–'B'

scale
1 : 5

GP	drawing no	rev
	D.5521	

17

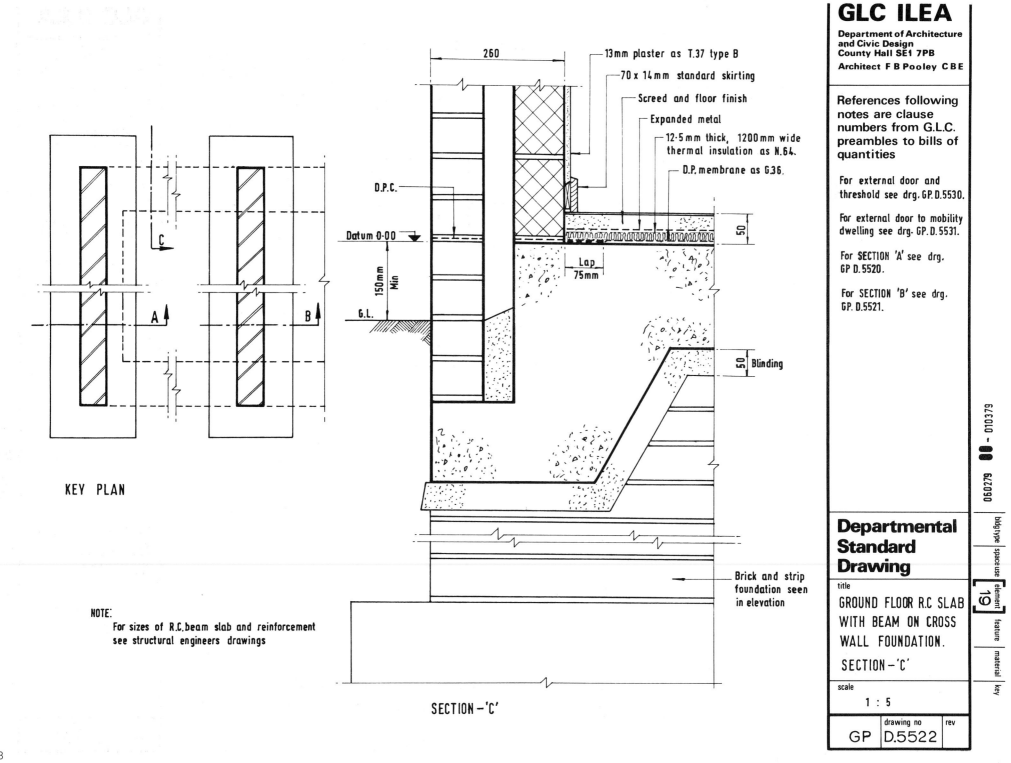

KEY PLAN

NOTE:
For sizes of R.C.beam slab and reinforcement
see structural engineers drawings

SECTION – 'C'

- 13mm plaster as T.37 type B
- 70 x 14mm standard skirting
- Screed and floor finish
- Expanded metal
- 12·5mm thick, 1200mm wide thermal insulation as N.64.
- D.P. membrane as G.36.

260

D.P.C.

Datum 0·00

150mm Min

G.L.

Lap 75mm

50

50 Blinding

Brick and strip foundation seen in elevation

GLC ILEA

Department of Architecture
and Civic Design
County Hall SE1 7PB
Architect F B Pooley CBE

References following
notes are clause
numbers from G.L.C.
preambles to bills of
quantities

For external door and
threshold see drg. GP. D.5530.

For external door to mobility
dwelling see drg. GP. D.5531.

For SECTION 'A' see drg.
GP D.5520.

For SECTION 'B' see drg.
GP. D.5521.

060279 ●● – 010379

**Departmental
Standard
Drawing**

bldg type | space use | element 19 | feature | material | key

title

GROUND FLOOR R.C SLAB
WITH BEAM ON CROSS
WALL FOUNDATION.

SECTION – 'C'

scale

1 : 5

GP | drawing no D.5522 | rev

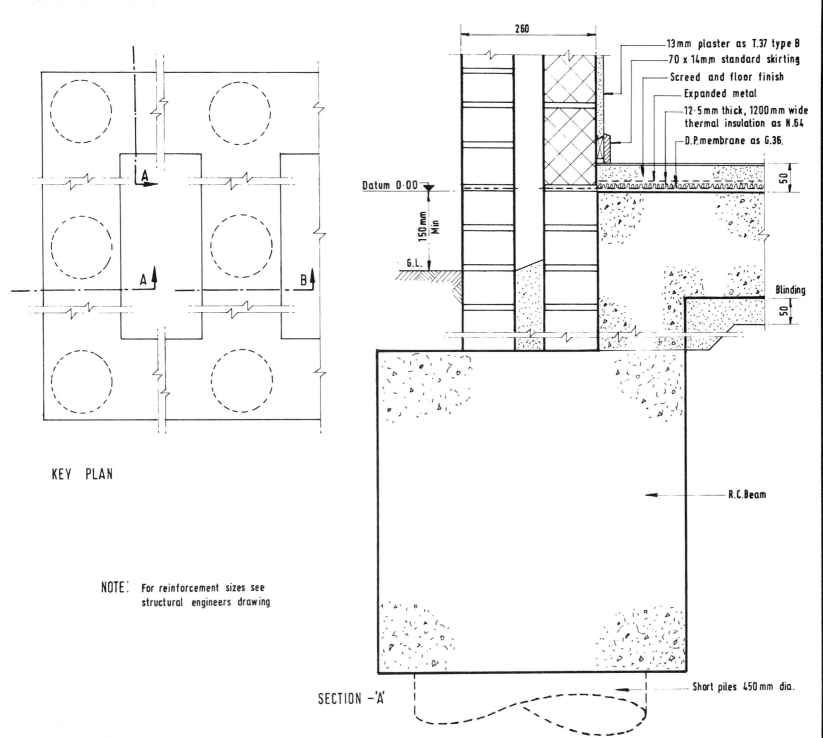

KEY PLAN

NOTE: For reinforcement sizes see structural engineers drawing

260

13mm plaster as T.37 type B
70 x 14mm standard skirting
Screed and floor finish
Expanded metal
12·5mm thick, 1200mm wide thermal insulation as N.64
D.P. membrane as G.36.

Datum 0·00

150 mm Min

G.L.

50

Blinding

50

R.C. Beam

Short piles 450 mm dia.

SECTION — 'A'

GLC ILEA

**Department of Architecture and Civic Design
County Hall SE1 7PB
Architect F B Pooley C B E**

References following notes are clause numbers from G.L.C. preambles to bills of quantities

For external door and threshold see drg. GP. D. 5530.

For external door to mobility dwelling see drg. GP. D. 5531.

For SECTION 'B' see drg. GP. D. 5527.

010379

060279

00

bldg type | space use

element **19**

feature

material

key

Departmental Standard Drawing

title

R.C. BEAMS AND SLAB ON SHORT PILE FOUNDATION. SECTION – 'A'

scale

1 : 5.

GP | drawing no D.5526 | rev

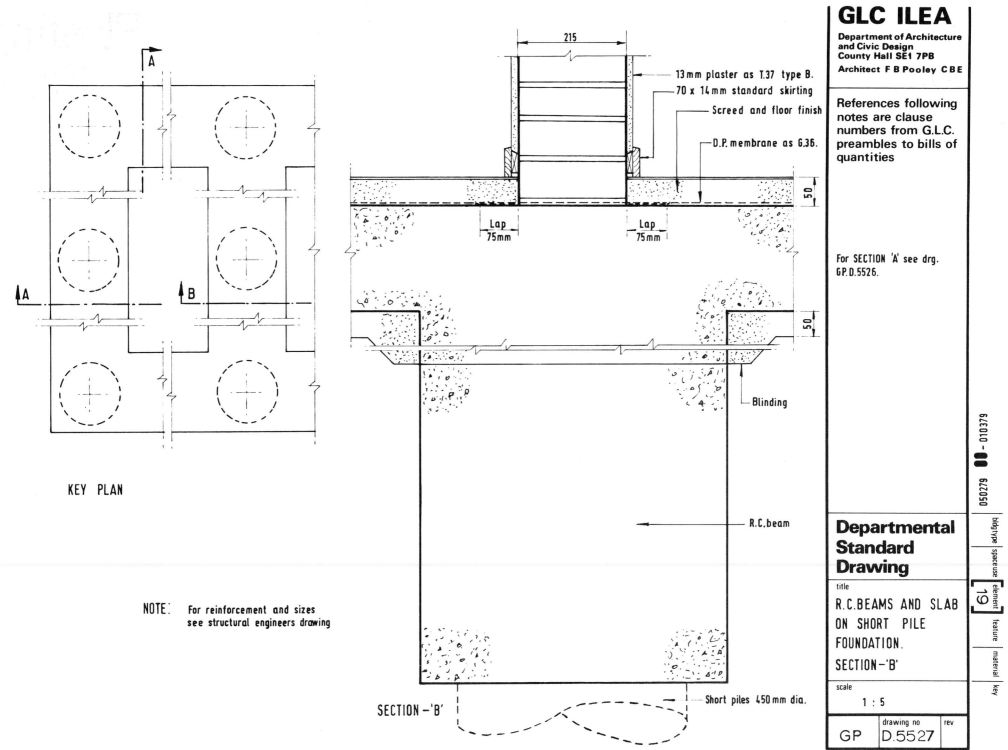

KEY PLAN

NOTE: For reinforcement and sizes
see structural engineers drawing

215

13 mm plaster as T.37 type B.

70 x 14mm standard skirting

Screed and floor finish

D.P. membrane as G.36.

Lap 75mm

Lap 75mm

50

50

Blinding

R.C.beam

SECTION –'B'

Short piles 450 mm dia.

GLC ILEA

Department of Architecture
and Civic Design
County Hall SE1 7PB

Architect F B Pooley C B E

References following
notes are clause
numbers from G.L.C.
preambles to bills of
quantities

For SECTION 'A' see drg.
GP.D.5526.

050279 **00** - 010379

**Departmental
Standard
Drawing**

bldg type | space use | element | feature | material | key

19

title

R.C.BEAMS AND SLAB
ON SHORT PILE
FOUNDATION.
SECTION-'B'

scale

1 : 5

GP	drawing no	rev
	D.5527	

20

Floating
Floor

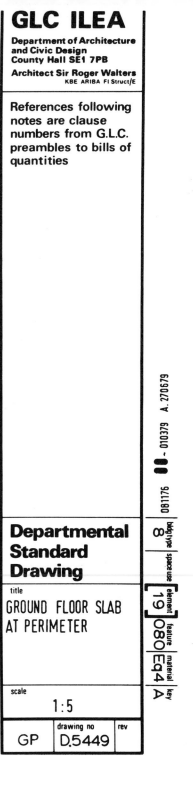

13 mm plaster. T.37. Type B.

50 x 13 mm ground.

70 x 14 mm standard skirting

finished floor level

50 mm screed and floor finish

Concrete slab (see job drawing for thickness)

D.P.M. as G 34, G 67.

25 mm sand blinding. D.12.

25 mm expanded polystyrene insulation

Hardcore

Max. level of cavity infill

D.P.C.

Datum

150mm. minimum

Fin. Grd Lvl.

3

2

1

NOTE :- For foundations see Structural Engineer.

A. 270679

A - 010379

081176

bldg type 8

space use

element 19

feature 080

material Eq4

key A

Departmental Standard Drawing

title
GROUND FLOOR SLAB AT PERIMETER

scale
1:5

GP

drawing no
D.5449

rev

22

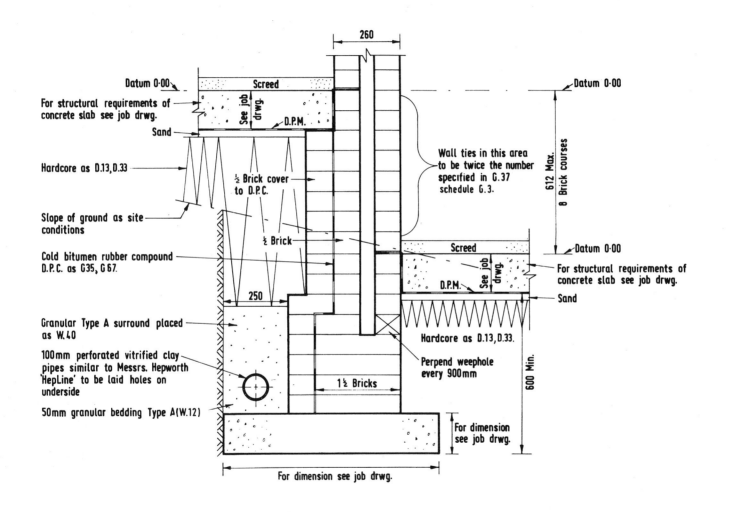

260

Datum 0·00

Screed

For structural requirements of concrete slab see job drwg.

See job drwg.

D.P.M.

Sand

Datum 0·00

Hardcore as D.13, D.33

½ Brick cover to D.P.C.

Wall ties in this area to be twice the number specified in G.37 schedule G.3.

612 Max.
8 Brick courses

Slope of ground as site conditions

½ Brick

Cold bitumen rubber compound D.P.C. as G35, G67.

Screed

Datum 0·00

See job drwg.

For structural requirements of concrete slab see job drwg.

D.P.M.

Sand

250

Granular Type A surround placed as W.40

Hardcore as D.13, D.33.

100mm perforated vitrified clay pipes similar to Messrs. Hepworth 'HepLine' to be laid holes on underside

Perpend weephole every 900mm

1½ Bricks

600 Min.

50mm granular bedding Type A(W.12)

For dimension see job drwg.

For dimension see job drwg.

GLC ILEA

Department of Architecture and Civic Design County Hall SE1 7PB

Architect Sir Roger Walters
KBE ARIBA FI Struct/E

References following notes are clause numbers from G.L.C. preambles to bills of quantities

To be read in conjunction with drwg. [19] D 5449.

G10379

00

bldg type | space use | element | feature | material | key

19

Departmental Standard Drawing

title

PARTY WALL AT 8 BRICK COURSES STEP IN LEVEL.

scale

1 : 10

drawing no | rev

GP D.5491

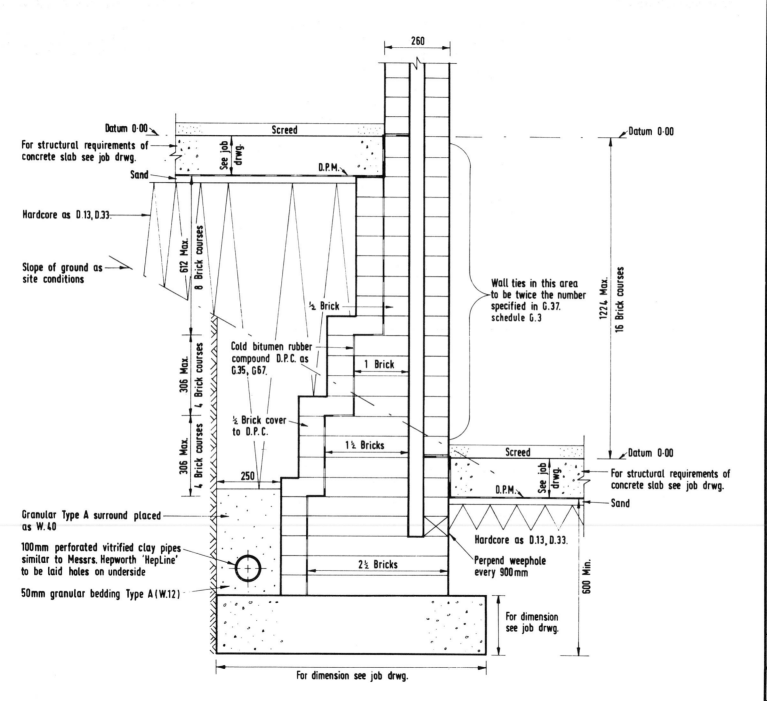

Datum 0·00

For structural requirements of concrete slab see job drwg.

Screed

See job drwg.

Sand

D.P.M.

Datum 0·00

Hardcore as D.13, D.33.

Slope of ground as site conditions

612 Max.

8 Brick courses

½ Brick

Wall ties in this area to be twice the number specified in G.37. schedule G.3

1224 Max.

16 Brick courses

Cold bitumen rubber compound D.P.C. as G.35, G.67.

1 Brick

306 Max.

4 Brick courses

½ Brick cover to D.P.C.

306 Max.

4 Brick courses

1½ Bricks

Screed

Datum 0·00

See job drwg.

D.P.M.

For structural requirements of concrete slab see job drwg.

Sand

250

Granular Type A surround placed as W.40

100mm perforated vitrified clay pipes similar to Messrs. Hepworth 'HepLine' to be laid holes on underside

50mm granular bedding Type A (W.12)

2½ Bricks

Hardcore as D.13, D.33.

Perpend weephole every 900mm

600 Min.

For dimension see job drwg.

For dimension see job drwg.

260

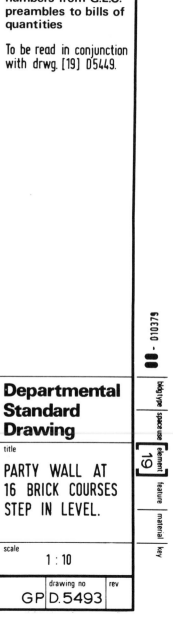

GLC ILEA

Department of Architecture and Civic Design County Hall SE1 7PB Architect Sir Roger Walters
KBE ARIBA FI Struct/E.

References following notes are clause numbers from G.L.C. preambles to bills of quantities

To be read in conjunction with drwg. [19] D5449.

D10379 - **00**

bldg type | space use | element | feature | material | key

19

Departmental Standard Drawing

title

PARTY WALL AT 16 BRICK COURSES STEP IN LEVEL.

scale

1 : 10

drawing no | rev

GP D.5493

Walls

In detailing the external walls the following principles have been followed :—

1 Wherever possible pressed steel lintols have been used. There are, however, differing requirements between the inner London Constructional Bye-laws and the National Building Regulations. Principally, in areas covered by the National Building Regulations pressed steel lintols can be used over all window openings (depending on span), whereas in inner London pressed steel lintols can only be used at the eaves or at intermediate levels where the lower window is not wider than the upper window. The pressed steel lintol shall be 3mm thick minimum, galvanised and painted with two coats of rubber/bitumen paint.

2 The detail of the flush brick cill is least favoured, and if used care must be taken to choose engineering or semi-engineering bricks for the cill.

3 When detailing stepped dwellings, the cavity wall is taken from top to bottom to avoid difficult detailing at the roof junction.

4 The porch details illustrated have been designed to be used with the GLC Preferred Dwelling Plans (previously published by The Architectural Press, ISBN : 0 85139 252 0).

5 Extreme care must be taken when designing the outside works in conjunction with mobility thresholds owing to the difficulty in making these completely watertight.

Co-ordinating Dimensions

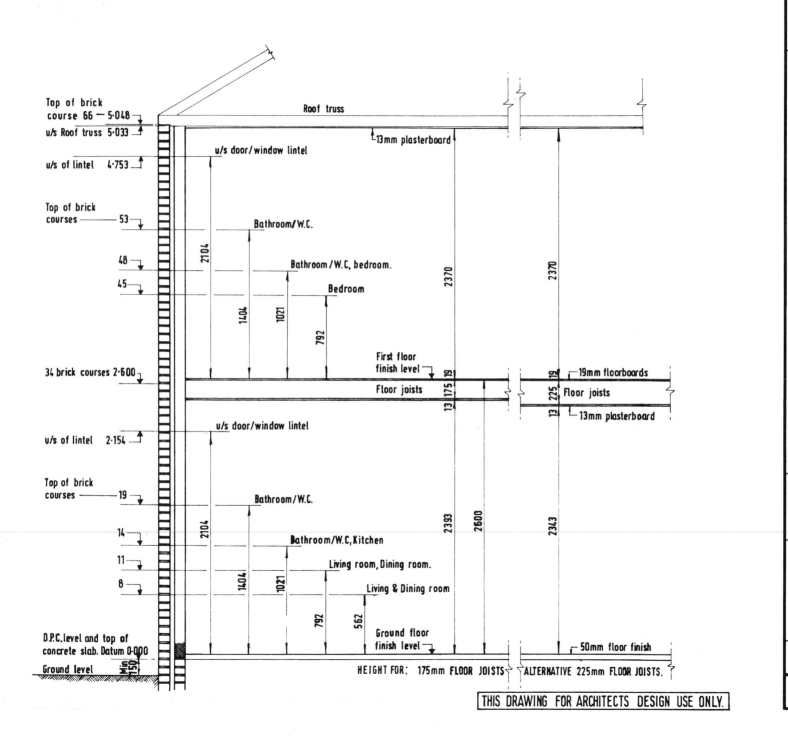

Top of brick course 66 — 5·048
u/s Roof truss 5·033
u/s of lintel 4·753
u/s door/window lintel
Roof truss
13mm plasterboard

Top of brick courses — 53

48

45

2104

Bathroom/W.C.

Bathroom/W.C, bedroom.

1404

1021

Bedroom

792

2370

2370

First floor finish level

34 brick courses 2·600

19

Floor joists

13 175

19mm floorboards

19 225 Floor joists

13

13mm plasterboard

u/s of lintel 2·154

u/s door/window lintel

Top of brick courses — 19

14

11

8

2104

Bathroom/W.C.

1404

1021

Bathroom/W.C, Kitchen

Living room, Dining room.

792

562

Living & Dining room

2393

2600

2343

Ground floor finish level

50mm floor finish

D.P.C. level and top of concrete slab. Datum 0·000

Ground level   Min 150

HEIGHT FOR: 175mm FLOOR JOISTS   ALTERNATIVE 225mm FLOOR JOISTS.

THIS DRAWING FOR ARCHITECTS DESIGN USE ONLY.

GLC ILEA

Department of Architecture and Civic Design
County Hall SE1 7PB
Architect F B Pooley C BE

References following notes are clause numbers from G.L.C. preambles to bills of quantities

D.O.E. Requirements
 2600 storey height
 2100 window/door height from finished floor level.

Brickwork coursing based on 215 x 103 x 65 brick.
 34 courses to 2600 see also drg. D.5246.

6270/0 - 00

bldg type | space use

Departmental Standard Drawing

element 21

feature | material | key

title

2 STOREY HOUSE
CO-ORDINATING DIMENSIONS

scale

1 : 25

GP | drawing no D. 2015 | rev B

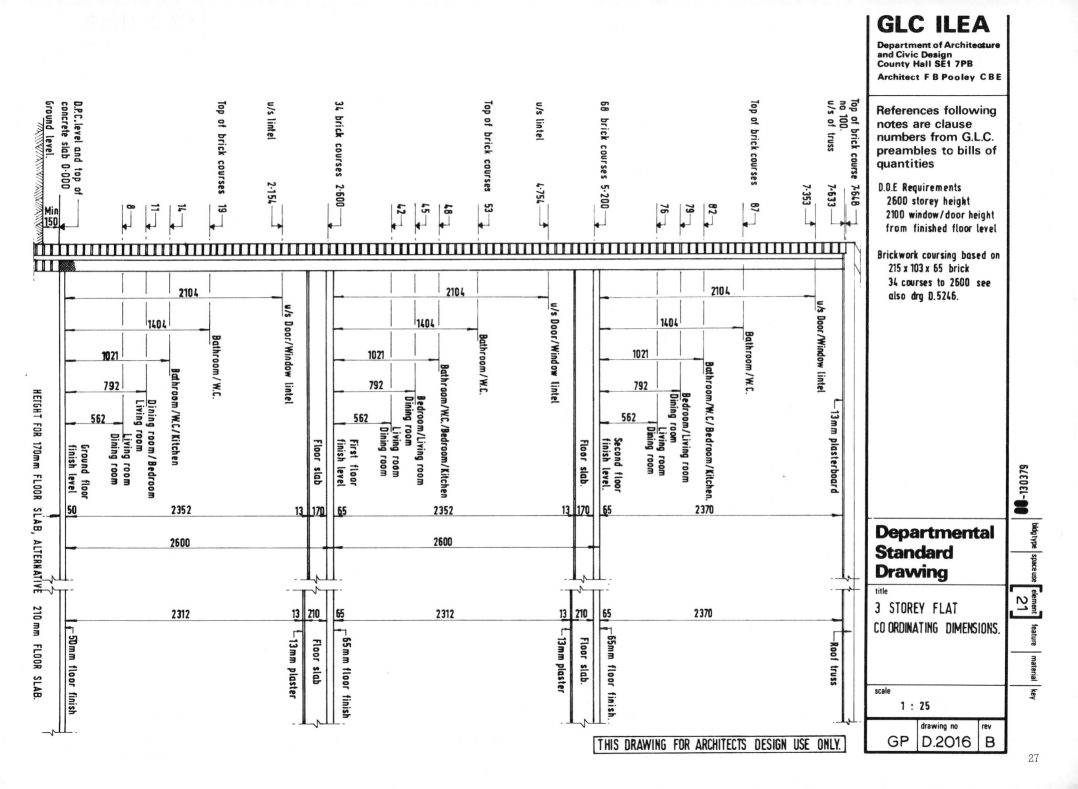

GLC ILEA

Department of Architecture
and Civic Design
County Hall SE1 7PB

Architect F B Pooley CBE

References following
notes are clause
numbers from G.L.C.
preambles to bills of
quantities

D.O.E Requirements
2600 storey height
2100 window/door height
from finished floor level

Brickwork coursing based on
215 x 103 x 65 brick
34 courses to 2600 see
also drg D.5246.

79/ED/ED-29

**Departmental
Standard
Drawing**

title

3 STOREY FLAT
CO ORDINATING DIMENSIONS.

bldg type

space use

element [21]

feature

material

key

scale

1 : 25

GP	D.2016	B
	drawing no	rev

THIS DRAWING FOR ARCHITECTS DESIGN USE ONLY.

27

Ground level.
D.P.C.level and top of
concrete slab 0·000
Min 150

Top of brick course 7·648
no 100.
u/s of truss 7·633

u/s of truss

Top of brick course 7·353

Top of brick courses

u/s lintel 2·154

34 brick courses 2·600

Top of brick courses

u/s lintel 4·754

68 brick courses 5·200

8
11
14
19
42
45
48
53
76
79
82
87

13mm plasterboard

u/s Door/Window lintel

Bathroom/W.C.

2104
1404
1021
792
562

Bedroom/W.C./Bedroom/Kitchen.
Living room
Dining room

Second floor
finish level.

u/s Door/Window lintel

Bathroom/W.C.

2104
1404
1021
792
562

Bedroom/W.C./Bedroom/Kitchen
Living room
Dining room

First floor
finish level

Floor slab

u/s Door/Window lintel

Bathroom/W.C.

2104
1404
1021
792
562

Dining room/Bedroom
Living room
Dining room

Bathroom/W.C./Kitchen
Living room
Dining room

Ground floor
finish level

HEIGHT FOR 170mm FLOOR SLAB, ALTERNATIVE 210mm FLOOR SLAB.

50mm floor finish

50 | 2352 | 13 | 170 | 65 | 2352 | 13 | 170 | 65 | 2370

2600 | 2600

13mm plaster
Floor slab
65mm floor finish

13mm plaster
Floor slab.
65mm floor finish.

Roof truss

2312 | 13 | 210 | 65 | 2312 | 13 | 210 | 65 | 2370

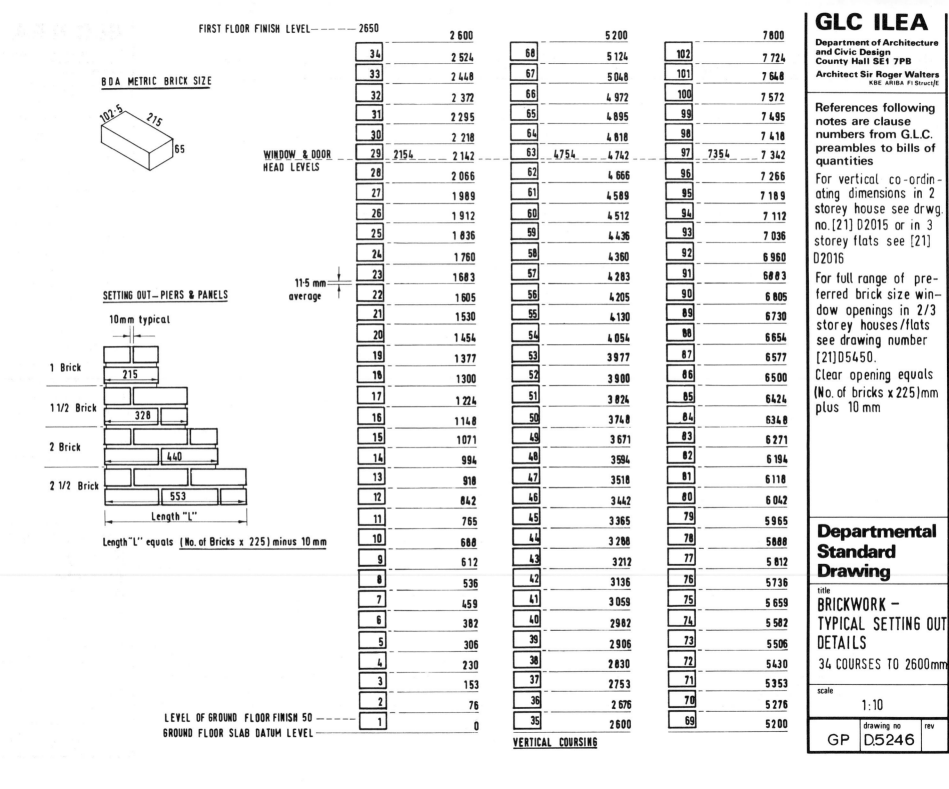

FIRST FLOOR FINISH LEVEL ──── 2650

BDA METRIC BRICK SIZE

102·5 215 65

SETTING OUT — PIERS & PANELS

10mm typical

1 Brick — 215
1 1/2 Brick — 328
2 Brick — 440
2 1/2 Brick — 553

Length "L"

Length "L" equals (No. of Bricks x 225) minus 10 mm

WINDOW & DOOR HEAD LEVELS

11·5 mm average

VERTICAL COURSING

Course		Height		Course		Height		Course		Height
		2 600				5 200				7 800
34		2 524		68		5 124		102		7 724
33		2 448		67		5 048		101		7 648
32		2 372		66		4 972		100		7 572
31		2 295		65		4 895		99		7 495
30		2 218		64		4 818		98		7 418
29	2154	2 142		63	4754	4 742		97	7354	7 342
28		2 066		62		4 666		96		7 266
27		1 989		61		4 589		95		7 189
26		1 912		60		4 512		94		7 112
25		1 836		59		4 436		93		7 036
24		1 760		58		4 360		92		6 960
23		1 683		57		4 283		91		6 883
22		1 605		56		4 205		90		6 805
21		1 530		55		4 130		89		6 730
20		1 454		54		4 054		88		6 654
19		1 377		53		3 977		87		6 577
18		1 300		52		3 900		86		6 500
17		1 224		51		3 824		85		6 424
16		1 148		50		3 748		84		6 348
15		1 071		49		3 671		83		6 271
14		994		48		3 594		82		6 194
13		918		47		3 518		81		6 118
12		842		46		3 442		80		6 042
11		765		45		3 365		79		5 965
10		688		44		3 288		78		5 888
9		612		43		3 212		77		5 812
8		536		42		3 136		76		5 736
7		459		41		3 059		75		5 659
6		382		40		2 982		74		5 582
5		306		39		2 906		73		5 506
4		230		38		2 830		72		5 430
3		153		37		2 753		71		5 353
2		76		36		2 676		70		5 276
1		0		35		2 600		69		5 200

LEVEL OF GROUND FLOOR FINISH 50 ─────
GROUND FLOOR SLAB DATUM LEVEL ─────

GLC ILEA

Department of Architecture and Civic Design
County Hall SE1 7PB
Architect Sir Roger Walters
KBE ARIBA FI Struct/E

References following notes are clause numbers from G.L.C. preambles to bills of quantities

For vertical co-ordinating dimensions in 2 storey house see drwg. no. [21] D2015 or in 3 storey flats see [21] D2016

For full range of preferred brick size window openings in 2/3 storey houses/flats see drawing number [21] D5450.

Clear opening equals (No. of bricks x 225) mm plus 10 mm

67/010-88

bldgtype 8
space use [21]
element 21

Departmental Standard Drawing

title
BRICKWORK – TYPICAL SETTING OUT DETAILS
34 COURSES TO 2600 mm

scale
1:10

GP | drawing no D.5246 | rev

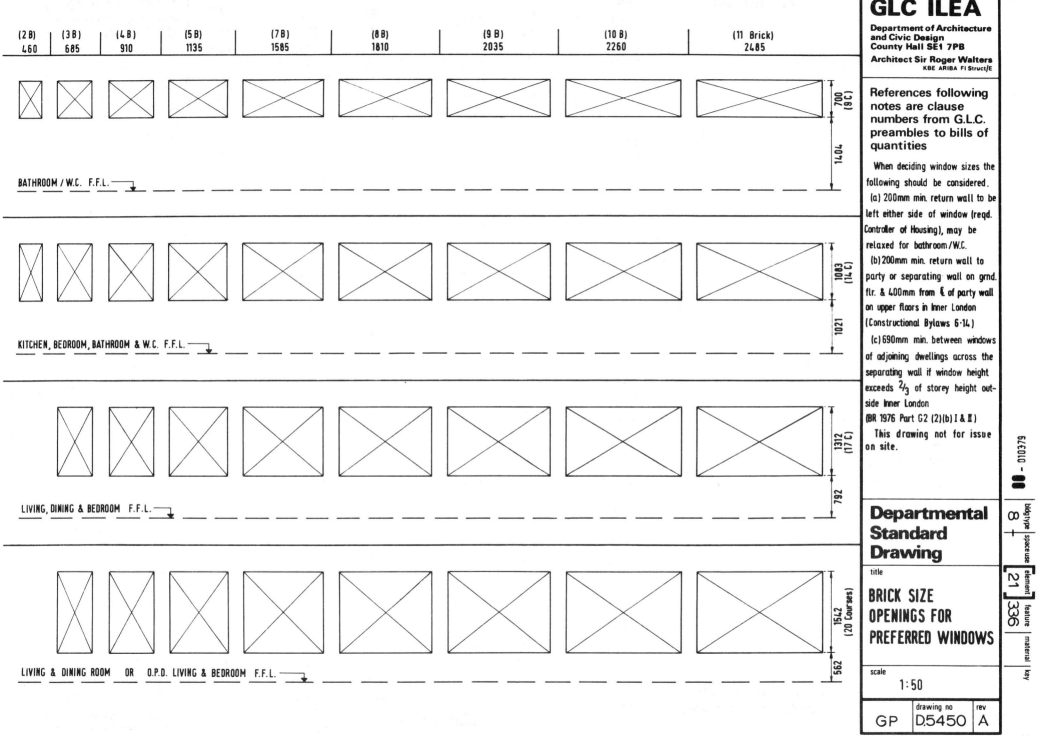

(2 B) 460	(3 B) 685	(4 B) 910	(5 B) 1135	(7 B) 1585	(8 B) 1810	(9 B) 2035	(10 B) 2260	(11 Brick) 2485

700 (9 C)

14.04

BATHROOM / W.C. F.F.L.

1083 (14 C)

1021

KITCHEN, BEDROOM, BATHROOM & W.C. F.F.L.

1312 (17 C)

792

LIVING, DINING & BEDROOM F.F.L.

1542 (20 Courses)

562

LIVING & DINING ROOM   OR   O.P.D. LIVING & BEDROOM F.F.L.

GLC ILEA

Department of Architecture and Civic Design
County Hall SE1 7PB
Architect Sir Roger Walters
KBE ARIBA FI Struct/E

References following notes are clause numbers from G.L.C. preambles to bills of quantities

When deciding window sizes the following should be considered.

(a) 200mm min. return wall to be left either side of window (reqd. Controller of Housing), may be relaxed for bathroom/W.C.

(b) 200mm min. return wall to party or separating wall on grnd. flr. & 400mm from ₵ of party wall on upper floors in Inner London (Constructional Bylaws 6·14)

(c) 690mm min. between windows of adjoining dwellings across the separating wall if window height exceeds $\frac{2}{3}$ of storey height outside Inner London
(BR 1976 Part G2 (2)(b) I & II)

This drawing not for issue on site.

Departmental Standard Drawing

title
BRICK SIZE OPENINGS FOR PREFERRED WINDOWS

scale
1:50

	drawing no	rev
GP	D.5450	A

9780101379

00 - 00   bldg type
8 +   space use
[21]   element
336   feature
material
key

Openings

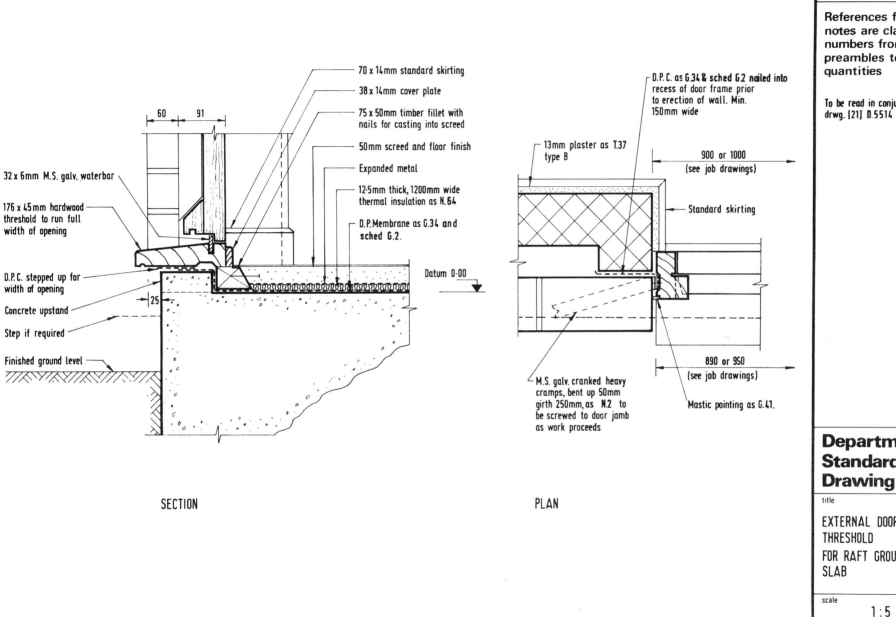

SECTION labels:

- 70 x 14mm standard skirting
- 38 x 14mm cover plate
- 75 x 50mm timber fillet with nails for casting into screed
- 50mm screed and floor finish
- Expanded metal
- 12·5mm thick, 1200mm wide thermal insulation as N.64
- D.P. Membrane as G.34 and sched G.2.
- 32 x 6mm M.S. galv. waterbar
- 176 x 45mm hardwood threshold to run full width of opening
- D.P.C. stepped up for width of opening
- Concrete upstand
- Step if required
- Finished ground level
- 60   91
- 25
- Datum 0·00

PLAN labels:

- D.P.C. as G.34 & sched G.2 nailed into recess of door frame prior to erection of wall. Min. 150mm wide
- 13mm plaster as T.37 type B
- 900 or 1000 (see job drawings)
- Standard skirting
- M.S. galv. cranked heavy cramps, bent up 50mm girth 250mm, as N.2 to be screwed to door jamb as work proceeds
- 890 or 950 (see job drawings)
- Mastic pointing as G.41.

SECTION   PLAN

GLC ILEA

Department of Architecture and Civic Design
County Hall SE1 7PB

Architect F B Pooley C B E.

References following notes are clause numbers from G.L.C. preambles to bills of quantities

To be read in conjunction with drwg. [21] D.5514

090479 · 00 · 010379

Departmental Standard Drawing

bldg type | space use | element | feature | material | key

21

title

EXTERNAL DOOR WITH THRESHOLD FOR RAFT GROUND FLOOR SLAB

scale

1 : 5

drawing no	rev
G P D.5528	

31

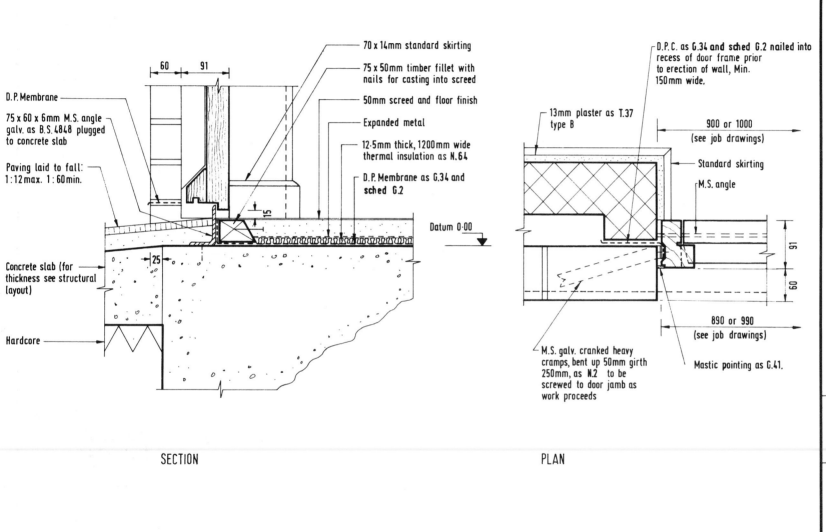

70 x 14mm standard skirting

75 x 50mm timber fillet with nails for casting into screed

50mm screed and floor finish

Expanded metal

12·5mm thick, 1200mm wide thermal insulation as N.64

D.P. Membrane as G.34 and sched G.2

D.P. Membrane

75 x 60 x 6mm M.S. angle galv. as B.S.4848 plugged to concrete slab

Paving laid to fall: 1:12 max. 1:60 min.

Concrete slab (for thickness see structural layout)

Hardcore

Datum 0·00

SECTION

D.P.C. as G.34 and sched G.2 nailed into recess of door frame prior to erection of wall, Min. 150mm wide.

13mm plaster as T.37 type B

900 or 1000 (see job drawings)

Standard skirting

M.S. angle

890 or 990 (see job drawings)

M.S. galv. cranked heavy cramps, bent up 50mm girth 250mm, as N.2 to be screwed to door jamb as work proceeds

Mastic pointing as G.41.

PLAN

GLC ILEA

Department of Architecture
and Civic Design
County Hall SE1 7PB
Architect F B Pooley C BE

References following notes are clause numbers from G.L.C. preambles to bills of quantities

To be read in conjunction with drwg. [21] D.5514

bldgtype | spaceuse | element | feature | material | key

21

**Departmental
Standard
Drawing**

title

EXTERNAL DOOR WITHOUT THRESHOLD.
FOR RAFT GROUND FLOOR SLAB –
MOBILITY DWELLING.

scale

1:5

G P | D.5529 | rev

32

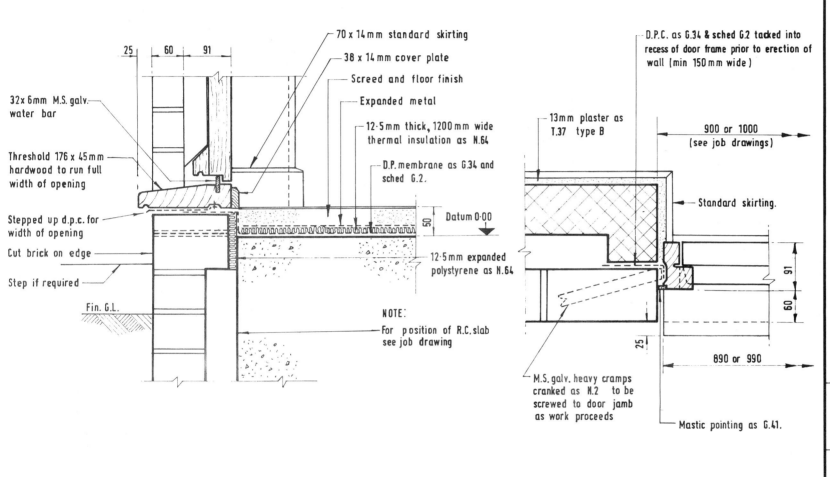

SECTION

- 70 x 14mm standard skirting
- 38 x 14mm cover plate
- Screed and floor finish
- Expanded metal
- 12·5mm thick, 1200 mm wide thermal insulation as N.64
- D.P. membrane as G.34 and sched G.2.

25   60   91

- 32 x 6mm M.S. galv. water bar
- Threshold 176 x 45mm hardwood to run full width of opening
- Stepped up d.p.c. for width of opening
- Cut brick on edge
- Step if required
- Fin. G.L.

Datum 0·00

50

- 12·5mm expanded polystyrene as N.64

NOTE:
For position of R.C. slab see job drawing

PLAN

- D.P.C. as G.34 & sched G.2 tacked into recess of door frame prior to erection of wall (min 150mm wide)
- 13mm plaster as T.37 type B
- Standard skirting.

900 or 1000
(see job drawings)

91
60
25

890 or 990

- M.S. galv. heavy cramps cranked as N.2 to be screwed to door jamb as work proceeds
- Mastic pointing as G.41.

GLC ILEA

Department of Architecture and Civic Design
County Hall SE1 7PB
Architect F B Pooley C B E

References following notes are clause numbers from G.L.C. preambles to bills of quantities

This drawing to be read in conjunction with :-

a) Raft ground floor slab type 2. drg. GP.D.5516

b) R.C. slab on strip foundation drg. GP.D.5518.

c) R.C. slab and slab on cross wall foundation drg. GP.D.5522.

d) R.C. slab and beams on short pile foundation drg. GP.D.5526.

637010 - **00**   020279

| bldg type | space use | element | feature | material | key |

Departmental Standard Drawing

title
EXTERNAL DOOR WITH THRESHOLD.
FOR R.C. SLAB WITH BRICK FACING.

element **21**

scale
1 : 5

| | drawing no | rev |
| GP | D.5530 | |

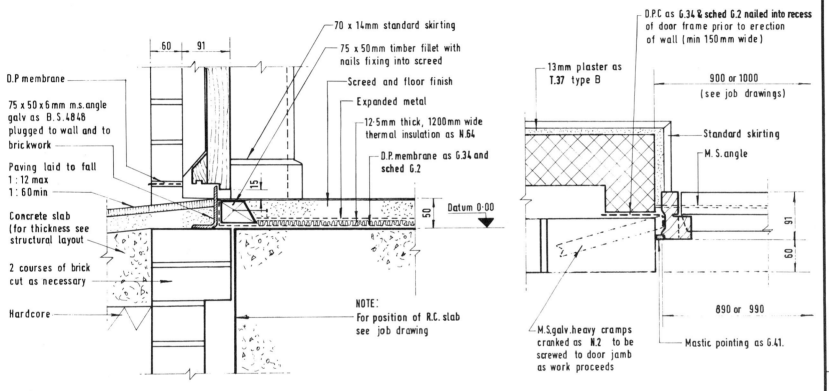

70 x 14mm standard skirting

75 x 50mm timber fillet with nails fixing into screed

Screed and floor finish

Expanded metal

12·5mm thick, 1200mm wide thermal insulation as N.64

D.P. membrane as G.34 and sched G.2

D.P membrane

75 x 50 x 6mm m.s.angle galv as B.S.4848 plugged to wall and to brickwork

Paving laid to fall 1:12 max 1:60min

Concrete slab (for thickness see structural layout

2 courses of brick cut as necessary

Hardcore

60   91

15

50   Datum 0·00

NOTE:
For position of R.C. slab see job drawing

SECTION

D.P.C as G.34 & sched G.2 nailed into recess of door frame prior to erection of wall (min 150mm wide)

13mm plaster as T.37 type B

900 or 1000
(see job drawings)

Standard skirting

M.S. angle

91

60

890 or 990

M.S.galv.heavy cramps cranked as N.2 to be screwed to door jamb as work proceeds

Mastic pointing as G.41.

PLAN

GLC ILEA

Department of Architecture and Civic Design
County Hall SE1 7PB
Architect F B Pooley C B E

References following notes are clause numbers from G.L.C. preambles to bills of quantities

This drawing to be read in conjunction with:-

a) Raft ground floor slab TYPE. 2. drg. GP.D.5516.

b) R.C.slab on strip foundation drg. GP.D.5518.

c) R.C.slab and beam on crosswall foundation drg. GP.D.5522.

d) R.C.slab and beams on short pile foundation drg. GP.D.5526.

Departmental Standard Drawing

title
EXTERNAL DOOR WITHOUT THRESHOLD
FOR R.C SLAB WITH BRICK FACING.
MOBILITY DWELLING.

scale
1 : 5

drawing no	rev
GP D.5531	

bldgtype | spaceuse | element 21 | feature | material | key

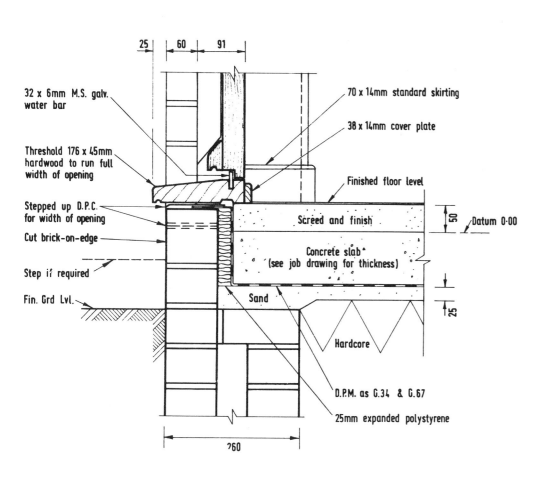

32 x 6mm M.S. galv. water bar

Threshold 176 x 45mm hardwood to run full width of opening

Stepped up D.P.C. for width of opening

Cut brick-on-edge

Step if required

Fin. Grd Lvl.

70 x 14mm standard skirting

38 x 14mm cover plate

Finished floor level

Screed and finish

Datum 0·00

Concrete slab
(see job drawing for thickness)

Sand

Hardcore

D.P.M. as G.34 & G.67

25mm expanded polystyrene

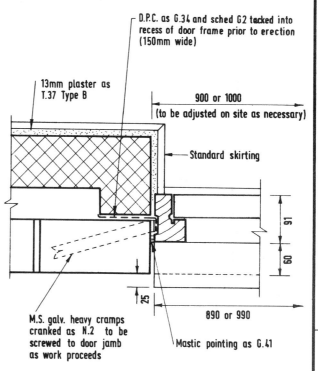

D.P.C. as G.34 and sched G2 tacked into recess of door frame prior to erection (150mm wide)

13mm plaster as T.37 Type B

900 or 1000
(to be adjusted on site as necessary)

Standard skirting

M.S. galv. heavy cramps cranked as N.2 to be screwed to door jamb as work proceeds

Mastic pointing as G.41

890 or 990

GLC ILEA

Department of Architecture and Civic Design
County Hall SE1 7PB
Architect Sir Roger Walters
KBE ARIBA FI Struct/E

References following notes are clause numbers from G.L.C. preambles to bills of quantities

Departmental Standard Drawing

title

EXTERNAL DOOR FIXING DETAIL.
(NOT MAIN ENTRANCE).

scale

1:5

G P | drawing no D.5490 | rev

bldg type -8-

space use

element 21

feature

material

key

010/379

35

GLC ILEA

**Department of Architecture
and Civic Design
County Hall SE1 7PB**

Architect Sir Roger Walters
KBE ARIBA FI Struct/E

References following
notes are clause
numbers from G.L.C.
preambles to bills of
quantities

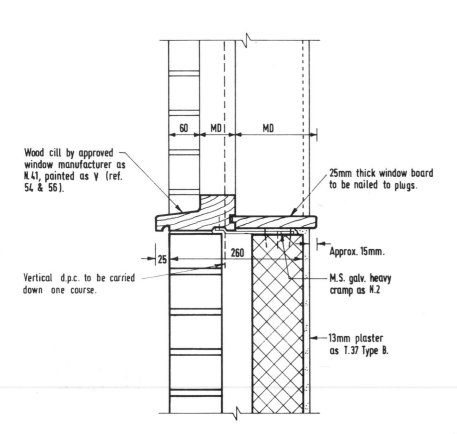

Wood cill by approved
window manufacturer as
N.41, painted as V (ref.
54 & 56).

60   MD   MD

25mm thick window board
to be nailed to plugs.

Approx. 15mm.

25   260

M.S. galv. heavy
cramp as N.2

Vertical d.p.c. to be carried
down one course.

13mm plaster
as T.37 Type B.

NOTES:

Jamb fixings:

2 points per side up to 1300mm high and
3 per side over 1300mm high.

Cill fixings:

For windows exceeding 900mm wide, fixings
to be at 600mm max. from each end and at
900mm max. centres.

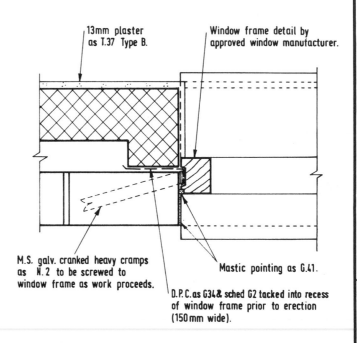

13mm plaster
as T.37 Type B.

Window frame detail by
approved window manufacturer.

M.S. galv. cranked heavy cramps
as N.2 to be screwed to
window frame as work proceeds.

Mastic pointing as G.41.

D.P.C. as G34 & sched G2 tacked into recess
of window frame prior to erection
(150mm wide).

NOTES:

Dimensions marked "MD" indicate window manufacturer's dimensions.

The frame sections and sizes (except those shown on the drawing)
may vary according to manufacturer.

GLC010-0379

00 -8-

21 336 Xi2 1

**Departmental
Standard
Drawing**

title

WOOD WINDOW-
BUILT-IN.
DETAIL OF JAMB AND
WOOD CILL.

scale

1 : 5

GP	drawing no	rev
	D.5451	

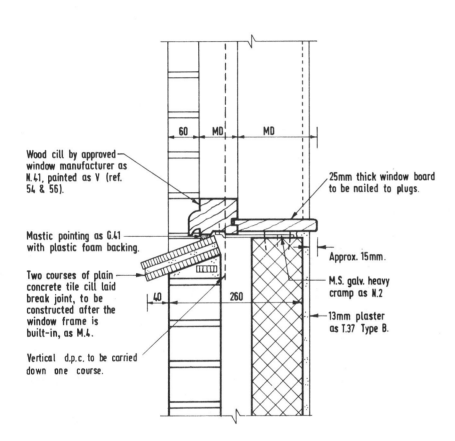

Wood cill by approved window manufacturer as N.41, painted as V (ref. 54 & 56).

Mastic pointing as G.41 with plastic foam backing.

Two courses of plain concrete tile cill laid break joint, to be constructed after the window frame is built-in, as M.4.

Vertical d.p.c. to be carried down one course.

25mm thick window board to be nailed to plugs.

Approx. 15mm.

M.S. galv. heavy cramp as N.2

13mm plaster as T.37 Type B.

60 | MD | MD

40 | 260

NOTES:

Jamb fixings:
2 points per side up to 1300mm high and 3 per side over 1300mm high.

Cill fixings:
For windows exceeding 900mm wide, fixings to be at 600mm max. from each end and at 900mm max. centres.

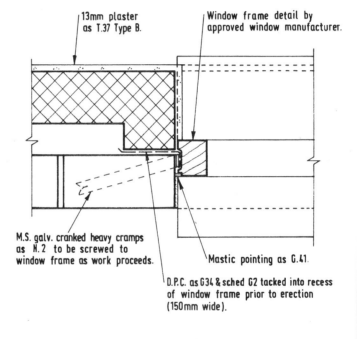

13mm plaster as T.37 Type B.

Window frame detail by approved window manufacturer.

M.S. galv. cranked heavy cramps as N.2 to be screwed to window frame as work proceeds.

Mastic pointing as G.41.

D.P.C. as G34 & sched G2 tacked into recess of window frame prior to erection (150mm wide).

NOTES:

Dimensions marked "MD" indicate window manufacturer's dimensions.

The frame sections and sizes (except those shown on the drawing) may vary according to manufacturer.

GLC ILEA

Department of Architecture and Civic Design
County Hall SE1 7PB

Architect Sir Roger Walters
KBE ARIBA FI Struct/E

References following notes are clause numbers from G.L.C. preambles to bills of quantities

9780851392429

bldg type | 8-
space use | 21
element | 336
feature | Xi2
material | 2
key

Departmental Standard Drawing

title
WOOD WINDOW-BUILT-IN.
DETAIL OF JAMB AND CONCRETE PLAIN TILE CILL.

scale
1:5

GP | drawing no **D.5452** | rev

37

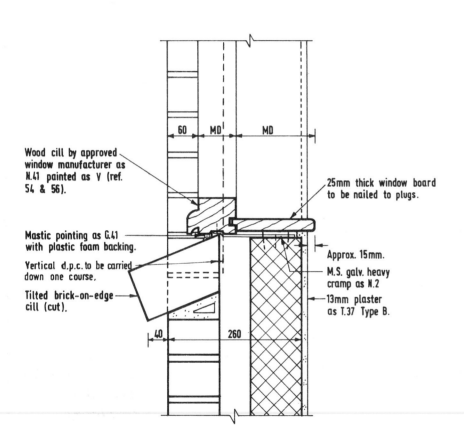

Wood cill by approved window manufacturer as N.41 painted as V (ref. 54 & 56).

Mastic pointing as G.41 with plastic foam backing.

Vertical d.p.c. to be carried down one course.

Tilted brick-on-edge cill (cut).

25mm thick window board to be nailed to plugs.

Approx. 15mm.

M.S. galv. heavy cramp as N.2

13mm plaster as T.37 Type B.

60   MD   MD

40   260

NOTES:

Jamb fixings:
2 points per side up to 1300mm high and 3 per side over 1300mm high.

Cill fixings:
For windows exceeding 900mm wide, fixings to be at 600mm max. from each end and at 900mm max. centres.

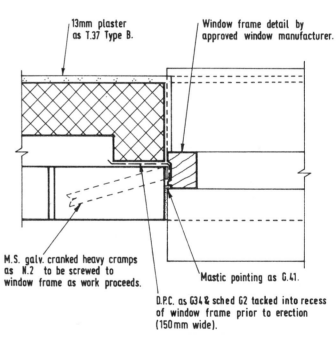

13mm plaster as T.37 Type B.

Window frame detail by approved window manufacturer.

M.S. galv. cranked heavy cramps as N.2 to be screwed to window frame as work proceeds.

Mastic pointing as G.41.

D.P.C. as G.34 & sched G2 tacked into recess of window frame prior to erection (150mm wide).

NOTES:

Dimensions marked "MD" indicate window manufacturer's dimensions.

The frame sections and sizes (except those shown on the drawing) may vary according to manufacturer.

Some facing bricks are not suitable for this type of cill.

GLC ILEA

Department of Architecture and Civic Design
County Hall SE1 7PB
Architect Sir Roger Walters
KBE ARIBA FI Struct/E

References following notes are clause numbers from G.L.C. preambles to bills of quantities

Departmental Standard Drawing

title
WOOD WINDOW-BUILT-IN.
DETAIL OF JAMB AND TILTED BRICK-ON-EDGE CILL.

scale
1 : 5

	drawing no	rev
GP	D.5453	

6.37079

88 - 010 - 0079

bldg type · space use · element · feature · material · key
8- · 21 · 336 · X12 · 3

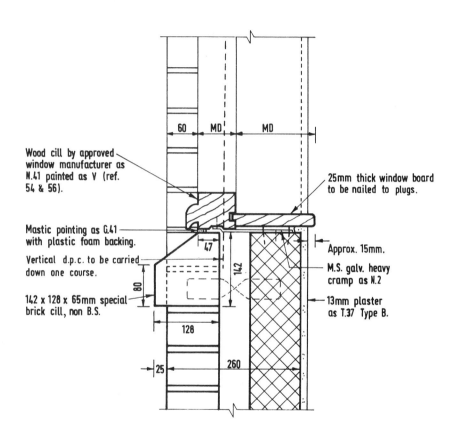

Wood cill by approved window manufacturer as N.41 painted as V (ref. 54 & 56).

Mastic pointing as G.41 with plastic foam backing.

Vertical d.p.c. to be carried down one course.

142 x 128 x 65mm special brick cill, non B.S.

60 MD MD

25mm thick window board to be nailed to plugs.

Approx. 15mm.

M.S. galv. heavy cramp as N.2

13mm plaster as T.37 Type B.

47 142 80 128 25 260

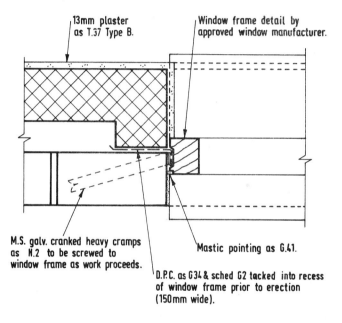

13mm plaster as T.37 Type B.

Window frame detail by approved window manufacturer.

M.S. galv. cranked heavy cramps as N.2 to be screwed to window frame as work proceeds.

Mastic pointing as G.41.

D.P.C. as G.34 & sched G2 tacked into recess of window frame prior to erection (150mm wide).

NOTES:

Jamb fixings:
2 points per side up to 1300mm high and 3 per side over 1300mm high.

Cill fixings:
For windows exceeding 900mm wide, fixings to be at 600mm max. from each end and at 900mm max. centres.

NOTES:

Dimensions marked "MD" indicate window manufacturer's dimensions.

The frame sections and sizes (except those shown on the drawing) may vary according to manufacturer.

Special bricks under window cill must be tied back securely to inner skin of blockwork with wall ties in each vertical joint.

Job architect to check with brick manufacturer for availability of the special brick. Only engineering or semi-engineering bricks suitable for this detail.

GLC ILEA

Department of Architecture and Civic Design County Hall SE1 7PB

Architect Sir Roger Walters
KBE ARIBA FI Struct/E

References following notes are clause numbers from G.L.C. preambles to bills of quantities

bldg type	space use	element	feature	material	key
00 - 010376/9	8-	21	336	Xi2	4

Departmental Standard Drawing

title

WOOD WINDOW-BUILT-IN.
DETAIL OF JAMB AND SPECIAL BRICK CILL.

scale
1:5

	drawing no	rev
GP	D.5454	

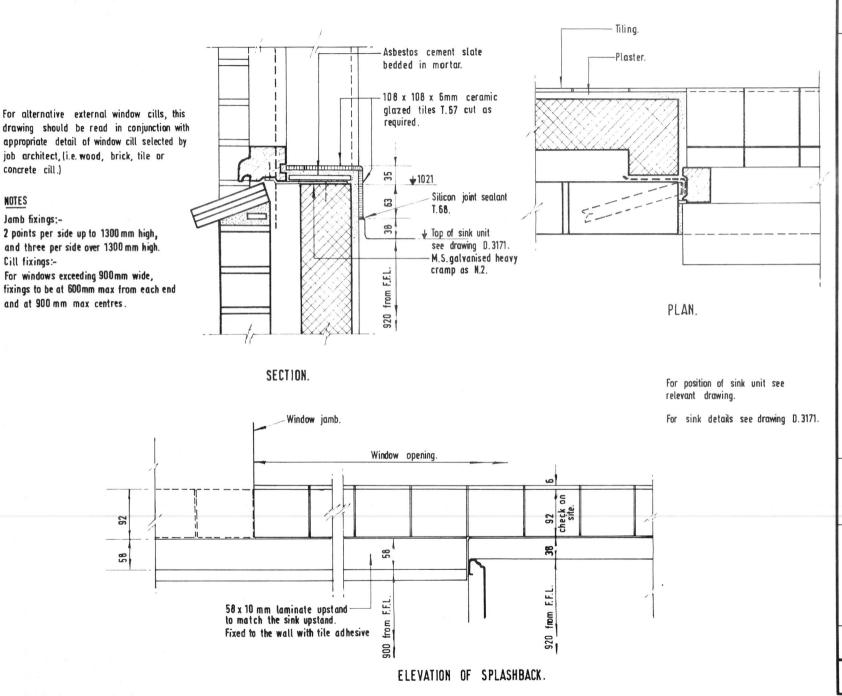

For alternative external window cills, this drawing should be read in conjunction with appropriate detail of window cill selected by job architect, (i.e. wood, brick, tile or concrete cill.)

NOTES

Jamb fixings:-
2 points per side up to 1300 mm high, and three per side over 1300 mm high.
Cill fixings:-
For windows exceeding 900mm wide, fixings to be at 600mm max from each end and at 900 mm max centres.

Asbestos cement slate bedded in mortar.

108 x 108 x 6mm ceramic glazed tiles T.67 cut as required.

35
↓1021
63
Silicon joint sealant T.68.
38
↓ Top of sink unit see drawing D.3171.
M.S. galvanised heavy cramp as N.2.

920 from F.F.L.

SECTION.

Tiling.

Plaster.

PLAN.

For position of sink unit see relevant drawing.

For sink details see drawing D.3171.

Window jamb.

Window opening.

92
58

6
92   check on site.
58
38
900 from F.F.L.
920 from F.F.L.

58 x 10 mm laminate upstand to match the sink upstand. Fixed to the wall with tile adhesive.

ELEVATION OF SPLASHBACK.

References following notes are clause numbers from G.L.C. preambles to bills of quantities

9370 010 - 9379

bldg type	space use	element	feature	material	key
8	8	21	336	Xi2	8

Departmental Standard Drawing

title
SPLASHBACK TILING TO SINK UNIT IN STANDARD KITCHEN.

scale
1 : 5

GP	drawing no D.5458	rev A

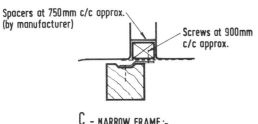

Spacers at 750mm c/c approx. (by manufacturer)

Screws at 900mm c/c approx.

C - NARROW FRAME:-
M.S. galv. heavy cramps as N.2(iii) screwed to timber battens.

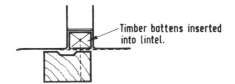

Timber battens inserted into lintel.

D - WIDER FRAME:-
Nailed at 900mm c/c approx. to timber battens.

HEAD FIXING DETAILS FOR WINDOWS 1800mm AND OVER

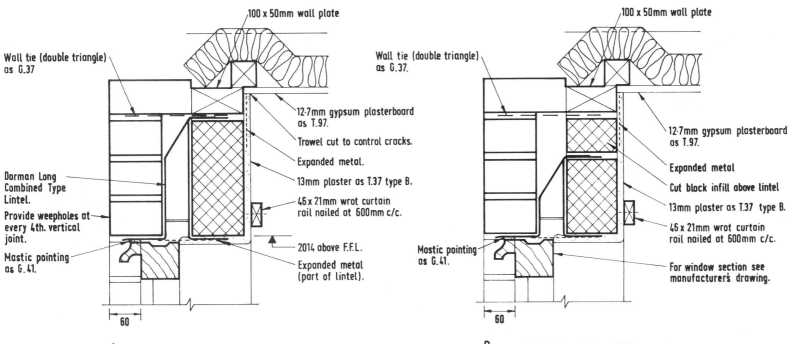

100 x 50mm wall plate

Wall tie (double triangle) as G.37

12·7mm gypsum plasterboard as T.97.

Trowel cut to control cracks.

Expanded metal.

13mm plaster as T.37 type B.

46 x 21mm wrot curtain rail nailed at 600mm c/c.

2014 above F.F.L.

Expanded metal (part of lintel).

Dorman Long Combined Type Lintel.

Provide weepholes at every 4th. vertical joint.

Mastic pointing as G.41.

60

A - 3 COURSE LINTEL: 229mm DEEP
(Coated with 2 coats of bitumen)

100 x 50mm wall plate

Wall tie (double triangle) as G.37.

12·7mm gypsum plasterboard as T.97.

Expanded metal

Cut block infill above lintel

13mm plaster as T.37 type B.

46 x 21mm wrot curtain rail nailed at 600mm c/c.

For window section see manufacturer's drawing.

Mastic pointing as G.41.

60

B - 2 COURSE LINTEL: 152mm DEEP
(Coated with 2 coats of bitumen)

GLC ILEA

Department of Architecture and Civic Design
County Hall SE1 7PB

Architect Sir Roger Walters
KBE ARIBA FI Struct/E.

References following notes are clause numbers from G.L.C. preambles to bills of quantities

To be read in conjunction with eaves detail drawings [27] D.5400 to D.5407 and cill and jamb detail drawings [21] D.5451 to D.5458 and [21] D.5450.

For size of lintel, see Structural Engineer's drawing.

1906078 A   00 - 010379

Departmental Standard Drawing	bldgtype	spaceuse
	element	21

title

WINDOW LINTEL.
(DORMAN LONG COMBINED TYPE) WITH NORMAL BRICK COURSES AT EAVES.

scale

1:5

drawing no	rev
G P D.5432	A

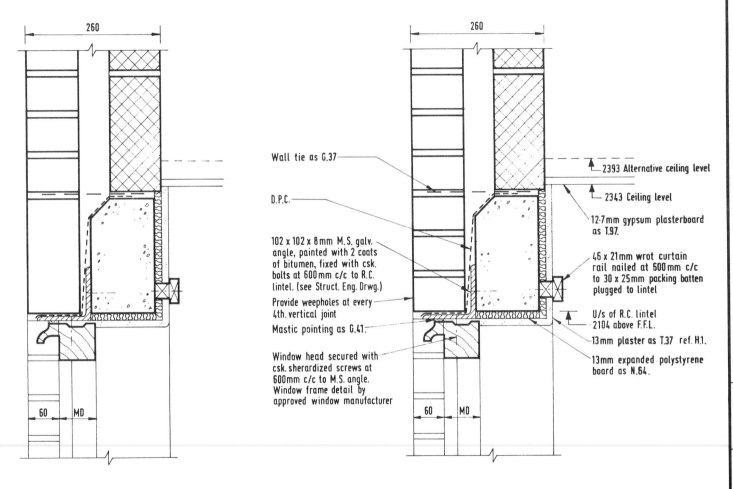

260

260

Wall tie as G.37

D.P.C.

102 x 102 x 8mm M.S. galv. angle, painted with 2 coats of bitumen, fixed with csk. bolts at 600mm c/c to R.C. lintel. (see Struct. Eng. Drwg.)

Provide weepholes at every 4th. vertical joint

Mastic pointing as G.41.

Window head secured with csk. sherardized screws at 600mm c/c to M.S. angle. Window frame detail by approved window manufacturer

2393 Alternative ceiling level

2343 Ceiling level

12·7mm gypsum plasterboard as T.97.

46 x 21mm wrot curtain rail nailed at 600mm c/c to 30 x 25mm packing batten plugged to lintel

U/s of R.C. lintel 2104 above F.F.L.

13mm plaster as T.37 ref. H.1.

13mm expanded polystyrene board as N.64.

60 MD

60 MD

SOLDIER COURSE – TYPE A

NORMAL COURSE – TYPE B

NOTES:

Dimensions marked "MD" indicate window manufacturer's dimensions

Frame sections and sizes (except those shown on the drawing) may vary according to manufacturer

No head fixing is required for windows under 1800mm width

GLC ILEA

Department of Architecture and Civic Design
County Hall SE1 7PB

Architect Sir Roger Walters
KBE ARIBA FI Struct/E.

References following notes are clause numbers from G.L.C. preambles to bills of quantities

To be read in conjunction with appropriate job drawing

301078 - 00 - 010379

Departmental Standard Drawing

bldg type | space use

element 21

feature | material | key

title

R.C. LINTEL – WITH M.S. ANGLE – 3 BRICK COURSES DEEP

scale

1 : 5

G P | drawing no D.5433 | rev

GLC ILEA

**Department of Architecture
and Civic Design
County Hall SE1 7PB**

Architect Sir Roger Walters
KBE ARIBA FI Struct/E.

References following
notes are clause
numbers from G.L.C.
preambles to bills of
quantities

To be read in conjunction with
appropriate job drawing

260

260

Wall tie as G.37

D.P.C.

102 x 102 x 8mm M.S. galv.
angle, painted with 2 coats
of bitumen, fixed with csk.
bolts at 600mm c/c to R.C.
lintel (see Struct. Eng. Drwg.)

Provide weepholes at every
4th. vertical joint

Mastic pointing as G.41.

Window head secured with
csk. sherardized screws at
600mm c/c to M.S. angle.
Window frame detail by
approved window manufacturer

2393 Alternative ceiling level

2343 Ceiling level

12·7mm gypsum plasterboard
as T.97.

46 x 21mm wrot curtain
rail nailed at 600mm c/c
to 30 x 25mm packing batten
plugged to lintel

U/s of R.C. lintel
2104 above F.F.L.

13mm plaster as T.37, ref. H.1.

13mm expanded polystyrene
board as N.64.

60   MD

60   MD

SOLDIER COURSE - TYPE C

NORMAL COURSE - TYPE D

<u>NOTES:</u>

Dimensions marked "MD" indicate window manufacturer's dimensions

Frame sections and sizes (except those shown on the drawing) may
vary according to manufacturer

No head fixing is required for windows under 1800mm width

30 01 78 00 - 010379

**Departmental
Standard
Drawing**

bldg type | space use

element [21]

feature | material | key

title

**R.C. LINTEL -
WITH M.S. ANGLE -
4 BRICK COURSES
DEEP**

scale
1 : 5

	drawing no	rev
G P	D.5435	

43

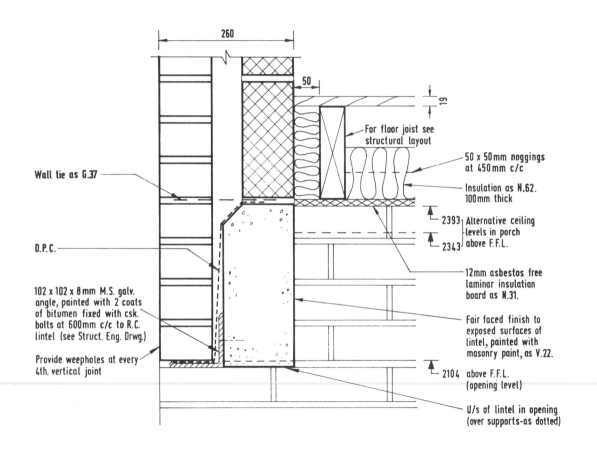

260

50

19

Wall tie as G.37

D.P.C.

102 x 102 x 8mm M.S. galv.
angle, painted with 2 coats
of bitumen fixed with csk.
bolts at 600mm c/c to R.C.
lintel (see Struct. Eng. Drwg.)

Provide weepholes at every
4th. vertical joint

For floor joist see
structural layout

50 x 50mm noggings
at 450mm c/c

Insulation as N.62.
100mm thick

2393 ⌐ Alternative ceiling
       ⌐levels in porch
2343 ⌐ above F.F.L.

12mm asbestos free
laminar insulation
board as N.31.

Fair faced finish to
exposed surfaces of
lintel, painted with
masonry paint, as V.22.

2104 above F.F.L.
     (opening level)

U/s of lintel in opening
(over supports-as dotted)

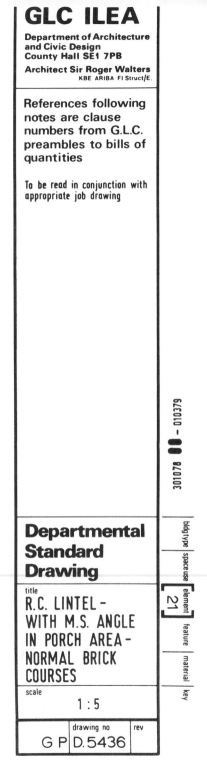

GLC ILEA

**Department of Architecture
and Civic Design
County Hall SE1 7PB**

Architect Sir Roger Walters
KBE ARIBA FI Struct/E.

References following
notes are clause
numbers from G.L.C.
preambles to bills of
quantities

To be read in conjunction with
appropriate job drawing

30107 8 00 - 010379

Departmental
Standard
Drawing

bldg type | space use | element | feature | material | key

21

title
R.C. LINTEL -
WITH M.S. ANGLE
IN PORCH AREA -
NORMAL BRICK
COURSES

scale
1 : 5

G P | drawing no D.5436 | rev

GLC ILEA

Department of Architecture and Civic Design
County Hall SE1 7PB

Architect Sir Roger Walters
KBE ARIBA FI Struct/E.

References following notes are clause numbers from G.L.C. preambles to bills of quantities

To be read in conjunction with appropriate job drawing

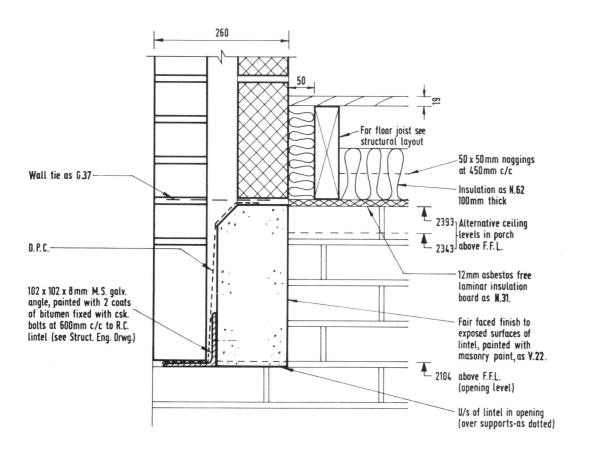

Wall tie as G.37

D.P.C.

102 x 102 x 8mm M.S. galv. angle, painted with 2 coats of bitumen fixed with csk. bolts at 600mm c/c to R.C. lintel (see Struct. Eng. Drwg.)

260

50

19

For floor joist see structural layout

50 x 50mm noggings at 450mm c/c

Insulation as N.62 100mm thick

2393 Alternative ceiling levels in porch
2343 above F.F.L.

12mm asbestos free laminar insulation board as N.31.

Fair faced finish to exposed surfaces of lintel, painted with masonry paint, as V.22.

2104 above F.F.L. (opening level)

U/s of lintel in opening (over supports-as dotted)

Departmental Standard Drawing

title

R.C. LINTEL – WITH M.S. ANGLE IN PORCH AREA – SOLDIER COURSE

scale
1 : 5

drawing no	rev
G P D.5437	

bldgtype | spaceuse | element | feature | material | key

[21]

311078 - 00 - 01079

45

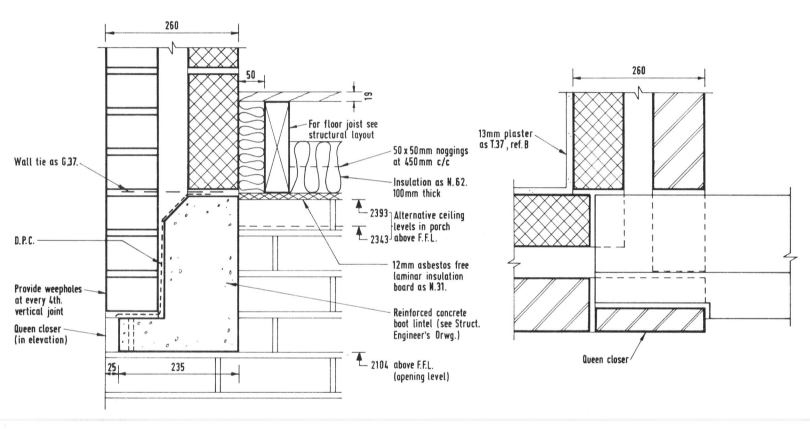

SECTION

260

50

19

Wall tie as G.37.

For floor joist see structural layout

50 x 50mm noggings at 450mm c/c

Insulation as N.62. 100mm thick

D.P.C.

2393 Alternative ceiling levels in porch
2343 above F.F.L.

12mm asbestos free laminar insulation board as N.31.

Provide weepholes at every 4th. vertical joint

Reinforced concrete boot lintel (see Struct. Engineer's Drwg.)

Queen closer (in elevation)

25   235

2104 above F.F.L. (opening level)

PLAN (at lintel level)

260

13mm plaster as T.37, ref.B

Queen closer

GLC ILEA

Department of Architecture and Civic Design
County Hall SE1 7PB

Architect Sir Roger Walters
KBE ARIBA FI Struct/E.

References following notes are clause numbers from G.L.C. preambles to bills of quantities

To be read in conjunction with appropriate job drawing

Exposed surfaces of lintel to have fair faced finish, painted with masonry paint, as V.22.

30 1030 - 00 - 010379

Departmental Standard Drawing

bldgtype | spaceuse | element [21] | feature | material | key

title
R. C. BOOT LINTEL IN PORCH AREA – 4 BRICK COURSES DEEP

scale
1 : 5

drawing no | rev
G P D.5438

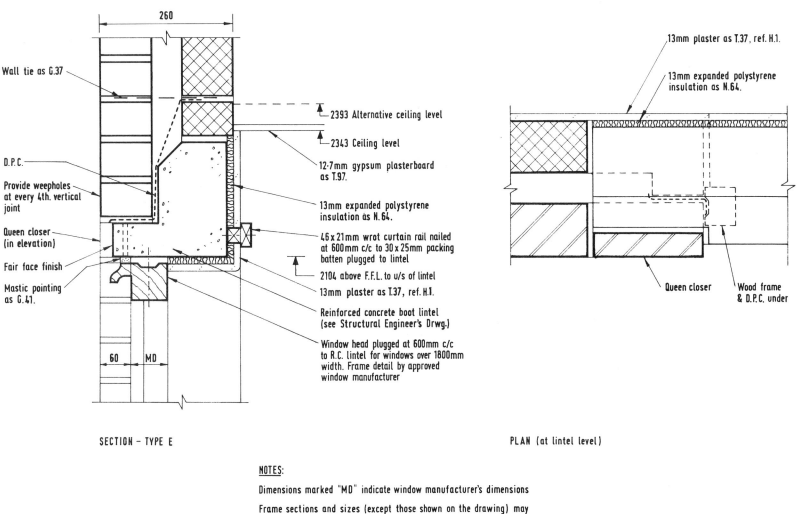

SECTION — TYPE E

260

60   MD

Wall tie as G.37

D.P.C.

Provide weepholes
at every 4th. vertical
joint

Queen closer
(in elevation)

Fair face finish

Mastic pointing
as G.41.

2393 Alternative ceiling level

2343 Ceiling level

12·7mm gypsum plasterboard
as T.97.

13mm expanded polystyrene
insulation as N.64.

46 x 21mm wrot curtain rail nailed
at 600mm c/c to 30 x 25mm packing
batten plugged to lintel

2104 above F.F.L. to u/s of lintel

13mm plaster as T.37, ref. H.1.

Reinforced concrete boot lintel
(see Structural Engineer's Drwg.)

Window head plugged at 600mm c/c
to R.C. lintel for windows over 1800mm
width. Frame detail by approved
window manufacturer

PLAN (at lintel level)

13mm plaster as T.37, ref. H.1.

13mm expanded polystyrene
insulation as N.64.

Queen closer

Wood frame
& D.P.C. under

NOTES:

Dimensions marked "MD" indicate window manufacturer's dimensions

Frame sections and sizes (except those shown on the drawing) may
vary according to manufacturer

Exposed surface of R.C. lintel to be painted with masonry paint, as V.22.

GLC ILEA

**Department of Architecture
and Civic Design
County Hall SE1 7PB**

Architect Sir Roger Walters
KBE ARIBA FI Struct/E.

References following
notes are clause
numbers from G.L.C.
preambles to bills of
quantities

To be read in conjunction with
appropriate job drawing

29010 - 010379

bldgtype   space use

element   **21**

feature

material

key

**Departmental
Standard
Drawing**

title
**R.C. BOOT LINTEL –
3 BRICK COURSES
DEEP**

scale
1 : 5

	drawing no	rev
G P	D.5446	

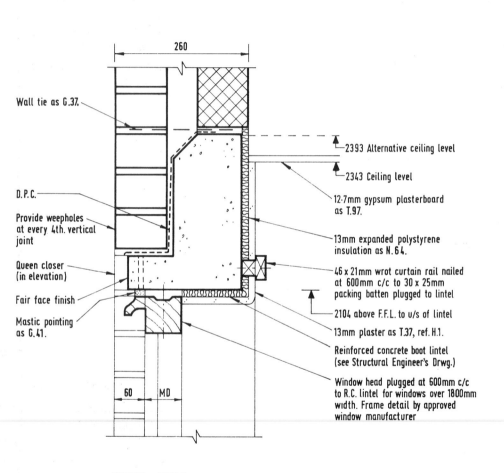

Wall tie as G.37.

D.P.C.

Provide weepholes at every 4th. vertical joint

Queen closer (in elevation)

Fair face finish

Mastic pointing as G.41.

260

60 MD

SECTION - TYPE F

2393 Alternative ceiling level

2343 Ceiling level

12·7mm gypsum plasterboard as T.97.

13mm expanded polystyrene insulation as N.64.

46 x 21mm wrot curtain rail nailed at 600mm c/c to 30 x 25mm packing batten plugged to lintel

2104 above F.F.L. to u/s of lintel

13mm plaster as T.37, ref. H.1.

Reinforced concrete boot lintel (see Structural Engineer's Drwg.)

Window head plugged at 600mm c/c to R.C. lintel for windows over 1800mm width. Frame detail by approved window manufacturer

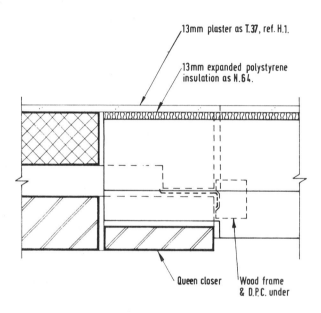

13mm plaster as T.37, ref. H.1.

13mm expanded polystyrene insulation as N.64.

Queen closer

Wood frame & D.P.C. under

PLAN (at lintel level)

NOTES:

Dimensions marked "MD" indicate window manufacturer's dimensions

Frame sections and sizes (except those shown on the drawing) may vary according to manufacturer

Exposed surface of R.C. lintel to be painted with masonry paint, as V.22.

GLC ILEA

**Department of Architecture and Civic Design
County Hall SE1 7PB
Architect Sir Roger Walters**
KBE ARIBA FI Struct/E.

References following notes are clause numbers from G.L.C. preambles to bills of quantities

To be read in conjunction with appropriate job drawing

31I078 - 010379

01I078 - 00

bldg type | space use

Departmental Standard Drawing

element | 21

title
R.C. BOOT LINTEL - 4 BRICK COURSES DEEP

feature | material | key

scale
1:5

G P | D.5447 | rev
drawing no

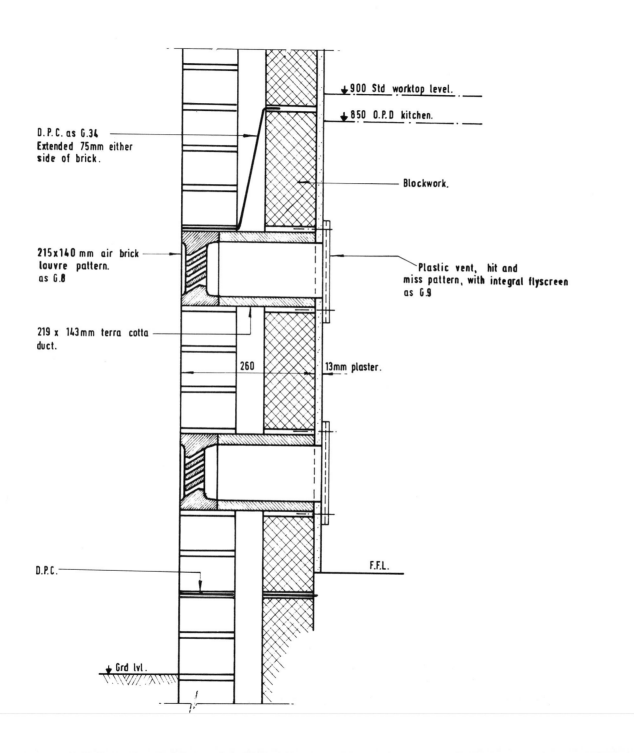

D.P.C. as G.34
Extended 75mm either
side of brick.

900 Std worktop level.

850 O.P.D kitchen.

Blockwork.

215x140 mm air brick
louvre pattern.
as G.8

Plastic vent, hit and
miss pattern, with integral flyscreen
as G.9

219 x 143mm terra cotta
duct.

260

13mm plaster.

D.P.C.

F.F.L.

Grd lvl.

GLC ILEA

**Department of Architecture
and Civic Design
County Hall SE1 7PB
Architect Sir Roger Walters**
KBE ARIBA FI Struct/E

References following
notes are clause
numbers from G.L.C.
preambles to bills of
quantities
**Some Local Authorities
will accept top vent
only. Job Architect to
check.**

673010 - **00**

8 -

| bldgtype | space use | element | feature | material | key |

Departmental Standard Drawing

21

title
**FOOD STORAGE CUPBOARD.
VENT UNDER KITCHEN WORKTOP.**
TERRA COTTA.

A

scale
1 : 5

| GP | drawing no | rev |
| | D.5478 | |

49

Linings

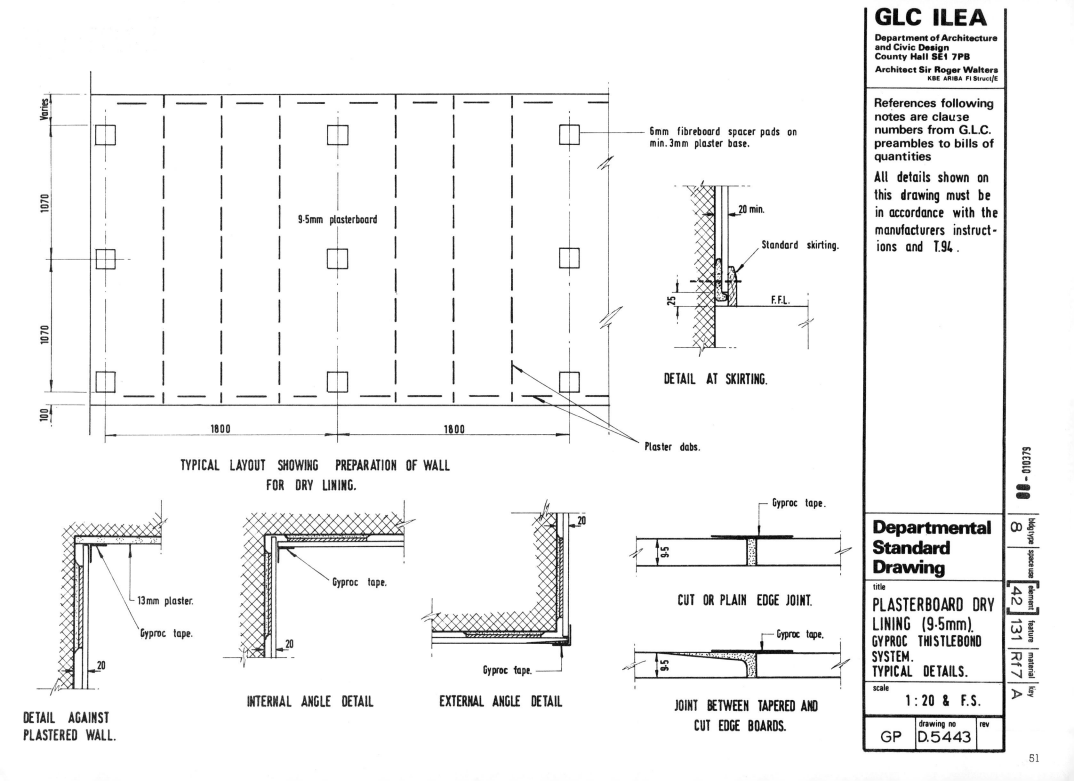

6mm fibreboard spacer pads on min. 3mm plaster base.

9·5mm plasterboard

Varies

1070

1070

100

1800

1800

Plaster dabs.

TYPICAL LAYOUT SHOWING PREPARATION OF WALL
FOR DRY LINING.

20 min.

Standard skirting.

25

F.F.L.

DETAIL AT SKIRTING.

13mm plaster.

Gyproc tape.

20

DETAIL AGAINST
PLASTERED WALL.

Gyproc tape.

20

20

Gyproc tape.

INTERNAL ANGLE DETAIL

EXTERNAL ANGLE DETAIL

Gyproc tape.

9·5

CUT OR PLAIN EDGE JOINT.

Gyproc tape.

9·5

JOINT BETWEEN TAPERED AND
CUT EDGE BOARDS.

GLC ILEA

**Department of Architecture
and Civic Design
County Hall SE1 7PB**

Architect Sir Roger Walters
KBE ARIBA FI Struct/E

References following
notes are clause
numbers from G.L.C.
preambles to bills of
quantities

All details shown on
this drawing must be
in accordance with the
manufacturers instruct-
ions and T.94.

010379 - 00

8   bldg type

42   space use

131   element

Rf7   feature

A   material key

**Departmental
Standard
Drawing**

title

PLASTERBOARD DRY
LINING (9·5mm).
GYPROC THISTLEBOND
SYSTEM.
TYPICAL DETAILS.

scale

1 : 20 & F.S.

GP   drawing no   D.5443   rev

51

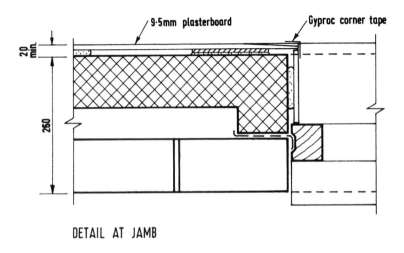

9·5mm plasterboard   Gyproc corner tape

20 min.

260

DETAIL AT JAMB

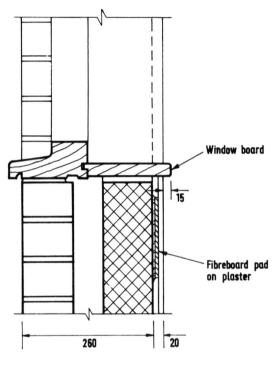

Window board

15

Fibreboard pad
on plaster

260   20

DETAIL AT CILL

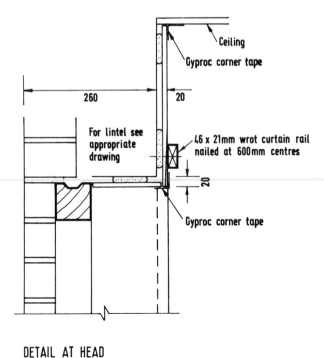

Ceiling

Gyproc corner tape

260   20

For lintel see
appropriate
drawing

46 x 21mm wrot curtain rail
nailed at 600mm centres

20

Gyproc corner tape

DETAIL AT HEAD

GLC ILEA

**Department of Architecture
and Civic Design
County Hall SE1 7PB**

Architect Sir Roger Walters
KBE ARIBA FI Struct/E.

References following
notes are clause
numbers from G.L.C.
preambles to bills of
quantities

Window cill for illustra-
tion only. Detail to be
read in conjunction with
chosen cill design.

All details shown on
this drawing must be in
accordance with manu-
facturers instructions
and T.94.

For fixing details of
window see appropriate
drawing.

9LE010 - 00

8-|

Departmental
Standard
Drawing

bldgtype	spaceuse	element	feature	material	key
8-		42	131	Rf7	C

title

**PLASTERBOARD DRY
LINING (9·5mm).**
GYPROC THISTLEBOND
SYSTEM.
WINDOW DETAILS.

scale

1 : 5

	drawing no	rev
GP	D.5445	

Party

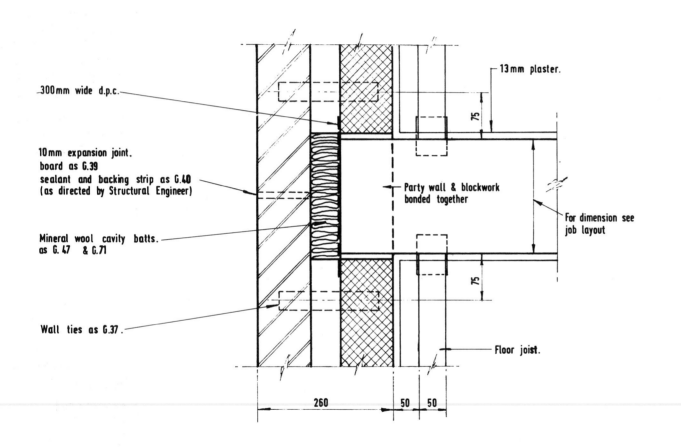

300mm wide d.p.c.

10mm expansion joint.
board as G.39
sealant and backing strip as G.40
(as directed by Structural Engineer)

Mineral wool cavity batts.
as G.47 & G.71

Wall ties as G.37.

13mm plaster.

75

Party wall & blockwork
bonded together

For dimension see
job layout

75

Floor joist.

260   50   50

GLC ILEA

**Department of Architecture
and Civic Design
County Hall SE1 7PB
Architect Sir Roger Walters**
KBE ARIBA FI Struct/E

References following
notes are clause
numbers from G.L.C.
preambles to bills of
quantities

To be read in conjunction
with the appropriate
details in series [21] 5460-
5475 for condition at
eaves.

The use of this detail is
limited to walls
7·5 m high (London build-
-ing bylaws). Job arch-
-itect to check with D.S.

00 - 010379

8 - | bldg type

21 | element

space use | feature | material | key

Departmental Standard Drawing

title
CAVITY AND PARTY
WALL JUNCTION.

scale
1 : 5

GP | drawing no
D.5459 | rev

54

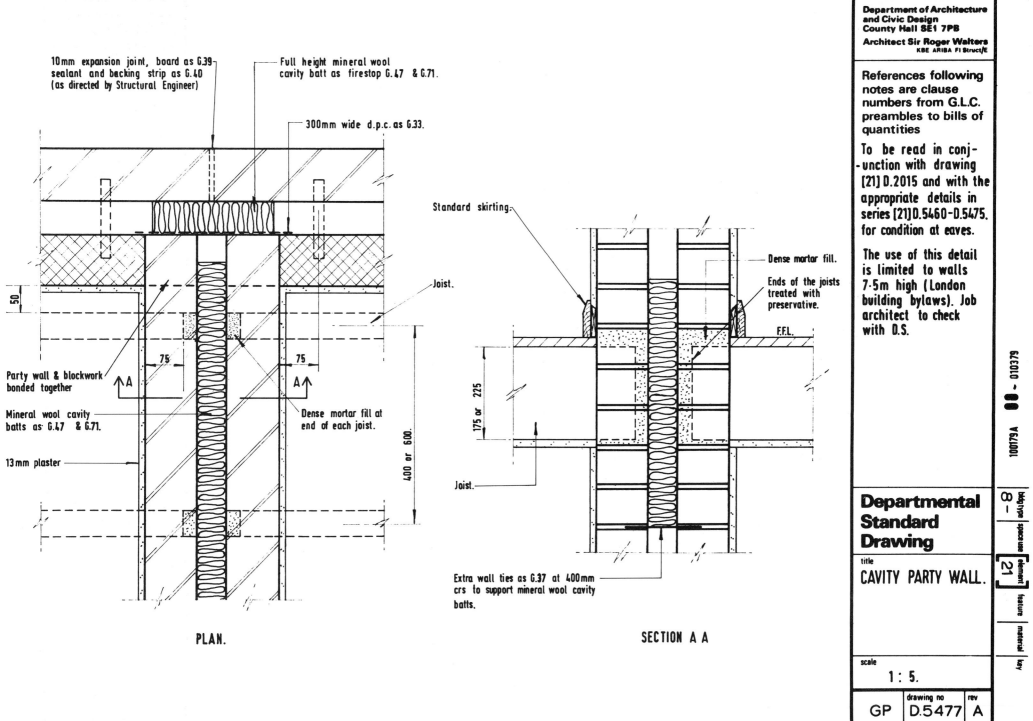

10mm expansion joint, board as G.39 sealant and backing strip as G.40 (as directed by Structural Engineer)

Full height mineral wool cavity batt as firestop G.47 & G.71.

300mm wide d.p.c. as G.33.

50

75

75

400 or 600.

Party wall & blockwork bonded together

Mineral wool cavity batts as G.47 & G.71.

13mm plaster

Dense mortar fill at end of each joist.

PLAN.

Standard skirting.

Joist.

Dense mortar fill.

Ends of the joists treated with preservative.

F.F.L.

175 or 225

Joist.

Extra wall ties as G.37 at 400mm crs to support mineral wool cavity batts.

SECTION A A

GLC ILEA

Department of Architecture and Civic Design County Hall SE1 7PB

Architect Sir Roger Walters
KBE ARIBA FI Struct/E

References following notes are clause numbers from G.L.C. preambles to bills of quantities

To be read in conjunction with drawing [21] D.2015 and with the appropriate details in series [21] D.5460-D.5475. for condition at eaves.

The use of this detail is limited to walls 7.5m high (London building bylaws). Job architect to check with D.S.

010376 100079A

8-   21

Departmental Standard Drawing

title
CAVITY PARTY WALL.

scale
1 : 5.

| GP | drawing no | rev |
| | D.5477 | A |

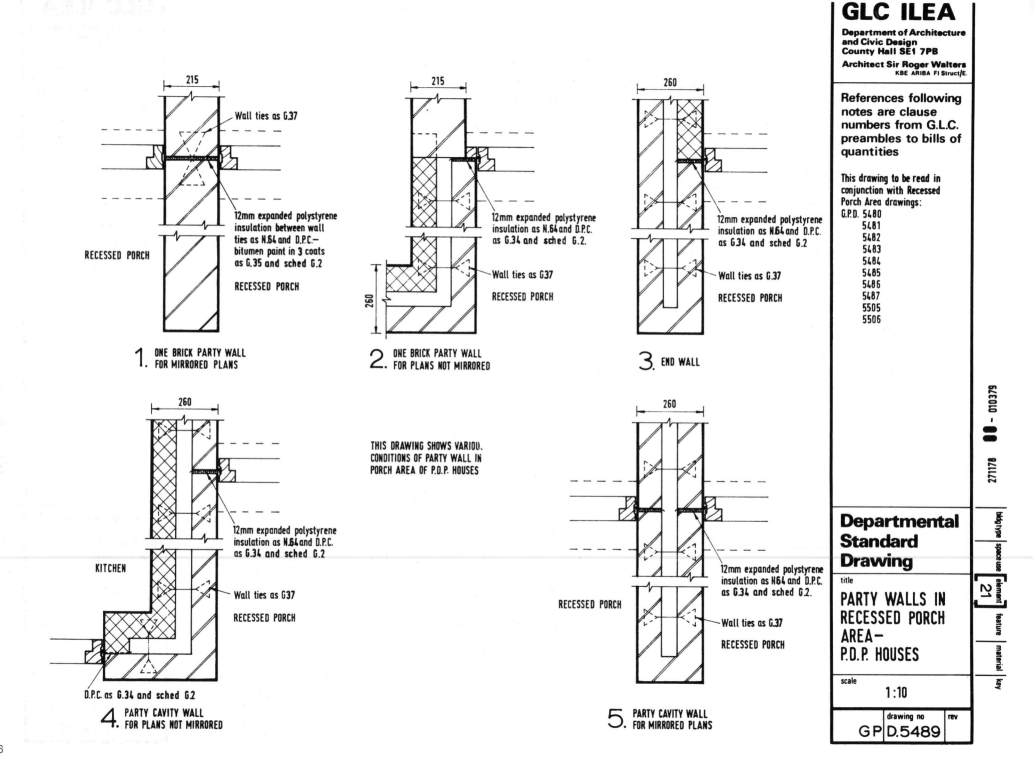

Wall ties as G.37

12mm expanded polystyrene insulation between wall ties as N.64 and D.P.C.— bitumen paint in 3 coats as G.35 and sched G.2

RECESSED PORCH

RECESSED PORCH

215

1. ONE BRICK PARTY WALL FOR MIRRORED PLANS

12mm expanded polystyrene insulation as N.64 and D.P.C. as G.34 and sched G.2.

Wall ties as G37

RECESSED PORCH

215

260

2. ONE BRICK PARTY WALL FOR PLANS NOT MIRRORED

12mm expanded polystyrene insulation as N.64 and D.P.C. as G.34 and sched G.2

Wall ties as G.37

RECESSED PORCH

260

3. END WALL

THIS DRAWING SHOWS VARIOUS CONDITIONS OF PARTY WALL IN PORCH AREA OF P.D.P. HOUSES

KITCHEN

260

12mm expanded polystyrene insulation as N.64 and D.P.C. as G.34 and sched G.2.

Wall ties as G37

RECESSED PORCH

D.P.C. as G.34 and sched G.2

4. PARTY CAVITY WALL FOR PLANS NOT MIRRORED

260

RECESSED PORCH

12mm expanded polystyrene insulation as N.64 and D.P.C. as G.34 and sched G.2.

Wall ties as G.37

RECESSED PORCH

5. PARTY CAVITY WALL FOR MIRRORED PLANS

GLC ILEA

Department of Architecture and Civic Design
County Hall SE1 7PB
Architect Sir Roger Walters
KBE ARIBA FI Struct/E.

References following notes are clause numbers from G.L.C. preambles to bills of quantities

This drawing to be read in conjunction with Recessed Porch Area drawings:
G.P.D. 5480
5481
5482
5483
5484
5485
5486
5487
5505
5506

6279 010379 00 - 271178

Departmental Standard Drawing

bldg type | space use | element | feature | material | key
21

title

PARTY WALLS IN RECESSED PORCH AREA— P.D.P. HOUSES

scale

1:10

GP | drawing no | rev
| D.5489 |

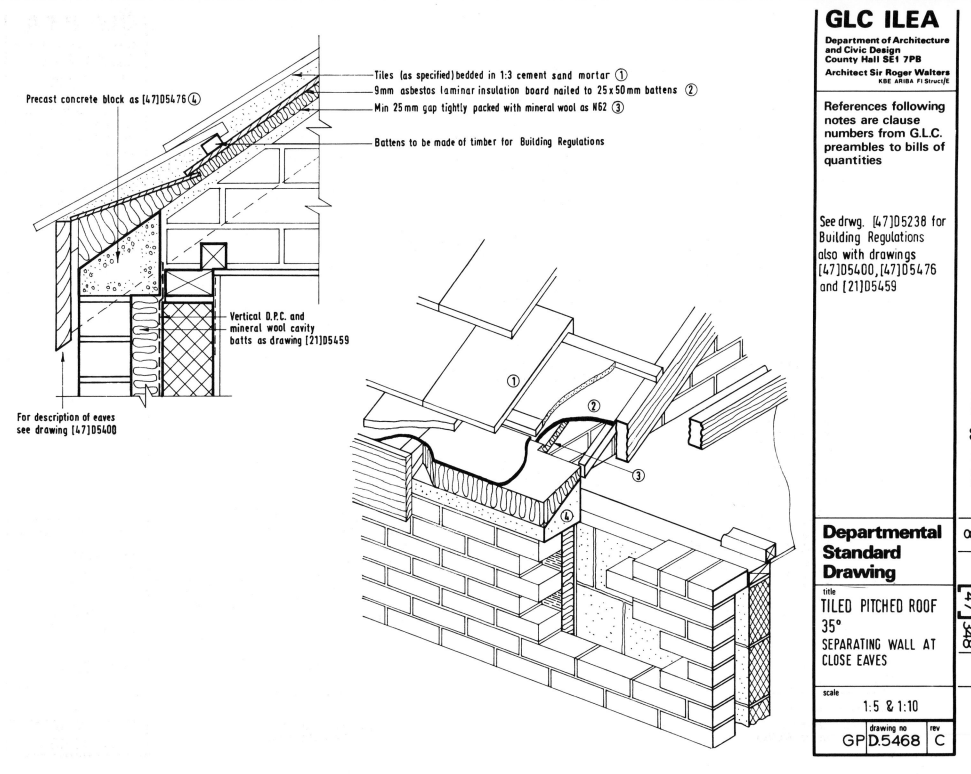

Tiles (as specified) bedded in 1:3 cement sand mortar ①
9mm asbestos laminar insulation board nailed to 25×50mm battens ②
Min 25mm gap tightly packed with mineral wool as N62 ③

Precast concrete block as [47]D5476 ④

Battens to be made of timber for Building Regulations

Vertical D.P.C. and mineral wool cavity batts as drawing [21]D5459

For description of eaves see drawing [47]D5400

GLC ILEA

Department of Architecture and Civic Design County Hall SE1 7PB

Architect Sir Roger Walters
KBE ARIBA FI Struct/E

References following notes are clause numbers from G.L.C. preambles to bills of quantities

See drwg. [47]D5238 for Building Regulations also with drawings [47]D5400, [47]D5476 and [21]D5459

J6/0376C

230279B **00**

	bldg type	space use	element	feature	material	key
	8		47	348		

Departmental Standard Drawing

title
TILED PITCHED ROOF 35°
SEPARATING WALL AT CLOSE EAVES

scale
1:5 & 1:10

	drawing no	rev
GP	D.5468	C

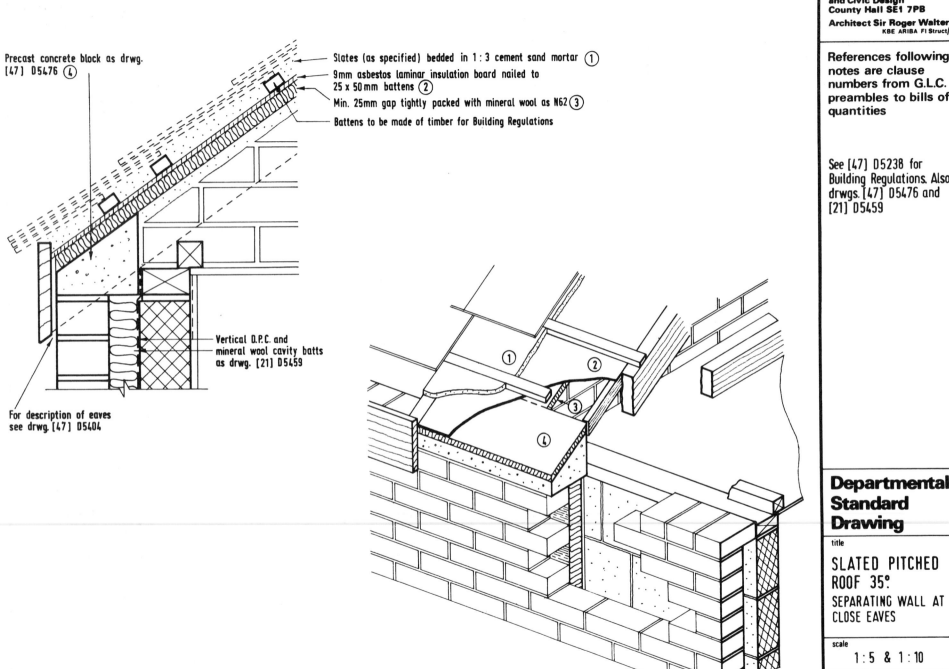

Precast concrete block as drwg.
[47] D5476 ④

Slates (as specified) bedded in 1:3 cement sand mortar ①
9mm asbestos laminar insulation board nailed to
25 x 50mm battens ②
Min. 25mm gap tightly packed with mineral wool as N62 ③
Battens to be made of timber for Building Regulations

Vertical D.P.C. and
mineral wool cavity batts
as drwg. [21] D5459

For description of eaves
see drwg. [47] D5404

GLC ILEA

**Department of Architecture
and Civic Design
County Hall SE1 7PB**

Architect Sir Roger Walters
KBE ARIBA FI Struct/E

**References following
notes are clause
numbers from G.L.C.
preambles to bills of
quantities**

See [47] D5238 for
Building Regulations. Also
drwgs. [47] D5476 and
[21] D5459

36/E0010 - **00**

022079 B

**Departmental
Standard
Drawing**

bldg type	space/use	element	feature	material	key
8		47	348		

title

SLATED PITCHED
ROOF 35°.
SEPARATING WALL AT
CLOSE EAVES

scale

1:5 & 1:10

	drawing no	rev
GP	D.5469	C

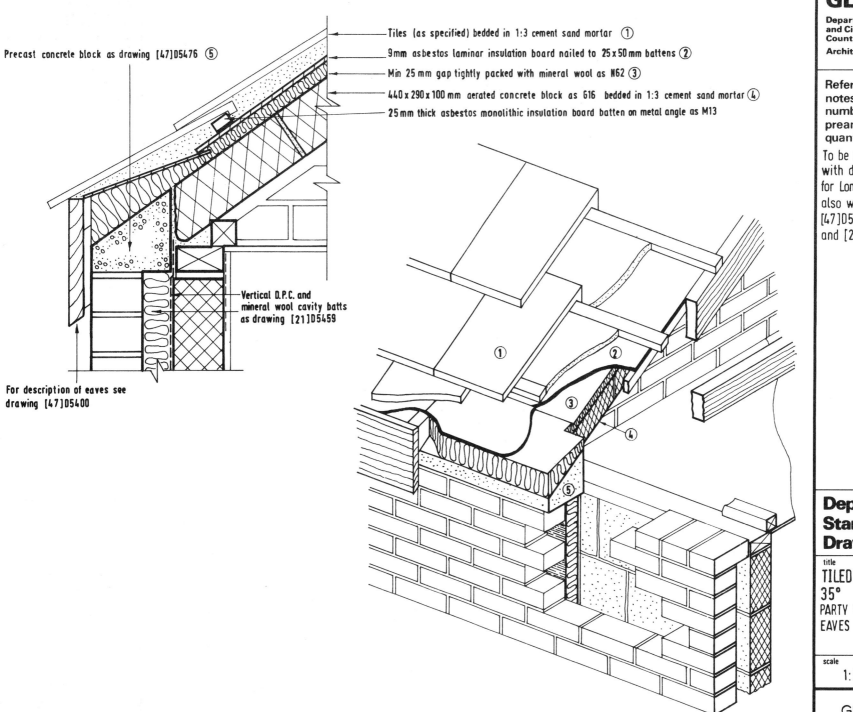

Precast concrete block as drawing [47]D5476 ⑤

Tiles (as specified) bedded in 1:3 cement sand mortar ①

9mm asbestos laminar insulation board nailed to 25 x 50 mm battens ②

Min 25 mm gap tightly packed with mineral wool as N62 ③

440 x 290 x 100 mm aerated concrete block as G16 bedded in 1:3 cement sand mortar ④

25 mm thick asbestos monolithic insulation board batten on metal angle as M13

Vertical D.P.C. and
mineral wool cavity batts
as drawing [21]D5459

For description of eaves see
drawing [47]D5400

GLC ILEA

**Department of Architecture
and Civic Design
County Hall SE1 7PB**

Architect Sir Roger Walters
KBE ARIBA FI Struct/E

**References following
notes are clause
numbers from G.L.C.
preambles to bills of
quantities**

To be read in conjunction
with drawings [47]D5237
for London Building Bylaws
also with drawings
[47]D5400,[47]D5476
and [21]D5459

036E010 - 00

Departmental
Standard
Drawing

bldgtype 8

space use

element 47

feature 348

material

key

title
TILED PITCHED ROOF
35°
PARTY WALL AT CLOSE
EAVES

scale
1:5 and 1:10

GP | drawing no D.5470 | rev C

Slates (as specified) bedded in 1:3 cement sand mortar ①

9mm asbestos laminar insulation board nailed to
25 x 50mm battens ②

Min. 25mm gap tightly packed with mineral wool as N62 ③

440 x 290 x 100mm aerated concrete blocks as G16 bedded
in 1:3 cement sand mortar ④

25mm thick asbestos monolithic insulation board batten on
metal angle as M13

Precast concrete block as drwg.
[47] D5476 ⑤

Vertical D.P.C. and
mineral wool cavity batts
as drwg. [21] D5459

For description of eaves
see drwg. [47] D5404

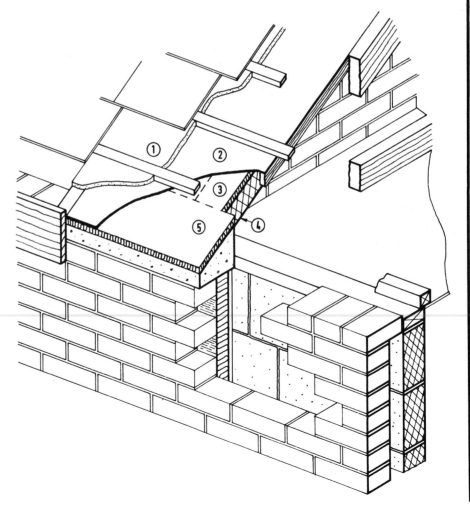

GLC ILEA

**Department of Architecture
and Civic Design
County Hall SE1 7PB**

Architect Sir Roger Walters
KBE ARIBA FI Struct/E

**References following
notes are clause
numbers from G.L.C.
preambles to bills of
quantities**

To be read in conjunction
with drwgs. [47] D5404
and [47] D5237 for
London Building Bylaws.
Also drwgs. [47] D5476
and [21] D5459.

9760310 - 00

220279 B

bldg type 8

space use

element [47]

feature 348

material

key

Departmental Standard Drawing

title

SLATED PITCHED
ROOF 35°
PARTY WALL AT CLOSE
EAVES

scale
1:5 & 1:10

G P | drawing no D.5471 | rev C

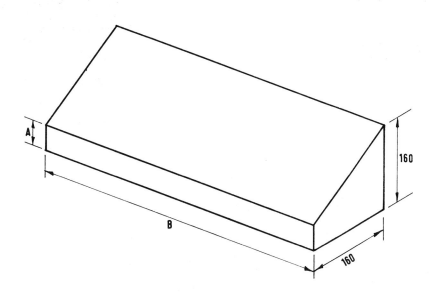

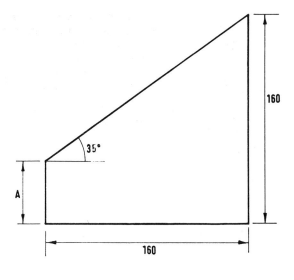

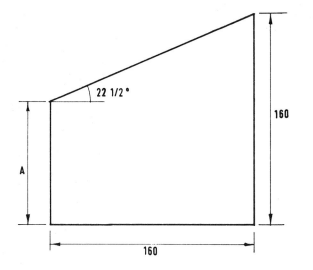

NOTE

Dimension A varies with the pitch of the roof, and should be obtained by measurement on site with the top of the block set at the appropriate pitch.

The length of the block, dimension B, should be such that the block fits inbetween the roof trusses, and should be measured on site.

GLC ILEA

Department of Architecture and Civic Design
County Hall SE1 7PB

Architect Sir Roger Walters
KBE ARIBA FI Struct/E

References following notes are clause numbers from G.L.C. preambles to bills of quantities

A.280679

00 - 010379

bldg type 8

space use

element 47

feature 348

material

key

Departmental Standard Drawing

title
SETTING OUT OF CONCRETE BLOCK FOR PARTY/SEPARATING WALL AT EAVES.

scale
1:2 & 1:5

GP | drawing no
D5476 | rev

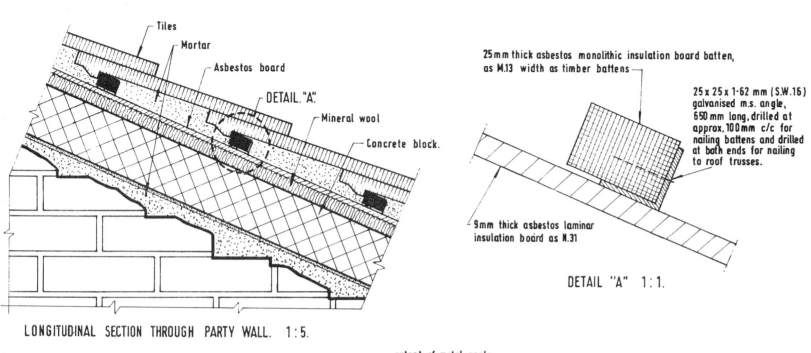

Tiles

Mortar

Asbestos board

DETAIL "A".

Mineral wool

Concrete block.

LONGITUDINAL SECTION THROUGH PARTY WALL. 1:5.

25mm thick asbestos monolithic insulation board batten, as M.13 width as timber battens

25 x 25 x 1·62 mm (S.W.16) galvanised m.s. angle, 650 mm long, drilled at approx. 100mm c/c for nailing battens and drilled at both ends for nailing to roof trusses.

9mm thick asbestos laminar insulation board as N.31

DETAIL "A" 1:1.

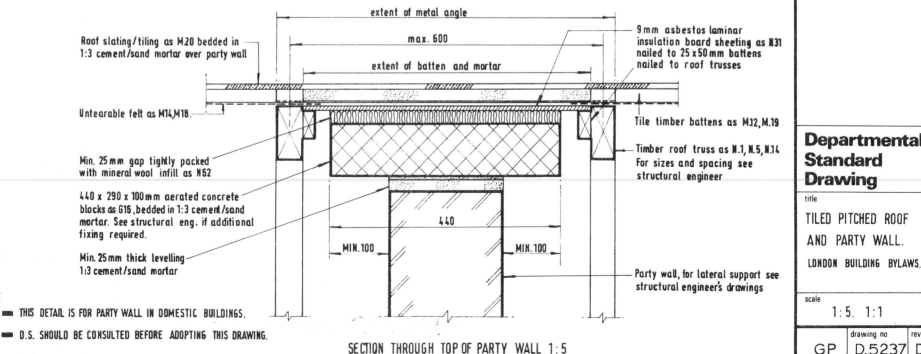

extent of metal angle

max. 600

extent of batten and mortar

9 mm asbestos laminar insulation board sheeting as N31 nailed to 25 x 50 mm battens nailed to roof trusses

Roof slating / tiling as M.20 bedded in 1:3 cement/sand mortar over party wall

Untearable felt as M14, M18.

Tile timber battens as M.12, M.19

Min. 25 mm gap tightly packed with mineral wool infill as N62

Timber roof truss as N.1, N.5, N.14 For sizes and spacing see structural engineer

440 x 290 x 100mm aerated concrete blocks as G16, bedded in 1:3 cement/sand mortar. See structural eng. if additional fixing required.

440

Min. 25 mm thick levelling 1:3 cement/sand mortar

MIN.100   MIN.100

Party wall, for lateral support see structural engineer's drawings

NOTE:

◼◼◼ THIS DETAIL IS FOR PARTY WALL IN DOMESTIC BUILDINGS.

◼◼◼ D.S. SHOULD BE CONSULTED BEFORE ADOPTING THIS DRAWING.

SECTION THROUGH TOP OF PARTY WALL 1:5

GLC ILEA

Department of Architecture and Civic Design
County Hall SE1 7PB
Architect F B Pooley C B E

References following notes are clause numbers from G.L.C. preambles to bills of quantities

This drawing to be read in conjunction with job drawings.

C 090578 D.140279. 01-0010

Departmental Standard Drawing

bldg type	space use	element	feature	material	key
		47			

title

TILED PITCHED ROOF AND PARTY WALL.

LONDON BUILDING BYLAWS.

scale
1:5. 1:1

	drawing no	rev
GP	D.5237	D

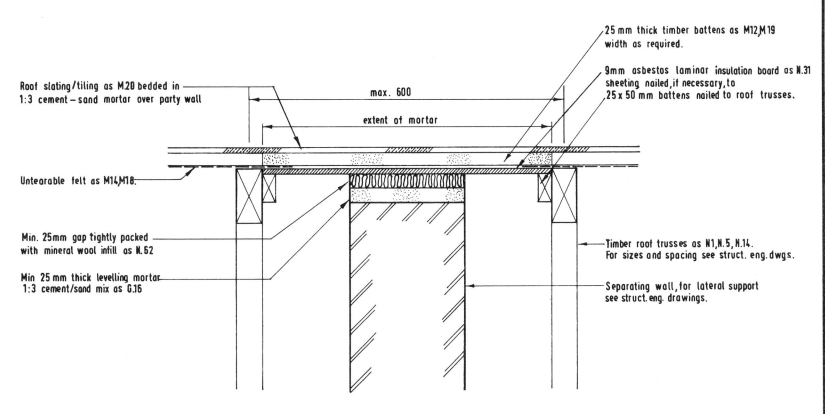

Roof slating/tiling as M.20 bedded in — 1:3 cement – sand mortar over party wall

25 mm thick timber battens as M.12,M.19 width as required.

9mm asbestos laminar insulation board as N.31 sheeting nailed, if necessary, to 25 x 50 mm battens nailed to roof trusses.

max. 600

extent of mortar

Untearable felt as M.14,M.18.

Min. 25mm gap tightly packed with mineral wool infill as N.62

Min 25 mm thick levelling mortar 1:3 cement/sand mix as G.16

Timber roof trusses as N.1,N.5,N.14. For sizes and spacing see struct. eng. dwgs.

Separating wall, for lateral support see struct. eng. drawings.

SECTION THROUGH TOP OF SEPARATING WALL 1:5

NOTE: THIS DETAIL IS FOR SEPARATING WALL IN DOMESTIC BUILDINGS (Outside London area)

GLC ILEA

Department of Architecture and Civic Design County Hall SE1 7PB

Architect Sir Roger Walters
KBE ARIBA FI Struct/E

References following notes are clause numbers from G.L.C. preambles to bills of quantities

This drawing is to be read in conjunction with job drawings.

C: 9/5/78   00 – 010379

Departmental Standard Drawing

bldg type	
space use	
element	47
feature	348
material	Sy
key	DID

title

TILED PITCHED ROOF AND SEPARATING WALL BUILDING REGULATIONS

scale   1:5

	drawing no	rev
GP	D.5238	C

63

Entrance
Porches

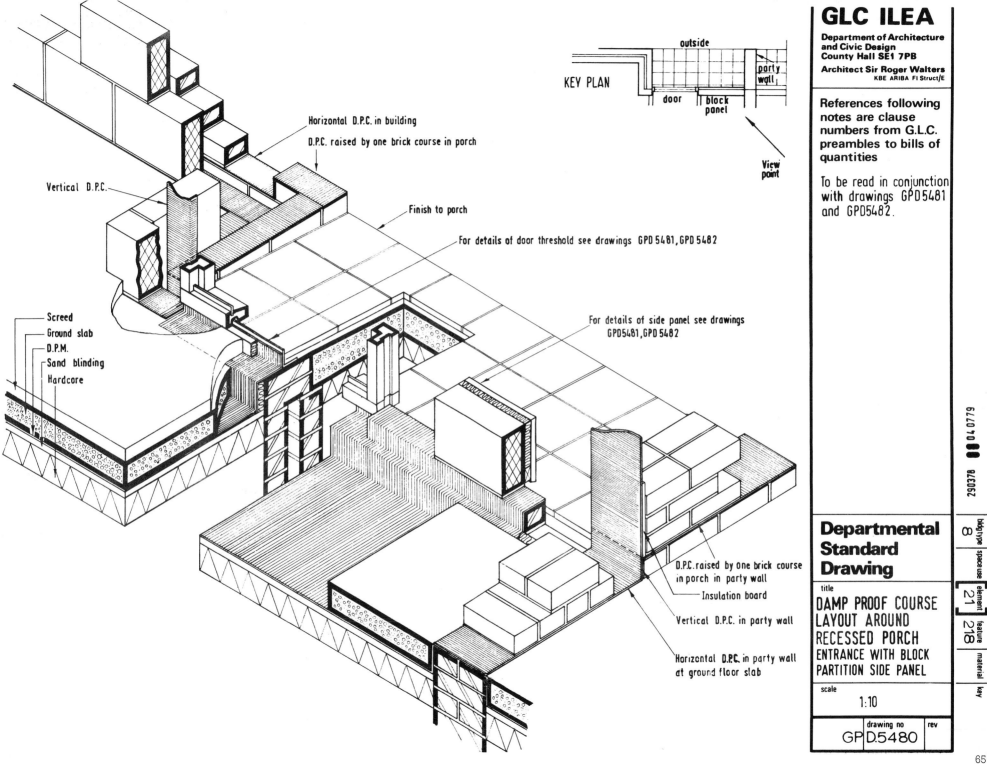

KEY PLAN

outside

door

block
panel

party
wall

View
point

Horizontal D.P.C. in building

D.P.C. raised by one brick course in porch

Vertical D.P.C.

Finish to porch

For details of door threshold see drawings GPD 5481, GPD 5482

For details of side panel see drawings GPD 5481, GPD 5482

Screed
Ground slab
D.P.M.
Sand blinding
Hardcore

D.P.C. raised by one brick course in porch in party wall

Insulation board

Vertical D.P.C. in party wall

Horizontal D.P.C. in party wall at ground floor slab

GLC ILEA

Department of Architecture and Civic Design
County Hall SE1 7PB

Architect Sir Roger Walters
KBE ARIBA FI Struct/E

References following notes are clause numbers from G.L.C. preambles to bills of quantities

To be read in conjunction with drawings GPD 5481 and GPD 5482.

2920410079

2920 8078

bldgtype 8

space use

element 21

feature 218

material

key

Departmental Standard Drawing

title
DAMP PROOF COURSE LAYOUT AROUND RECESSED PORCH ENTRANCE WITH BLOCK PARTITION SIDE PANEL

scale
1:10

drawing no
GPD 5480

rev

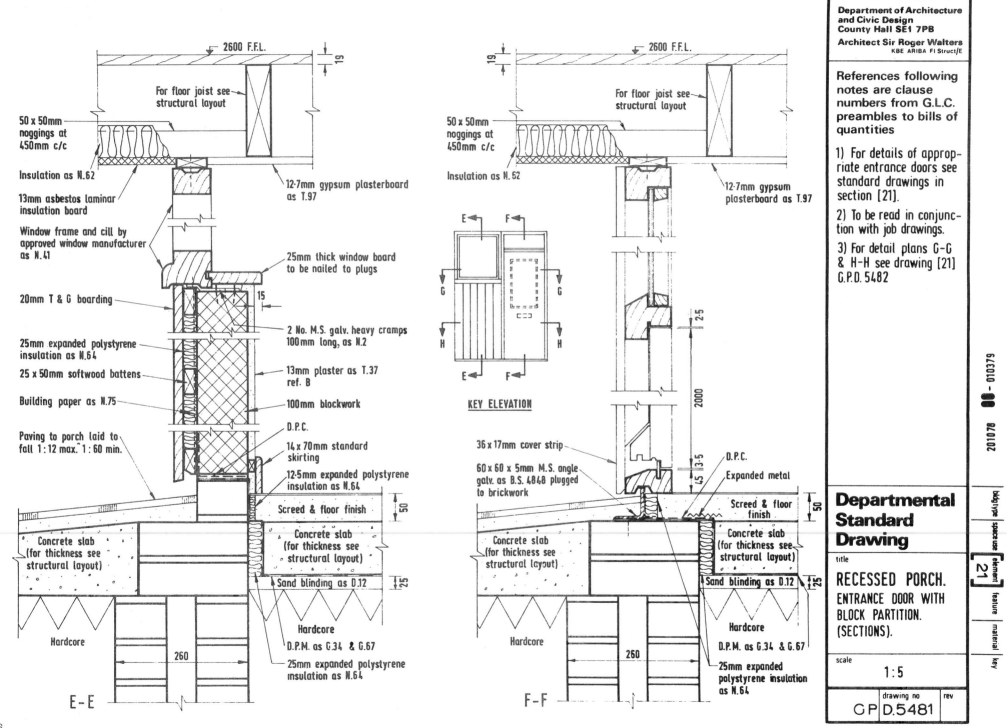

E-E section labels

2600 F.F.L.

19

For floor joist see structural layout

50 x 50mm noggings at 450mm c/c

Insulation as N.62

13mm asbestos laminar insulation board

Window frame and cill by approved window manufacturer as N.41

20mm T & G boarding

25mm expanded polystyrene insulation as N.64

25 x 50mm softwood battens

Building paper as N.75

Paving to porch laid to fall 1:12 max. 1:60 min.

12·7mm gypsum plasterboard as T.97

25mm thick window board to be nailed to plugs

15

2 No. M.S. galv. heavy cramps 100mm long, as N.2

13mm plaster as T.37 ref. B

100mm blockwork

D.P.C.

14 x 70mm standard skirting

12·5mm expanded polystyrene insulation as N.64

Screed & floor finish

50

Concrete slab (for thickness see structural layout)

Concrete slab (for thickness see structural layout)

Sand blinding as D.12

25

Hardcore

Hardcore

260

D.P.M. as G.34 & G.67

25mm expanded polystyrene insulation as N.64

E-E

KEY ELEVATION

E   F

G   G

H   H

E   F

KEY ELEVATION

F-F section labels

2600 F.F.L.

19

For floor joist see structural layout

50 x 50mm noggings at 450mm c/c

Insulation as N.62

12·7mm gypsum plasterboard as T.97

2·5

2000

3·5

45

36 x 17mm cover strip

60 x 60 x 5mm M.S. angle galv. as B.S. 4848 plugged to brickwork

D.P.C.

Expanded metal

Screed & floor finish

50

Concrete slab (for thickness see structural layout)

Concrete slab (for thickness see structural layout)

Sand blinding as D.12

25

Hardcore

Hardcore

260

D.P.M. as G.34 & G.67

25mm expanded polystyrene insulation as N.64

F-F

GLC ILEA

Department of Architecture and Civic Design
County Hall SE1 7PB
Architect Sir Roger Walters
KBE ARIBA FI Struct/E

References following notes are clause numbers from G.L.C. preambles to bills of quantities

1) For details of appropriate entrance doors see standard drawings in section [21].

2) To be read in conjunction with job drawings.

3) For detail plans G-G & H-H see drawing [21] G.P.D. 5482

00 - 010379

201078

Departmental Standard Drawing

bldg type | space use | element | feature | material | key

21

title

RECESSED PORCH. ENTRANCE DOOR WITH BLOCK PARTITION. (SECTIONS).

scale
1:5

drawing no | rev
G P D.5481

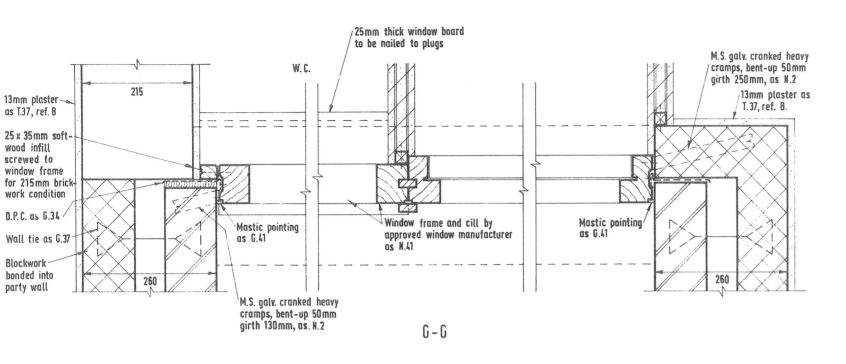

25mm thick window board
to be nailed to plugs

W.C.

M.S. galv. cranked heavy
cramps, bent-up 50mm
girth 250mm, as N.2

13mm plaster as
T.37, ref. B.

13mm plaster
as T.37, ref. B

215

25 x 35mm soft-
wood infill
screwed to
window frame
for 215mm brick-
work condition

D.P.C. as G.34

Wall tie as G.37

Blockwork
bonded into
party wall

Mastic pointing
as G.41

260

M.S. galv. cranked heavy
cramps, bent-up 50mm
girth 130mm, as. N.2

Window frame and cill by
approved window manufacturer
as N.41

Mastic pointing
as G.41

260

G-G

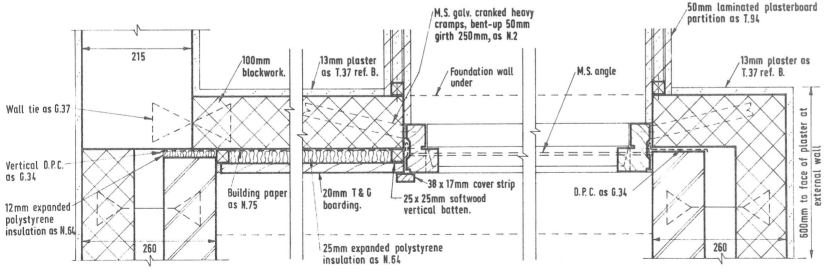

M.S. galv. cranked heavy
cramps, bent-up 50mm
girth 250mm, as N.2

50mm laminated plasterboard
partition as T.94

215

100mm
blockwork.

13mm plaster
as T.37 ref. B.

Foundation wall
under

M.S. angle

13mm plaster as
T.37 ref. B.

Wall tie as G.37

Vertical D.P.C.
as G.34

12mm expanded
polystyrene
insulation as N.64

Building paper
as N.75

20mm T & G
boarding.

38 x 17mm cover strip

25 x 25mm softwood
vertical batten.

D.P.C. as G.34

600mm to face of plaster at
external wall

260

25mm expanded polystyrene
insulation as N.64

260

H-H

GLC ILEA

**Department of Architecture
and Civic Design
County Hall SE1 7PB
Architect Sir Roger Walters**
KBE ARIBA FI Struct/E.

References following
notes are clause
numbers from G.L.C.
preambles to bills of
quantities

1) For details of approp-
riate entrance doors see
standard drawings in
section [21].

2) To be read in conjunc-
tion with job drawings.

3) To be read in conjunc-
tion with drawing [21]
G.P.D. 5481 (Sections).

25 1074 00 08 - 013379

bldg type	space use	element	feature	material	key

**Departmental
Standard
Drawing**

[21]

title

**RECESSED PORCH.
ENTRANCE DOOR WITH
BLOCK PARTITION
(PLANS)**

scale
1:5

drawing no	rev
GP D.5482	

67

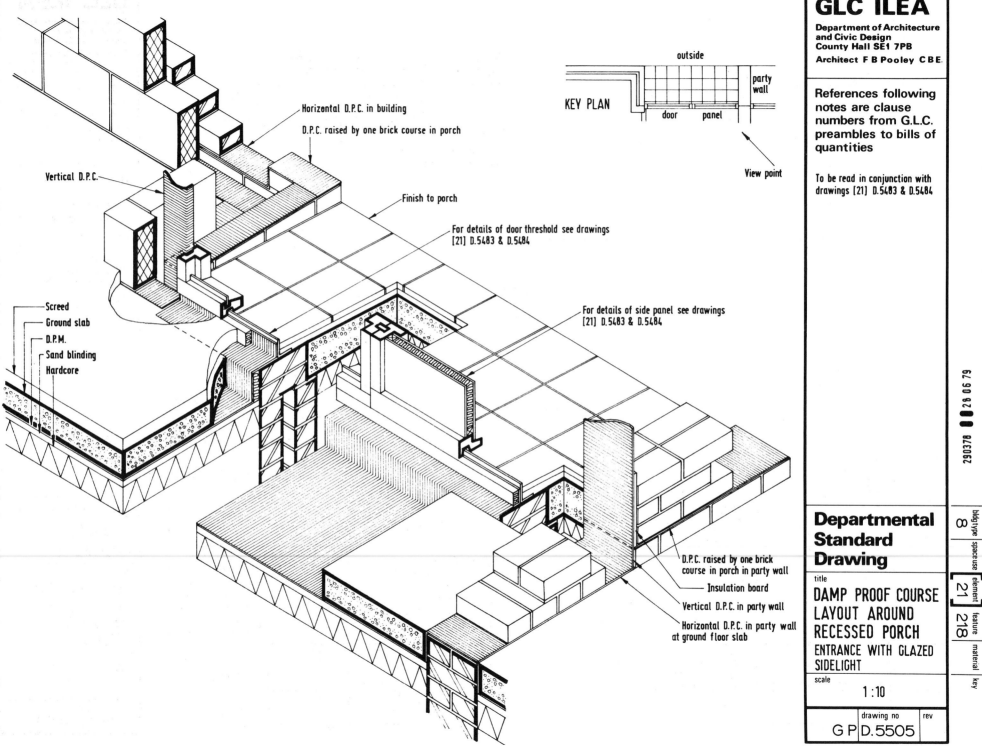

KEY PLAN

outside

party wall

door   panel

View point

Horizontal D.P.C. in building

D.P.C. raised by one brick course in porch

Vertical D.P.C.

Finish to porch

For details of door threshold see drawings [21] D.5483 & D.5484

For details of side panel see drawings [21] D.5483 & D.5484

Screed
Ground slab
D.P.M.
Sand blinding
Hardcore

D.P.C. raised by one brick course in porch in party wall

Insulation board

Vertical D.P.C. in party wall

Horizontal D.P.C. in party wall at ground floor slab

GLC ILEA

Department of Architecture and Civic Design
County Hall SE1 7PB
Architect F B Pooley C B E.

References following notes are clause numbers from G.L.C. preambles to bills of quantities

To be read in conjunction with drawings [21] D.5483 & D.5484

Departmental Standard Drawing

bldg type 8

space use

title

DAMP PROOF COURSE LAYOUT AROUND RECESSED PORCH ENTRANCE WITH GLAZED SIDELIGHT

element 21

feature 218

material

key

scale

1:10

	drawing no	rev
G P	D.5505	

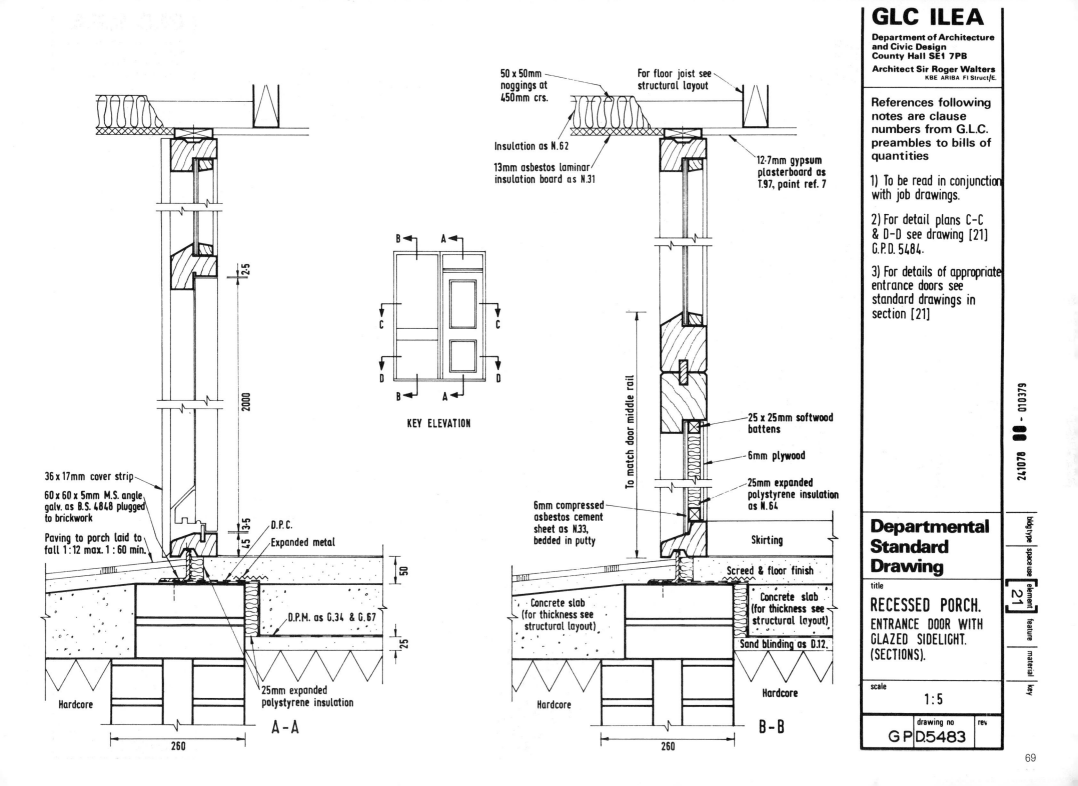

50 x 50mm noggings at 450mm crs.

For floor joist see structural layout

Insulation as N.62

13mm asbestos laminar insulation board as N.31

12·7mm gypsum plasterboard as T.97, paint ref. 7

KEY ELEVATION

B — A
C — C
D — D
B — A

2·5

2000

36 x 17mm cover strip

60 x 60 x 5mm M.S. angle galv. as B.S. 4848 plugged to brickwork

Paving to porch laid to fall 1:12 max. 1:60 min.

D.P.C.

Expanded metal

4·5 3·5

50

25

D.P.M. as G.34 & G.67

25mm expanded polystyrene insulation

Hardcore

260

A - A

To match door middle rail

25 x 25mm softwood battens

6mm plywood

25mm expanded polystyrene insulation as N.64

6mm compressed asbestos cement sheet as N.33, bedded in putty

Skirting

Screed & floor finish

Concrete slab (for thickness see structural layout)

Concrete slab (for thickness see structural layout)

Sand blinding as D.12.

Hardcore

Hardcore

260

B - B

GLC ILEA

Department of Architecture and Civic Design
County Hall SE1 7PB

Architect Sir Roger Walters
KBE ARIBA FI Struct/E.

References following notes are clause numbers from G.L.C. preambles to bills of quantities

1) To be read in conjunction with job drawings.

2) For detail plans C-C & D-D see drawing [21] G.P.D. 5484.

3) For details of appropriate entrance doors see standard drawings in section [21]

6·3·079

2·41078 · 00 - 010·079

Departmental Standard Drawing

bldg type | space use | element | feature | material | key

[21]

title

RECESSED PORCH. ENTRANCE DOOR WITH GLAZED SIDELIGHT. (SECTIONS).

scale

1:5

drawing no | rev

G P D.5483

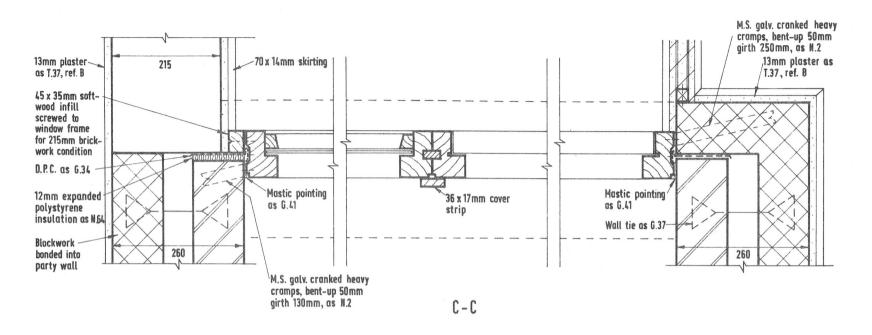

C-C

13mm plaster as T.37, ref. B

215

70 x 14mm skirting

45 x 35mm softwood infill screwed to window frame for 215mm brickwork condition

D.P.C. as G.34

12mm expanded polystyrene insulation as N.64

Blockwork bonded into party wall

260

Mastic pointing as G.41

M.S. galv. cranked heavy cramps, bent-up 50mm girth 130mm, as N.2

36 x 17mm cover strip

M.S. galv. cranked heavy cramps, bent-up 50mm girth 250mm, as N.2

13mm plaster as T.37, ref. B

Mastic pointing as G.41

Wall tie as G.37

260

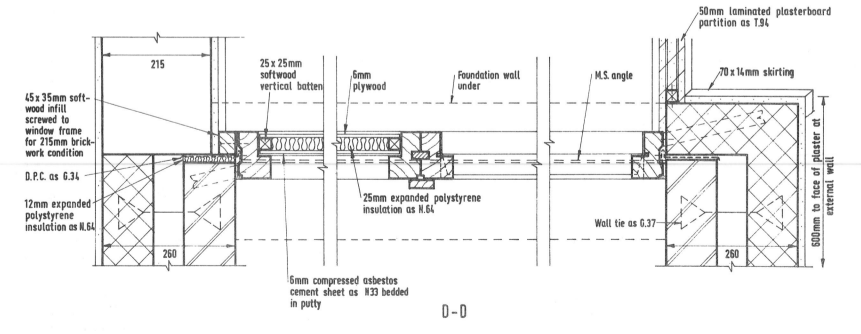

D-D

215

45 x 35mm softwood infill screwed to window frame for 215mm brickwork condition

D.P.C. as G.34

12mm expanded polystyrene insulation as N.64

260

25 x 25mm softwood vertical batten

6mm plywood

6mm compressed asbestos cement sheet as N.33 bedded in putty

25mm expanded polystyrene insulation as N.64

Foundation wall under

M.S. angle

50mm laminated plasterboard partition as T.94

70 x 14mm skirting

Wall tie as G.37

260

600mm to face of plaster at external wall

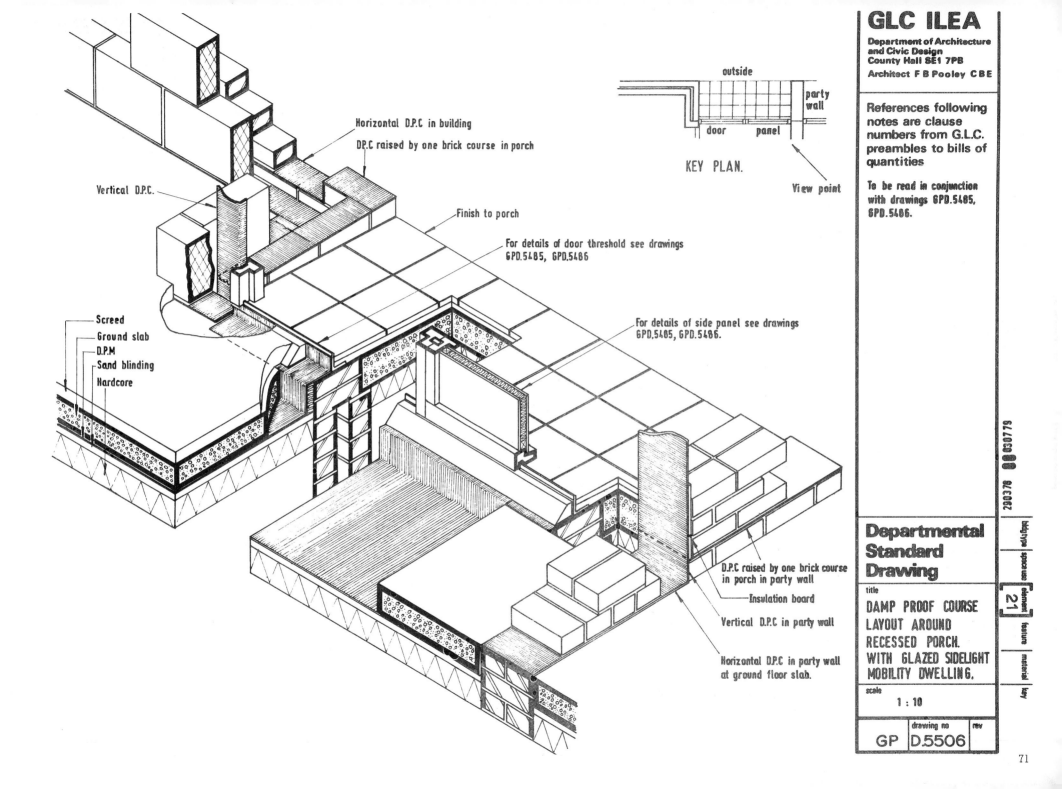

Horizontal D.P.C in building

D.P.C raised by one brick course in porch

Vertical D.P.C.

Finish to porch

For details of door threshold see drawings GPD.5485, GPD.5486.

For details of side panel see drawings GPD.5485, GPD.5486.

Screed
Ground slab
D.P.M
Sand blinding
Hardcore

D.P.C raised by one brick course in porch in party wall

Insulation board

Vertical D.P.C in party wall

Horizontal D.P.C in party wall at ground floor slab.

outside

party wall

door   panel

KEY PLAN.

View point

GLC ILEA

Department of Architecture and Civic Design
County Hall SE1 7PB
Architect F B Pooley CBE

References following notes are clause numbers from G.L.C. preambles to bills of quantities

To be read in conjunction with drawings GPD.5485, GPD.5486.

29037B 00 030779

Departmental Standard Drawing

bldgtype | spaceuse | element | feature | material | key

title
DAMP PROOF COURSE
LAYOUT AROUND
RECESSED PORCH.
WITH GLAZED SIDELIGHT
MOBILITY DWELLING.

element **21**

scale
1 : 10

	drawing no	rev
GP	D.5506	

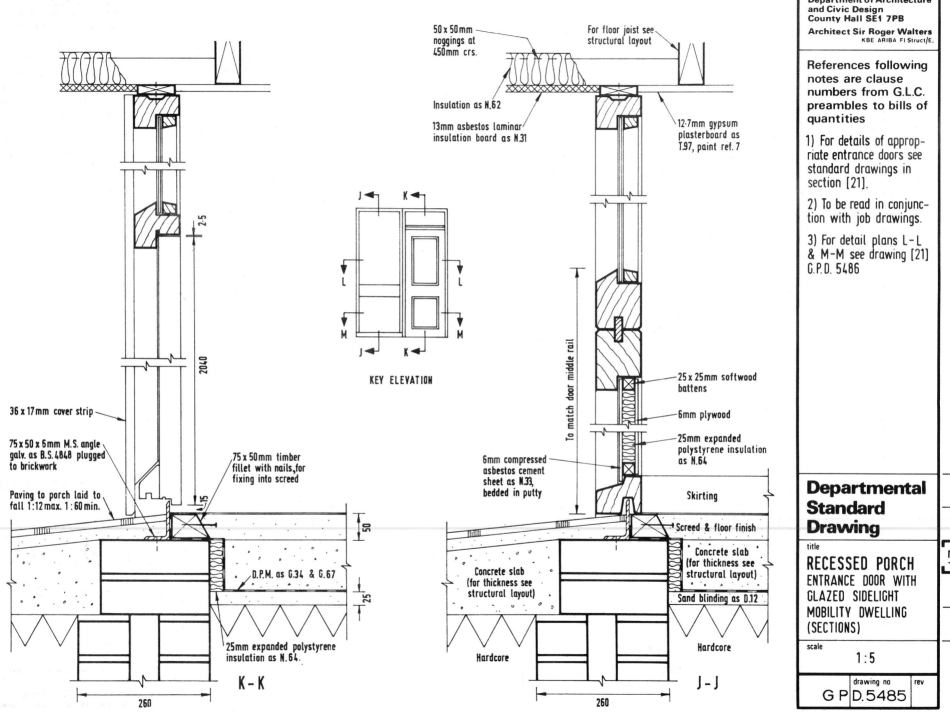

KEY ELEVATION

50 x 50mm noggings at 450mm crs.

For floor joist see structural layout

Insulation as N.62

13mm asbestos laminar insulation board as N.31

12·7mm gypsum plasterboard as T.97, paint ref. 7

36 x 17mm cover strip

75 x 50 x 6mm M.S. angle galv. as B.S. 4848 plugged to brickwork

Paving to porch laid to fall 1:12 max. 1:60 min.

75 x 50mm timber fillet with nails, for fixing into screed

D.P.M. as G.34 & G.67

25mm expanded polystyrene insulation as N.64.

To match door middle rail

25 x 25mm softwood battens

6mm plywood

25mm expanded polystyrene insulation as N.64

6mm compressed asbestos cement sheet as N.33, bedded in putty

Skirting

Screed & floor finish

Concrete slab (for thickness see structural layout)

Concrete slab (for thickness see structural layout)

Sand blinding as D.12

Hardcore

Hardcore

2040

2·5

15

50

25

260

260

K - K

J - J

GLC ILEA

Department of Architecture
and Civic Design
County Hall SE1 7PB
Architect Sir Roger Walters
KBE ARIBA FI Struct/E.

References following notes are clause numbers from G.L.C. preambles to bills of quantities

1) For details of appropriate entrance doors see standard drawings in section [21].

2) To be read in conjunction with job drawings.

3) For detail plans L - L & M-M see drawing [21] G.P.D. 5486

9379 - 010 .251

00 251042 0B

bldgtype | spaceuse | element [21] | feature | material | key

Departmental Standard Drawing

title
RECESSED PORCH ENTRANCE DOOR WITH GLAZED SIDELIGHT MOBILITY DWELLING (SECTIONS)

scale
1:5

drawing no | rev
G P D.5485 |

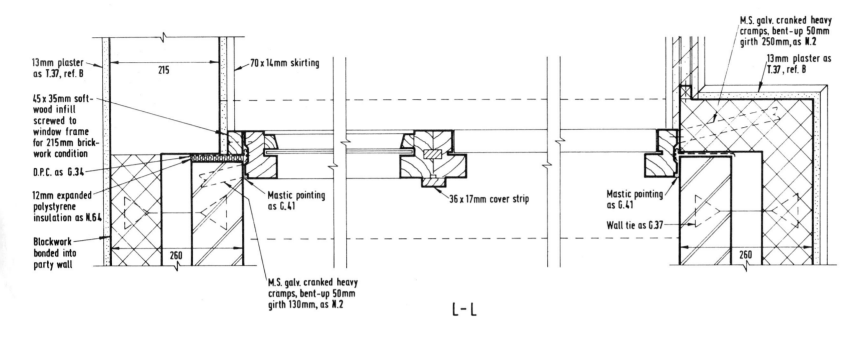

13mm plaster as T.37, ref. B

215

70 x 14mm skirting

M.S. galv. cranked heavy cramps, bent-up 50mm girth 250mm, as N.2

13mm plaster as T.37, ref. B

45 x 35mm softwood infill screwed to window frame for 215mm brickwork condition

D.P.C. as G.34

12mm expanded polystyrene insulation as N.64

Blockwork bonded into party wall

Mastic pointing as G.41

36 x 17mm cover strip

Mastic pointing as G.41

Wall tie as G.37

260

260

M.S. galv. cranked heavy cramps, bent-up 50mm girth 130mm, as N.2

L-L

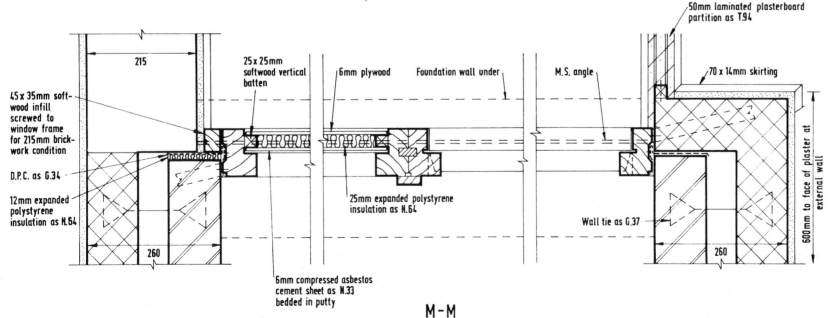

215

45 x 35mm softwood infill screwed to window frame for 215mm brickwork condition

D.P.C. as G.34

12mm expanded polystyrene insulation as N.64

25 x 25mm softwood vertical batten

6mm plywood

Foundation wall under

M.S. angle

50mm laminated plasterboard partition as T.94

70 x 14mm skirting

25mm expanded polystyrene insulation as N.64

Wall tie as G.37

260

600mm to face of plaster at external wall

260

6mm compressed asbestos cement sheet as N.33 bedded in putty

M-M

73

GLC ILEA

Department of Architecture and Civic Design
County Hall SE1 7PB
Architect F B Pooley C B E.

References following notes are clause numbers from G.L.C. preambles to bills of quantities

1) For details of appropriate entrance doors see standard drawings in section [21]

2) To be read in conjunction with job drawings

3) To be read in conjunction with drawing [21] D.5485 (Sections)

20013/79 - 00 - 013/79

20013/78

Departmental Standard Drawing

bldg type

space use

element **21**

feature

material

key

title
RECESSED PORCH ENTRANCE DOOR WITH GLAZED SIDELIGHT MOBILITY DWELLING (PLANS)

scale **1:5**

| G P | drawing no D.5486 | rev |

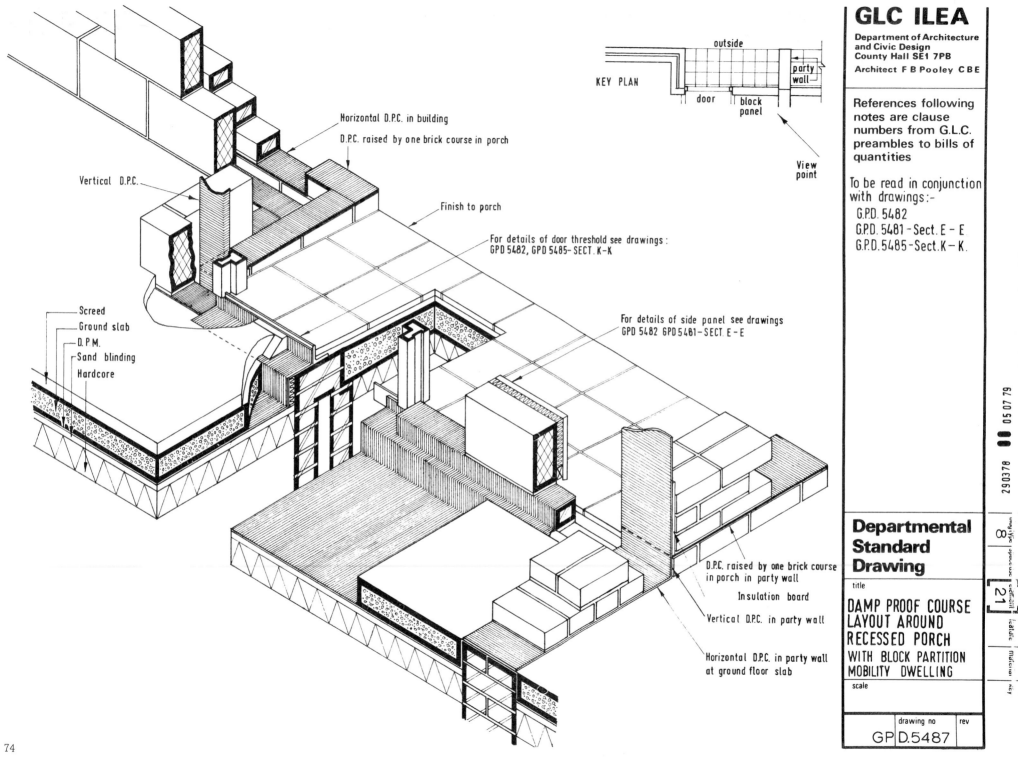

GLC ILEA
Department of Architecture
and Civic Design
County Hall SE1 7PB
Architect F B Pooley CBE

References following
notes are clause
numbers from G.L.C.
preambles to bills of
quantities

To be read in conjunction
with drawings:-
G.P.D. 5482
G.P.D. 5481-Sect. E - E
G.P.D. 5485-Sect. K - K.

KEY PLAN

outside

party wall

door

block panel

View point

Departmental Standard Drawing

title

DAMP PROOF COURSE
LAYOUT AROUND
RECESSED PORCH
WITH BLOCK PARTITION
MOBILITY DWELLING

scale

drawing no | rev

GP D.5487

Horizontal D.P.C. in building

D.P.C. raised by one brick course in porch

Vertical D.P.C.

Finish to porch

For details of door threshold see drawings:
GPD 5482, GPD 5485-SECT. K-K

For details of side panel see drawings
GPD 5482 GPD 5481-SECT. E-E

Screed
Ground slab
D.P.M.
Sand blinding
Hardcore

D.P.C. raised by one brick course
in porch in party wall

Insulation board

Vertical D.P.C. in party wall

Horizontal D.P.C. in party wall
at ground floor slab

74

Roofs

Pitches of $22\frac{1}{2}°$ and 35° are shown as falling within the average range recommended for asbestos cement slates and concrete tiles. $22\frac{1}{2}°$ is the minimum pitch recommended in the GLC for housing work. Pre-made trusses @ 600 mm C/S are assumed. Trusses rest on a standard 100 mm x 50 mm wall plate nailed down. Certain Local Authorities may require additional fixings and this should be checked by the Architect. The last truss should be placed as near to the gable as possible (50 mm) even if the adjoining bay will be less than 600 mm. It is important to space the trusses at 600 mm over party walls to avoid humping.

The main principles in roof design are :—

1 The roof space must be ventilated through the eaves and the special requirements for monopitch roofs should be noted.

2 Cavity walls must be closed to prevent moist air from the cavity entering the roof space.

3 Insulation should be carefully laid at the eaves to prevent blocking of the ventilation.

4 Noggings must be provided between trusses at the perimeter securely nailed to the wall plate to prevent the ceiling board from curling upwards.

5 The bottom edges of fascias should be splayed.

Eaves
Ridge
Ventilation Pipe
Verge
Gable End

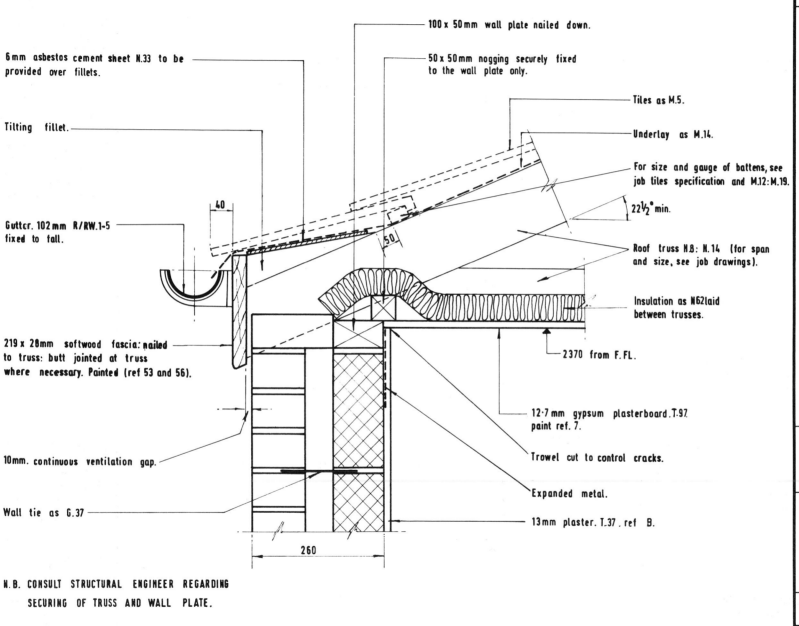

6mm asbestos cement sheet N.33 to be provided over fillets.

Tilting fillet.

Gutter. 102mm R/RW.1-5 fixed to fall.

219 x 28mm softwood fascia: nailed to truss: butt jointed at truss where necessary. Painted (ref 53 and 56).

10mm. continuous ventilation gap.

Wall tie as G.37

40

260

100 x 50mm wall plate nailed down.

50 x 50mm nogging securely fixed to the wall plate only.

Tiles as M.5.

Underlay as M.14.

For size and gauge of battens, see job tiles specification and M.12:M.19.

50

$22\frac{1}{2}°$ min.

Roof truss N.8: N.14 (for span and size, see job drawings).

Insulation as N62 laid between trusses.

2370 from F.FL.

12·7mm gypsum plasterboard.T.97. paint ref. 7.

Trowel cut to control cracks.

Expanded metal.

13mm plaster. T.37. ref B.

N.B. CONSULT STRUCTURAL ENGINEER REGARDING SECURING OF TRUSS AND WALL PLATE.

GLC ILEA

Department of Architecture and Civic Design
County Hall SE1 7PB
Architect Sir Roger Walters
KBE ARIBA FI Struct/E

References following notes are clause numbers from G.L.C. preambles to bills of quantities

To be read in conjunction with drwgs. [47] D5412 and D5420 or D5422- Verge detail or D5414- Verge barge board. D5415 or D5416-Stepped flashing at junction. D5425-Ridge D5430 Vent or D5429- Ridge vent/Flue.

Departmental Standard Drawing

title

CLOSE EAVES.
FOR PITCHED ROOF $22\frac{1}{2}°$
TILED- SINGLE LAP.

scale
1: 5

GP   drawing no   rev
       D5401   A

6Z010-00
8-
bldg type | space use | element | feature | material | key
47 | 176 | N | A21

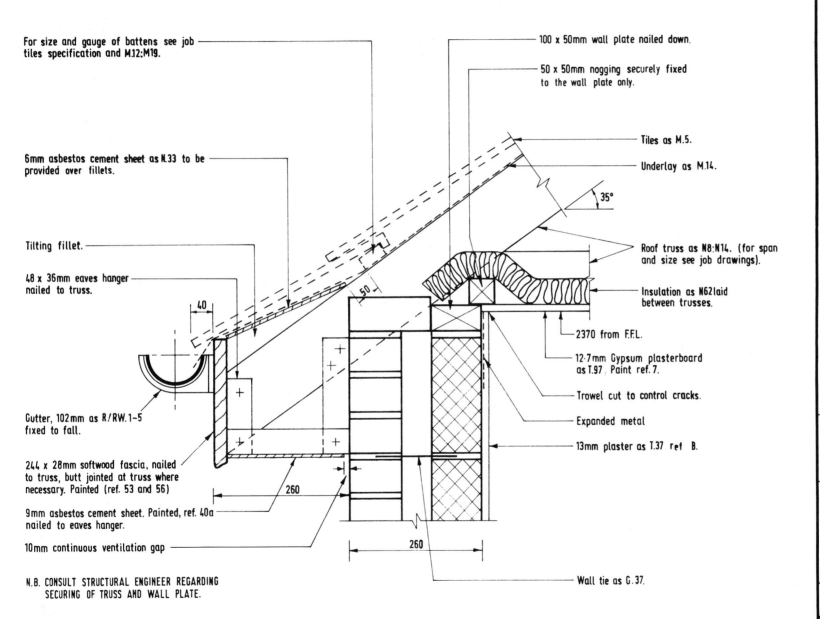

For size and gauge of battens see job tiles specification and M.12:M.19.

6mm asbestos cement sheet as N.33 to be provided over fillets.

Tilting fillet.

48 x 36mm eaves hanger nailed to truss.

40

Gutter, 102mm as R/RW.1-5 fixed to fall.

244 x 28mm softwood fascia, nailed to truss, butt jointed at truss where necessary. Painted (ref. 53 and 56)

9mm asbestos cement sheet. Painted, ref. 40a nailed to eaves hanger.

10mm continuous ventilation gap

N.B. CONSULT STRUCTURAL ENGINEER REGARDING
SECURING OF TRUSS AND WALL PLATE.

100 x 50mm wall plate nailed down.

50 x 50mm nogging securely fixed to the wall plate only.

Tiles as M.5.

Underlay as M.14.

35°

Roof truss as N8:N14. (for span and size see job drawings).

Insulation as N62 laid between trusses.

2370 from F.F.L.

12·7mm Gypsum plasterboard as T.97. Paint ref. 7.

Trowel cut to control cracks.

Expanded metal

13mm plaster as T.37 ref B.

Wall tie as G.37.

50

260

260

GLC ILEA

Department of Architecture and Civic Design
County Hall SE1 7PB
Architect Sir Roger Walters
KBE ARIBA FI Struct/E

References following notes are clause numbers from G.L.C. preambles to bills of quantities

To be read in conjunction with drwgs. [47] D5408 and D5409 – Stopped ends. D5419 or D5421 – Verge detail. D5415 or D5416 – Stepped flashing at junction D5425 – Ridge. D5429 – Ridge vent/flue. D5430 – Vent.

Departmental Standard Drawing

title

BOX EAVES.
FOR PITCHED ROOF 35°
TILED. – SINGLE LAP.

scale

1 : 5

GP	drawing no	rev
GP	D.5402	A

GP/010 - 9/79

bldg type -8

space use

element 47

feature 176

material N

key B11

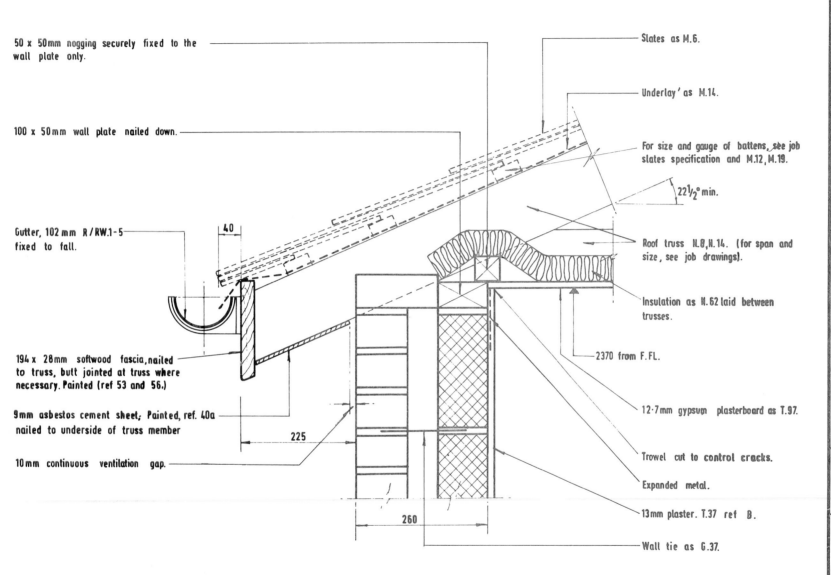

50 x 50mm nogging securely fixed to the wall plate only.

100 x 50mm wall plate nailed down.

Gutter, 102 mm R/RW.1-5 fixed to fall.

40

194 x 28mm softwood fascia, nailed to truss, butt jointed at truss where necessary. Painted (ref 53 and 56.)

9mm asbestos cement sheet; Painted, ref. 40a nailed to underside of truss member

10mm continuous ventilation gap.

225

260

N.B. CONSULT STRUCTURAL ENGINEER REGARDING SECURING OF TRUSS AND WALL PLATE.

Slates as M.6.

Underlay' as M.14.

For size and gauge of battens, see job slates specification and M.12, M.19.

22 1/2° min.

Roof truss N.8, N.14. (for span and size, see job drawings).

Insulation as N.62 laid between trusses.

2370 from F.FL.

12·7mm gypsum plasterboard as T.97.

Trowel cut to control cracks.

Expanded metal.

13mm plaster. T.37 ref B.

Wall tie as G.37.

GLC ILEA

Department of Architecture and Civic Design
County Hall SE1 7PB
Architect Sir Roger Walters
KBE ARIBA FI Struct/E

References following notes are clause numbers from G.L.C. preambles to bills of quantities

To be read in conjunction with drwgs. [47] D5410 and D5411 - Stopped ends.
D5417 - Stepped flashing at junction.
D5424 - Verge detail.
D5426 - Ridge.
D5431 - Vent
D5428 - Ridge vent/flue.

100/0379 00-010.379

bldg type | space use | element | feature | material | key
8- | | 47 | 176 | N | C.22.

Departmental Standard Drawing

title
SLOPING EAVES SOFFIT
FOR PITCHED ROOF 22½°
ASBESTOS CEMENT SLATES.

scale
1 : 5.

| | drawing no | rev |
| GP | D.5407 | B |

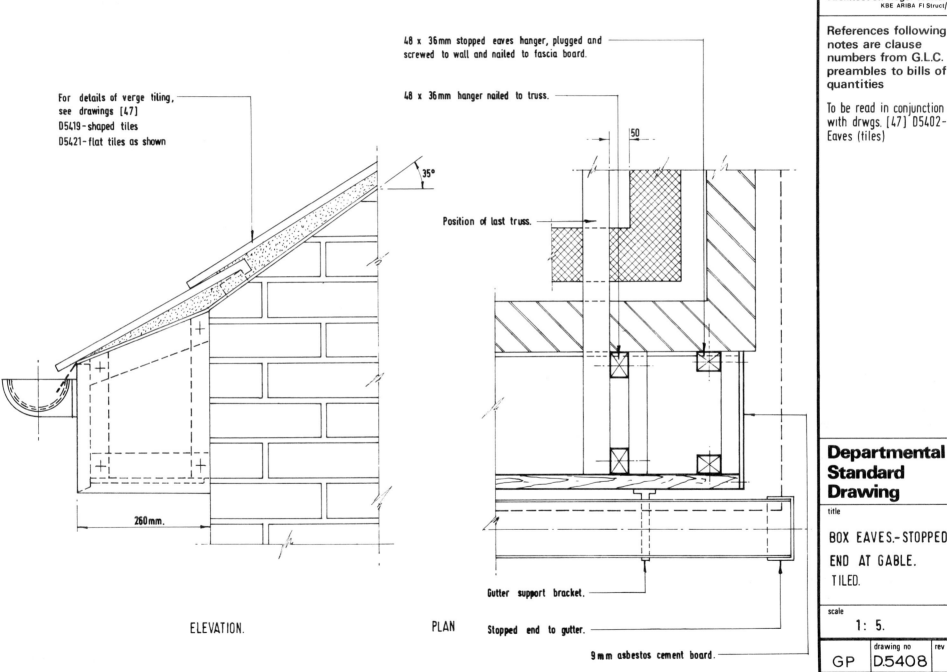

For details of verge tiling,
see drawings [47]
D5419-shaped tiles
D5421-flat tiles as shown

35°

260mm.

ELEVATION.

48 x 36mm stopped eaves hanger, plugged and
screwed to wall and nailed to fascia board.

48 x 36mm hanger nailed to truss.

50

Position of last truss.

PLAN

Gutter support bracket.

Stopped end to gutter.

9mm asbestos cement board.

GLC ILEA

**Department of Architecture
and Civic Design
County Hall SE1 7PB**
Architect Sir Roger Walters
KBE ARIBA FI Struct/E

References following
notes are clause
numbers from G.L.C.
preambles to bills of
quantities

To be read in conjunction
with drwgs. [47] D5402-
Eaves (tiles)

01039 - **00**

8 -

bldg type	space use

**Departmental
Standard
Drawing**

element	[47]	176	N	B.11

title

BOX EAVES.-STOPPED
END AT GABLE.
TILED.

scale

1: 5.

GP	drawing no	rev
	D.5408	

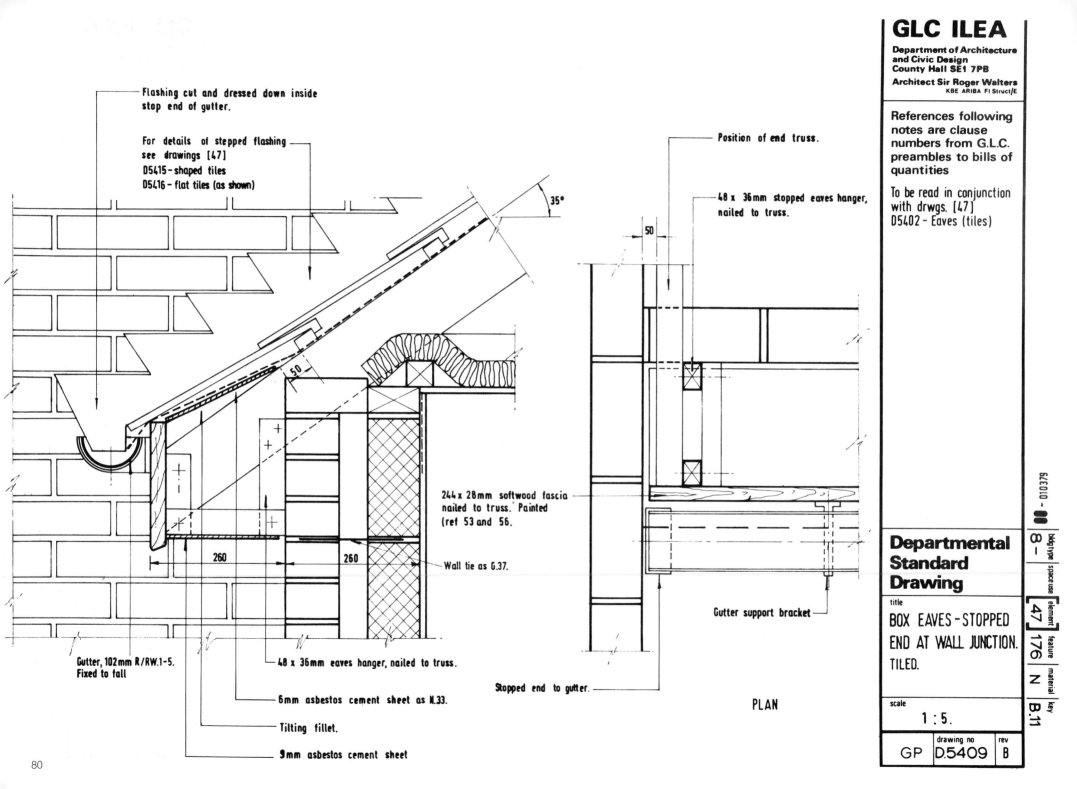

Flashing cut and dressed down inside stop end of gutter.

For details of stepped flashing see drawings [47]
D5415 - shaped tiles
D5416 - flat tiles (as shown)

35°

50

260

260

Gutter, 102mm R/RW.1-5. Fixed to fall

48 x 36mm eaves hanger, nailed to truss.

6mm asbestos cement sheet as N.33.

Tilting fillet.

9mm asbestos cement sheet

244 x 28mm softwood fascia nailed to truss. Painted (ref 53 and 56.

Wall tie as G.37.

Position of end truss.

48 x 36mm stopped eaves hanger, nailed to truss.

50

Gutter support bracket

Stopped end to gutter.

PLAN

GLC ILEA

Department of Architecture and Civic Design
County Hall SE1 7PB
Architect Sir Roger Walters
KBE ARIBA FI Struct/E

References following notes are clause numbers from G.L.C. preambles to bills of quantities

To be read in conjunction with drwgs. [47]
D5402 - Eaves (tiles)

6379010 - 00

bldgtype 8 -

space use [47]

element 176

feature N

material B.11

key

Departmental Standard Drawing

title
BOX EAVES - STOPPED END AT WALL JUNCTION. TILED.

scale
1 : 5.

GP | drawing no D.5409 | rev B

80

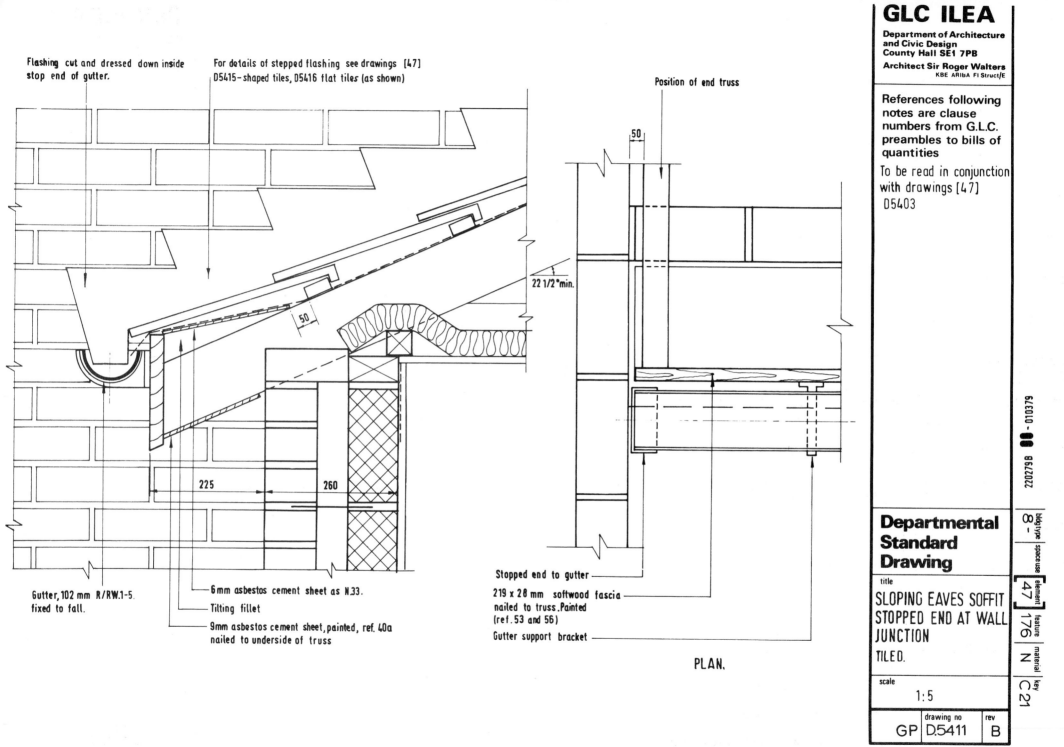

Flashing cut and dressed down inside stop end of gutter.

For details of stepped flashing see drawings [47] D5415-shaped tiles, D5416 flat tiles (as shown)

Position of end truss

50

22 1/2°min.

50

Gutter, 102 mm R/RW.1-5. fixed to fall.

225

260

6 mm asbestos cement sheet as N.33.

Tilting fillet

9mm asbestos cement sheet, painted, ref. 40a nailed to underside of truss

Stopped end to gutter

219 x 28 mm softwood fascia nailed to truss. Painted (ref. 53 and 56)

Gutter support bracket

PLAN.

GLC ILEA

Department of Architecture and Civic Design
County Hall SE1 7PB
Architect Sir Roger Walters
KBE ARIBA FI Struct/E

References following notes are clause numbers from G.L.C. preambles to bills of quantities

To be read in conjunction with drawings [47] D5403

6/E010-0M 86/20202

bldg type 8 -

space use

Departmental Standard Drawing

element 47

title
SLOPING EAVES SOFFIT STOPPED END AT WALL JUNCTION
TILED.

feature 176

material N

key C 21

scale
1:5

GP | drawing no D.5411 | rev B

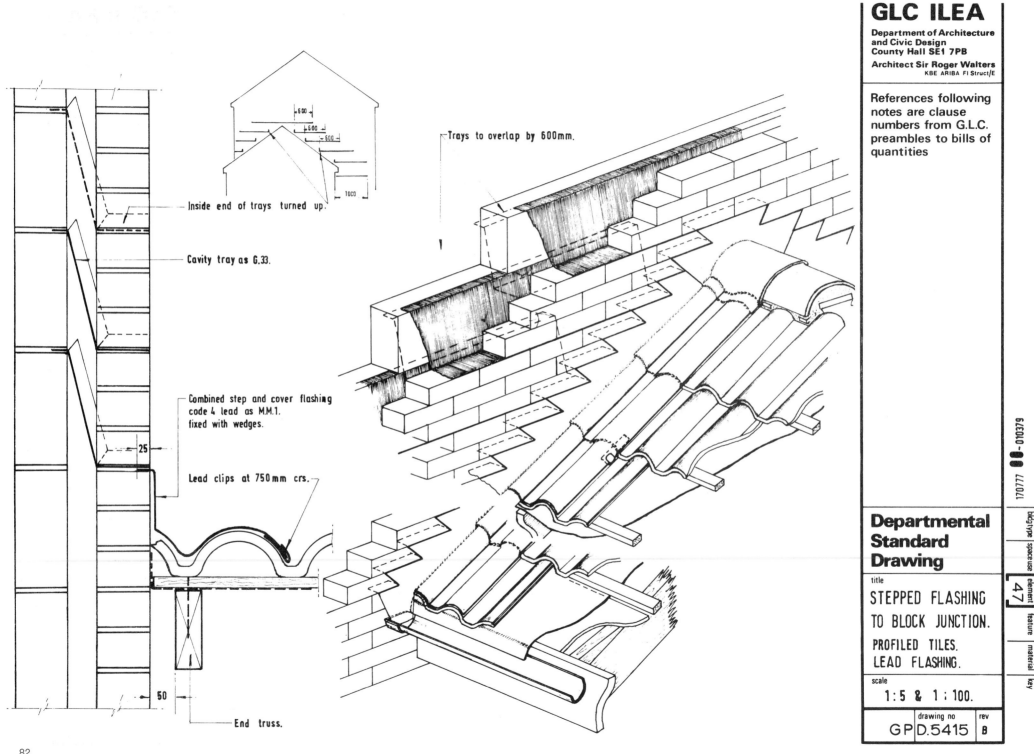

Inside end of trays turned up.

Cavity tray as G.33.

Combined step and cover flashing code 4 lead as M.M.1. fixed with wedges.

25

Lead clips at 750mm crs.

50

End truss.

Trays to overlap by 600mm.

600
600
600
1000

GLC ILEA

Department of Architecture and Civic Design
County Hall SE1 7PB
Architect Sir Roger Walters
KBE ARIBA FI Struct/E

References following notes are clause numbers from G.L.C. preambles to bills of quantities

1-010379
170777
bldg type
space use
47 element
feature
material
key

Departmental Standard Drawing

title
STEPPED FLASHING TO BLOCK JUNCTION. PROFILED TILES. LEAD FLASHING.

scale
1:5 & 1:100.

drawing no	rev
GPD.5415	B

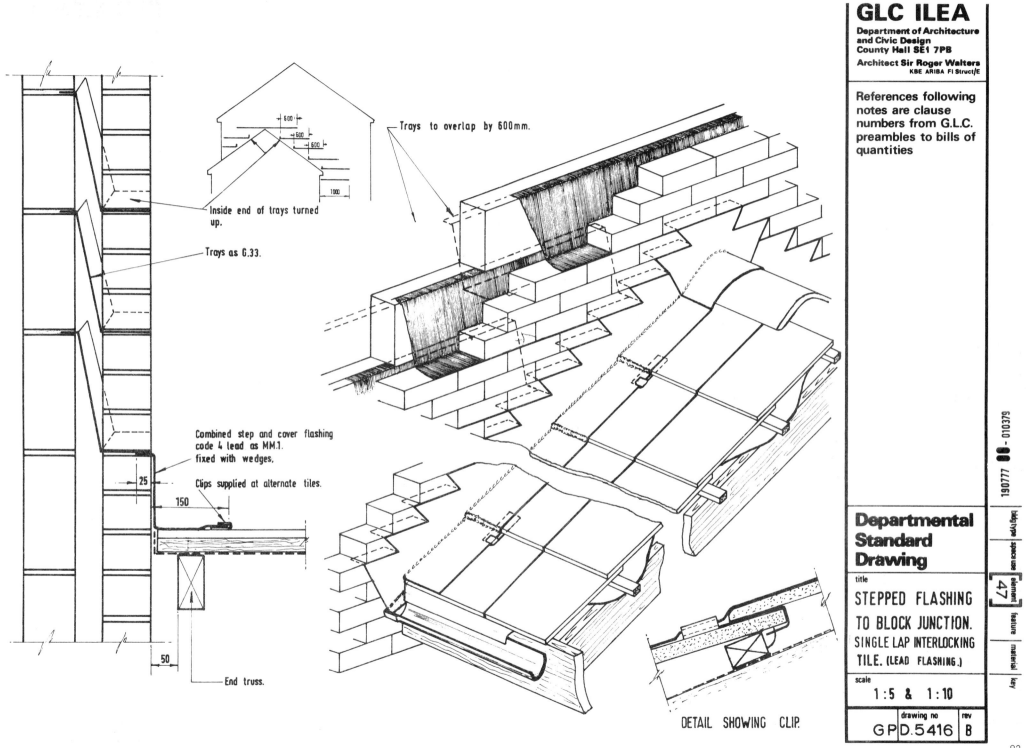

Trays to overlap by 600mm.

Inside end of trays turned up.

Trays as G.33.

Combined step and cover flashing code 4 lead as MM.1. fixed with wedges,

Clips supplied at alternate tiles.

25

150

50

End truss.

DETAIL SHOWING CLIP.

GLC ILEA

**Department of Architecture and Civic Design
County Hall SE1 7PB**

Architect Sir Roger Walters
KBE ARIBA FI Struct/E

References following notes are clause numbers from G.L.C. preambles to bills of quantities

190777 00 - 010379

bldg type	space use	element	feature	material	key

Departmental Standard Drawing

title
STEPPED FLASHING TO BLOCK JUNCTION. SINGLE LAP INTERLOCKING TILE. (LEAD FLASHING.)

scale
1:5 & 1:10

drawing no	rev
G P D. 5416	B

47

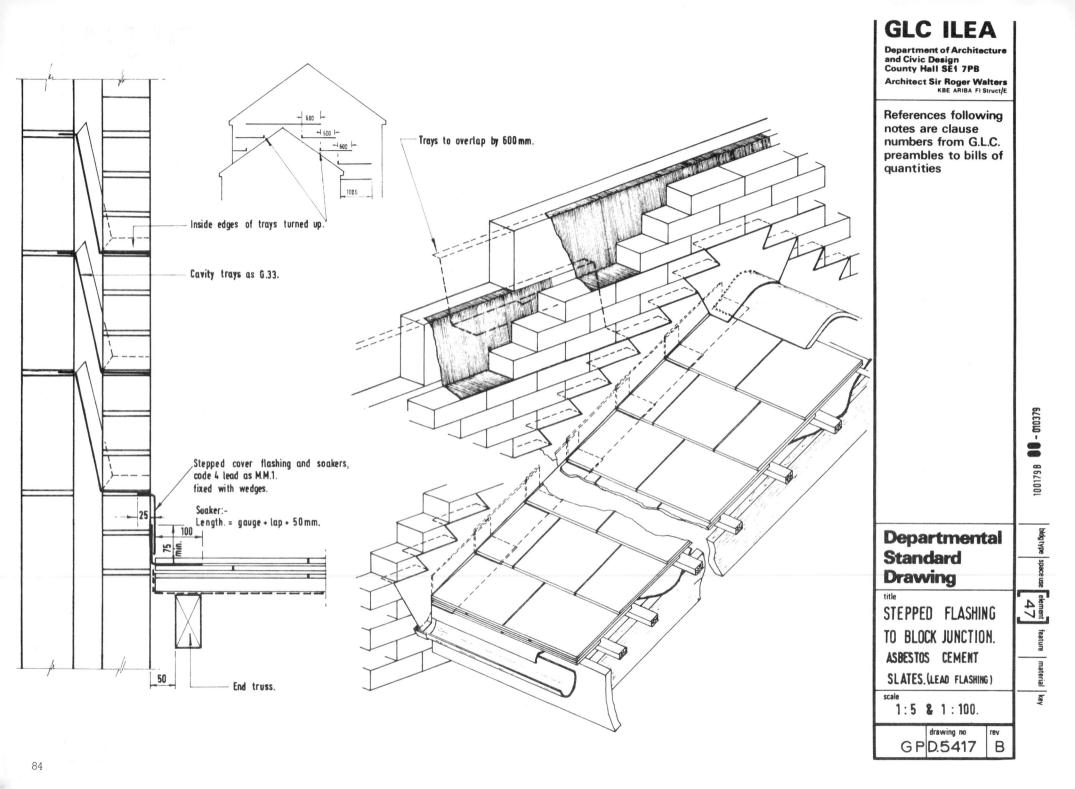

Trays to overlap by 600mm.

Inside edges of trays turned up.

Cavity trays as G.33.

Stepped cover flashing and soakers,
code 4 lead as M.M.1.
fixed with wedges.

Soaker:-
Length. = gauge + lap + 50mm.

End truss.

600

600

600

1000

25

100

75 min.

50

GLC ILEA

**Department of Architecture
and Civic Design
County Hall SE1 7PB**

Architect Sir Roger Walters
KBE ARIBA FI Struct/E

References following
notes are clause
numbers from G.L.C.
preambles to bills of
quantities

100179 B 98 - 01010/79

bldgtype | space use | element | feature | material | key

47

Departmental
Standard
Drawing

title

**STEPPED FLASHING
TO BLOCK JUNCTION.
ASBESTOS CEMENT
SLATES.** (LEAD FLASHING)

scale
1:5 & 1:100.

drawing no	rev
G P D.5417	B

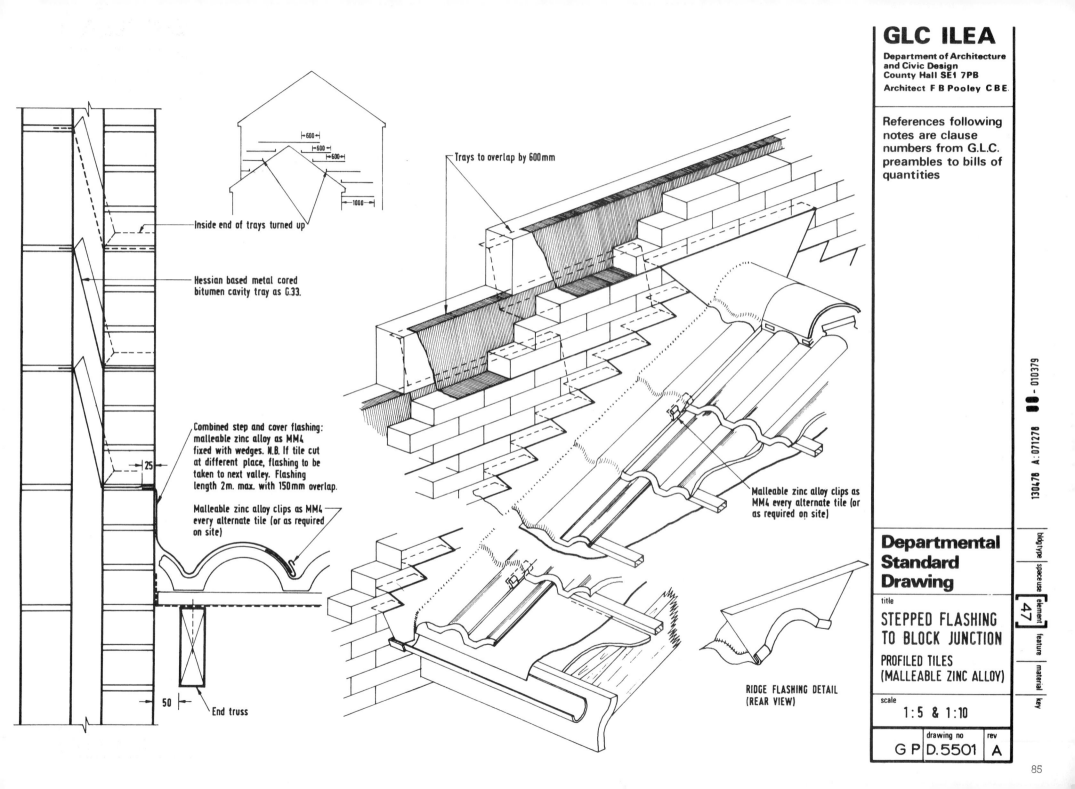

Inside end of trays turned up

Hessian based metal cored bitumen cavity tray as G.33.

Combined step and cover flashing: malleable zinc alloy as MM4 fixed with wedges. N.B. If tile cut at different place, flashing to be taken to next valley. Flashing length 2m. max. with 150mm overlap.

Malleable zinc alloy clips as MM4 every alternate tile (or as required on site)

25

50   End truss

Trays to overlap by 600mm

600
600
600
1000

Malleable zinc alloy clips as MM4 every alternate tile (or as required on site)

RIDGE FLASHING DETAIL
(REAR VIEW)

GLC ILEA

Department of Architecture and Civic Design
County Hall SE1 7PB
Architect F B Pooley C B E.

References following notes are clause numbers from G.L.C. preambles to bills of quantities

6Z£010 - 010379

130478 A:071278

130478 B:071278

Departmental Standard Drawing

	bldg type
	space use
47	element
	feature
	material
	key

title
STEPPED FLASHING TO BLOCK JUNCTION

PROFILED TILES (MALLEABLE ZINC ALLOY)

scale
1:5 & 1:10

	drawing no	rev
G P	D.5501	A

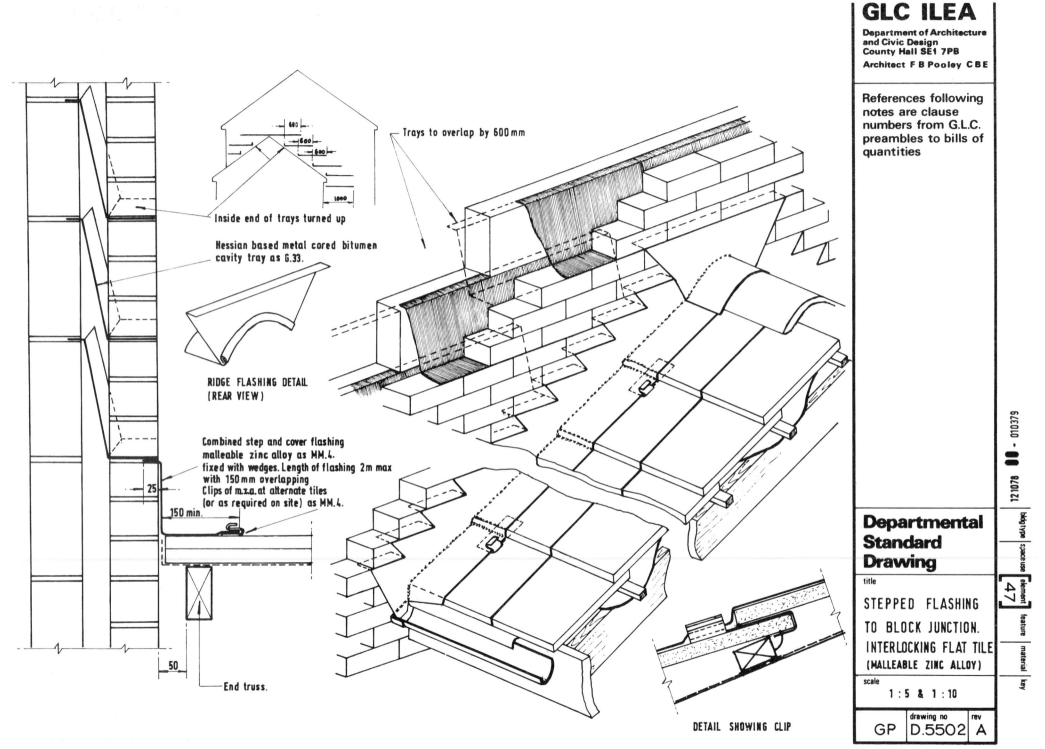

GLC ILEA

Department of Architecture
and Civic Design
County Hall SE1 7PB

Architect F B Pooley C BE

References following
notes are clause
numbers from G.L.C.
preambles to bills of
quantities

Trays to overlap by 600 mm

Inside end of trays turned up

Hessian based metal cored bitumen
cavity tray as G.33.

RIDGE FLASHING DETAIL
(REAR VIEW)

Combined step and cover flashing
malleable zinc alloy as MM.4.
fixed with wedges. Length of flashing 2m max
with 150 mm overlapping
Clips of m.z.a. at alternate tiles
(or as required on site) as MM.4.

25

150 min.

50

End truss.

DETAIL SHOWING CLIP

**Departmental
Standard
Drawing**

title

STEPPED FLASHING
TO BLOCK JUNCTION.
INTERLOCKING FLAT TILE
(MALLEABLE ZINC ALLOY)

scale

1 : 5 & 1 : 10

GP | drawing no D.5502 | rev A

121078   010379

bldg type | space use | element | feature | material | key

47

86

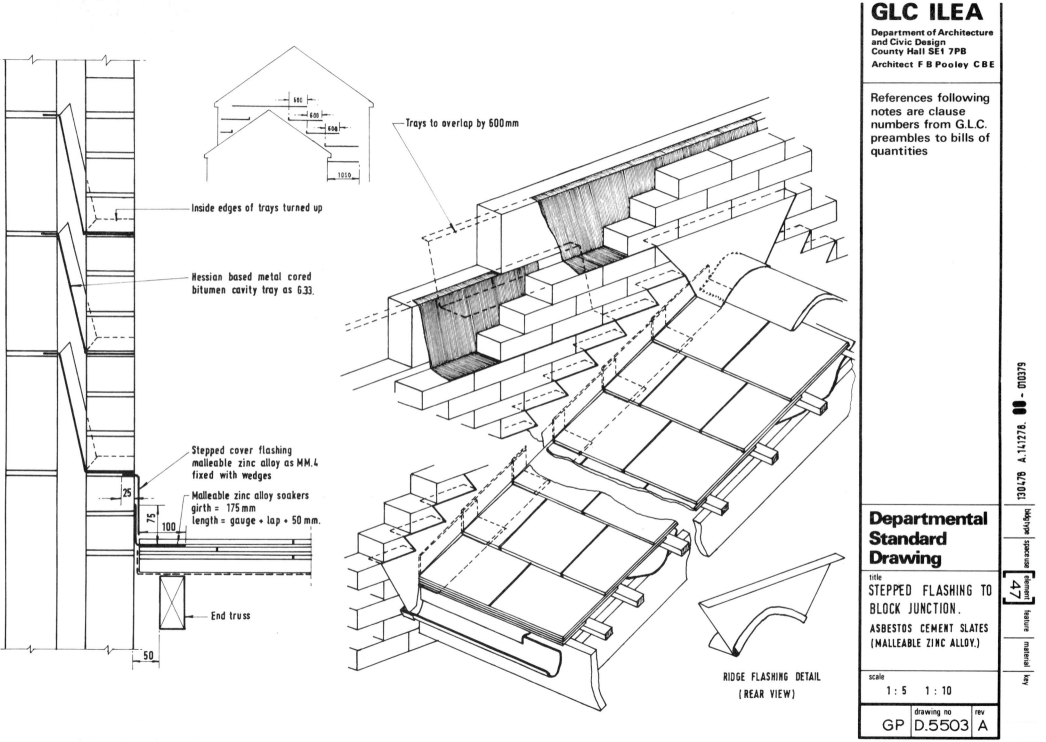

Trays to overlap by 600mm

Inside edges of trays turned up

Hessian based metal cored bitumen cavity tray as 6.33.

Stepped cover flashing malleable zinc alloy as MM.4 fixed with wedges

Malleable zinc alloy soakers
girth = 175 mm
length = gauge + lap + 50 mm.

End truss

25
75
100
50

600
600
600
1000

RIDGE FLASHING DETAIL
(REAR VIEW)

GLC ILEA

Department of Architecture and Civic Design
County Hall SE1 7PB
Architect F B Pooley C B E

References following notes are clause numbers from G.L.C. preambles to bills of quantities

6379 · 00 - 010379
A.141278.
13018 · 87Z1478

bldg type | space use | element | feature | material | key

Departmental Standard Drawing

title
STEPPED FLASHING TO BLOCK JUNCTION.
ASBESTOS CEMENT SLATES
(MALLEABLE ZINC ALLOY.)

element 47

scale
1 : 5   1 : 10

GP | drawing no D.5503 | rev A

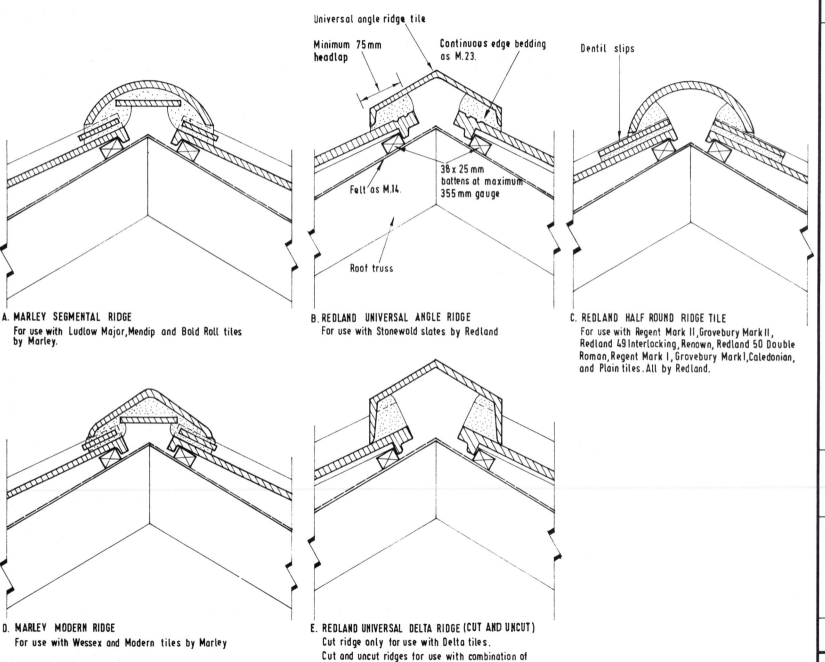

Universal angle ridge tile

Minimum 75mm headlap

Continuous edge bedding as M.23.

Dentil slips

Felt as M.14.

38 x 25 mm battens at maximum 355 mm gauge

Roof truss

A. MARLEY SEGMENTAL RIDGE
For use with Ludlow Major,Mendip and Bold Roll tiles by Marley.

B. REDLAND UNIVERSAL ANGLE RIDGE
For use with Stonewold slates by Redland

C. REDLAND HALF ROUND RIDGE TILE
For use with Regent Mark II,Grovebury Mark II, Redland 49 Interlocking, Renown, Redland 50 Double Roman,Regent Mark I, Grovebury Mark I,Caledonian, and Plain tiles. All by Redland.

D. MARLEY MODERN RIDGE
For use with Wessex and Modern tiles by Marley

E. REDLAND UNIVERSAL DELTA RIDGE (CUT AND UNCUT)
Cut ridge only for use with Delta tiles.
Cut and uncut ridges for use with combination of Stonewold slates and Delta tiles. All by Redland.

GLC ILEA

**Department of Architecture and Civic Design
County Hall SE1 7PB**

Architect Sir Roger Walters
KBE ARIBA FI Struct/E

References following notes are clause numbers from G.L.C. preambles to bills of quantities

For details of ridge flue see drawings [47] D5429 and D5427

01 0379

00

8 -

Departmental Standard Drawing

title
RIDGE TILES
FIXING DETAILS

element 47
feature 141
material N
key A

scale
1 : 5

GP	drawing no	rev
	D.5425	A

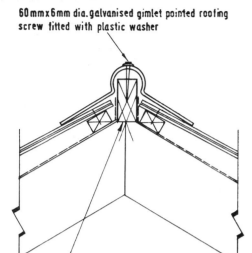

60mm×6mm dia. galvanised gimlet pointed roofing screw fitted with plastic washer

75×40 mm ridge batten skew nailed to truss

A: ETERNIT ROLL TOP ANGULAR RIDGE

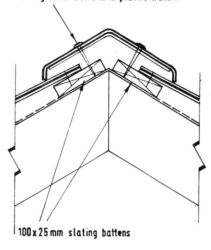

60mm×6mm dia. galvanised gimlet pointed roofing screw fitted with plastic washer

100×25mm slating battens

B: ETERNIT INTERNALLY SOCKETED RIDGE

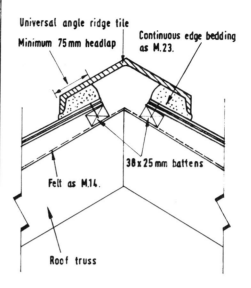

Universal angle ridge tile

Minimum 75mm headlap

Continuous edge bedding as M.23.

38×25mm battens

Felt as M.14.

Roof truss

E: REDLAND UNIVERSAL ANGLE RIDGE

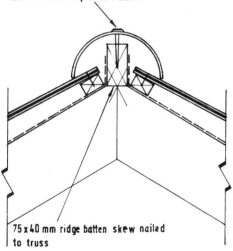

60mm×6mm dia. galvanised gimlet pointed roofing screw fitted with plastic washer

75×40 mm ridge batten skew nailed to truss

C: ETERNIT HALF ROUND TAPERING RIDGE

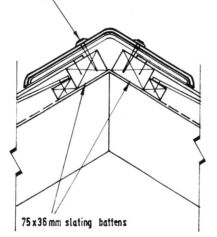

50mm×16sg galvanised roofing screws fitted with 'Sealit' plastic washer.

75×36mm slating battens

D: TAC RIDGE COVERING

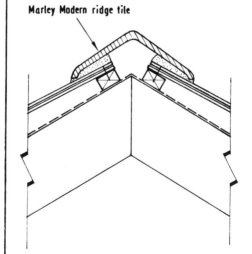

Marley Modern ridge tile

F: MARLEY MODERN RIDGE
(Alternative Segmental ridge not illustrated)

SLATE CAPPINGS (ASBESTOS CEMENT)

TILE CAPPINGS

GLC ILEA

Department of Architecture and Civic Design
County Hall SE1 7PB
Architect Sir Roger Walters
KBE ARIBA FI Struct/E

References following notes are clause numbers from G.L.C. preambles to bills of quantities

For details of ridge flue see drawings [47]D5427 and [47]D5428

670100·00

bldg type 8
space use
element 47
feature
material
key

Departmental Standard Drawing

title
RIDGE CAPPINGS FOR SLATED ROOFS (ASB. CEM.) FIXING DETAILS

scale 1:5

GP D5426   rev

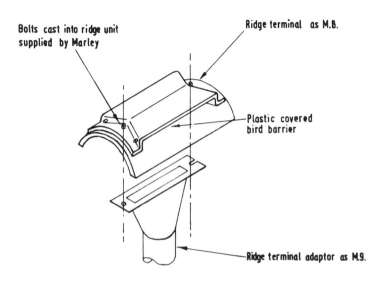

Bolts cast into ridge unit supplied by Marley

Ridge terminal as M.B.

Plastic covered bird barrier

Ridge terminal adaptor as M.9.

A: MARLEY GAS VENT RIDGE TERMINAL
for use with Marley Segmental and Modern ridges

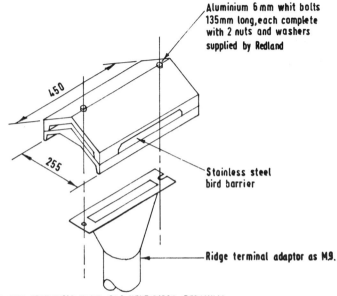

Aluminium 6 mm whit bolts 135 mm long, each complete with 2 nuts and washers supplied by Redland

450

255

Stainless steel bird barrier

Ridge terminal adaptor as M.9.

B: REDLAND STONEWOLD TYPE GAS VENT RIDGE TERMINAL
for use with Redland Universal Angle ridge

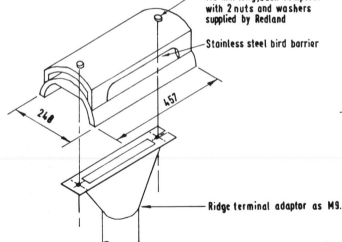

6mm aluminium whit bolts 110 mm long, each complete with 2 nuts and washers supplied by Redland

Stainless steel bird barrier

457

248

Ridge terminal adaptor as M.9.

C: REDLAND HALF ROUND TYPE GAS VENT RIDGE TERMINAL
for use with Redland Half Round Ridge

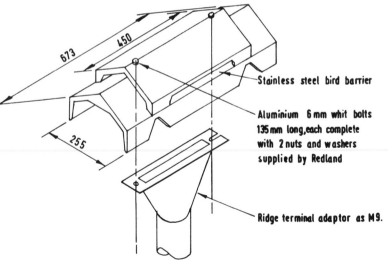

673

450

255

Stainless steel bird barrier

Aluminium 6 mm whit bolts 135 mm long, each complete with 2 nuts and washers supplied by Redland

Ridge terminal adaptor as M.9.

D: REDLAND DELTA TYPE GAS VENT RIDGE TERMINAL
for use with Redland Universal Delta ridge

GLC ILEA

Department of Architecture and Civic Design
County Hall SE1 7PB
Architect Sir Roger Walters
KBE ARIBA FI Struct/E

References following notes are clause numbers from G.L.C. preambles to bills of quantities

To be read in conjunction with drawings [47]D5428 and D5429

01.0379 – **00**

8 bldg type

[47] element

Departmental Standard Drawing

title
RIDGE TERMINALS FOR GAS FLUES

ISOMETRIC DRAWINGS

scale
1:10

GP | drawing no D.5427 | rev

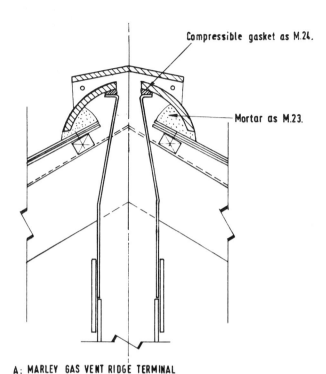

Compressible gasket as M.24.

Mortar as M.23.

A: MARLEY GAS VENT RIDGE TERMINAL
for use with Marley Segmental and Modern ridges

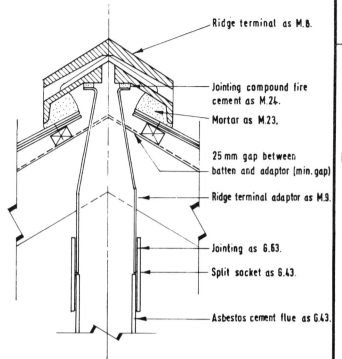

Ridge terminal as M.8.

Jointing compound fire cement as M.24.

Mortar as M.23.

25 mm gap between batten and adaptor (min. gap)

Ridge terminal adaptor as M.9.

Jointing as 6.63.

Split socket as 6.43.

Asbestos cement flue as 6.43.

B: REDLAND STONEWOLD TYPE GAS VENT RIDGE TERMINAL
for use with Redland Universal Angle ridge

GLC ILEA

**Department of Architecture and Civic Design
County Hall SE1 7PB
Architect Sir Roger Walters**
KBE ARIBA FI Struct/E

References following notes are clause numbers from G.L.C. preambles to bills of quantities
To be read in conjunction with drawings [47] D5426 and D5427

Departmental Standard Drawing

title
RIDGE TERMINALS
FOR GAS FLUES
SLATED ROOFS (ASB. CEM.)

SECTIONS

scale
1:5

GP | drawing no D.5428 | rev

bldg type | 00
space use | 8
element | [47]
feature |
material |
key |

6/£010 - 01037.9

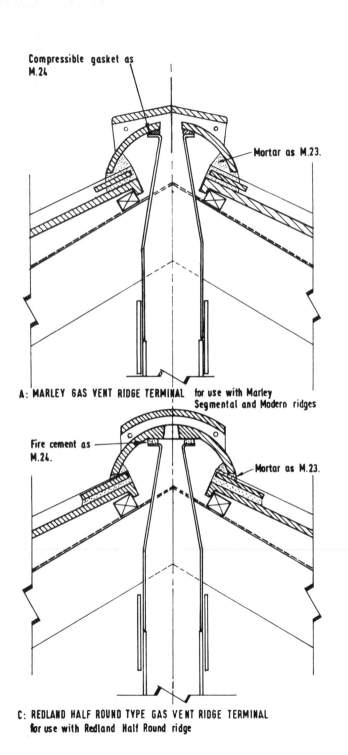

Compressible gasket as M.24

Mortar as M.23.

A: MARLEY GAS VENT RIDGE TERMINAL for use with Marley Segmental and Modern ridges

Fire cement as M.24.

Mortar as M.23.

C: REDLAND HALF ROUND TYPE GAS VENT RIDGE TERMINAL for use with Redland Half Round ridge

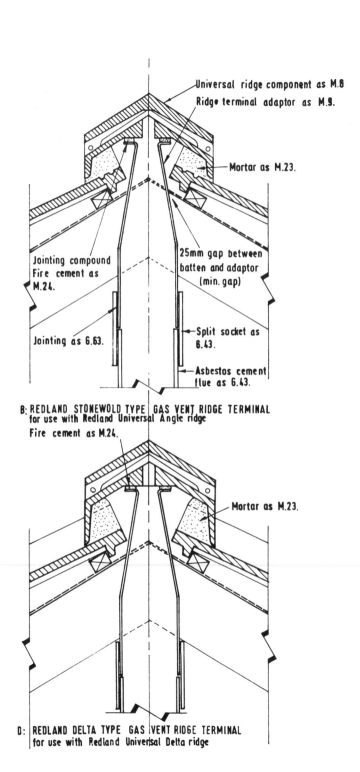

Universal ridge component as M.8
Ridge terminal adaptor as M.9.

Mortar as M.23.

Jointing compound Fire cement as M.24.

25mm gap between batten and adaptor (min. gap)

Jointing as 6.63.

Split socket as 6.43.

Asbestos cement flue as 6.43.

B: REDLAND STONEWOLD TYPE GAS VENT RIDGE TERMINAL for use with Redland Universal Angle ridge

Fire cement as M.24.

Mortar as M.23.

D: REDLAND DELTA TYPE GAS VENT RIDGE TERMINAL for use with Redland Universal Delta ridge

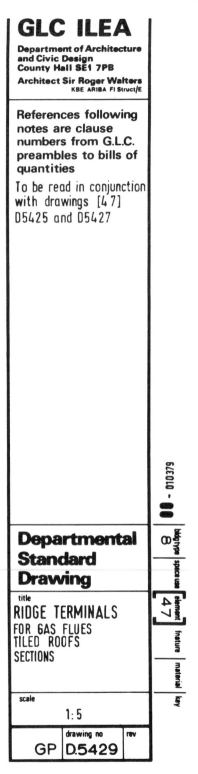

GLC ILEA

Department of Architecture and Civic Design
County Hall SE1 7PB
Architect Sir Roger Walters
KBE ARIBA FI Struct/E

References following notes are clause numbers from G.L.C. preambles to bills of quantities

To be read in conjunction with drawings [47] D5425 and D5427

drawing no D.0379

Departmental Standard Drawing

bldg type 00 | space use 8 | element 47 | feature | material | key

title
RIDGE TERMINALS
FOR GAS FLUES
TILED ROOFS
SECTIONS

scale 1:5

GP | drawing no D.5429 | rev

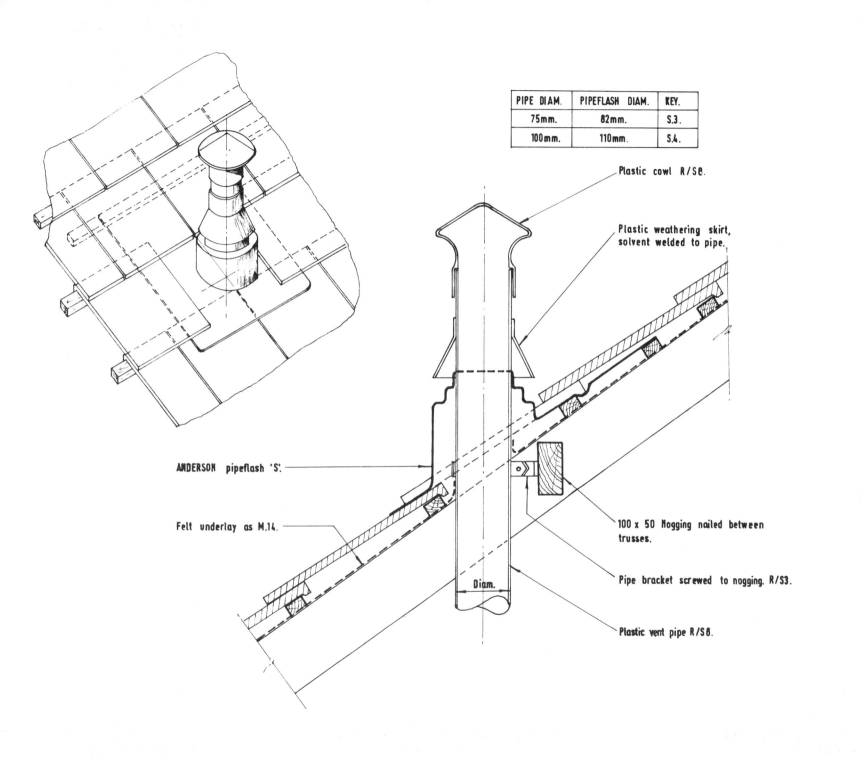

PIPE DIAM.	PIPEFLASH DIAM.	KEY.
75mm.	82mm.	S.3.
100mm.	110mm.	S.4.

Plastic cowl R/S8.

Plastic weathering skirt, solvent welded to pipe.

ANDERSON pipeflash 'S'.

Felt underlay as M.14.

100 x 50 Nogging nailed between trusses.

Pipe bracket screwed to nogging. R/S3.

Plastic vent pipe R/S8.

Diam.

GLC ILEA

**Department of Architecture
and Civic Design
County Hall SE1 7PB**

Architect Sir Roger Walters
KBE ARIBA FI Struct/E

References following notes are clause numbers from G.L.C. preambles to bills of quantities

Anderson pipeflash 'S' flexible to adjust between 22½° or 35°. (It is pre-made to 27°).

Departmental Standard Drawing

title

VENTILATING PIPE THROUGH TILED ROOF. (BROKEN BOND - SINGLE LAP).

scale

1 : 5. & 1 : 10.

	drawing no	rev
GP	D.5430	

010379

8-   52   470 Xn6

bldg type | space use | element | feature | material | key

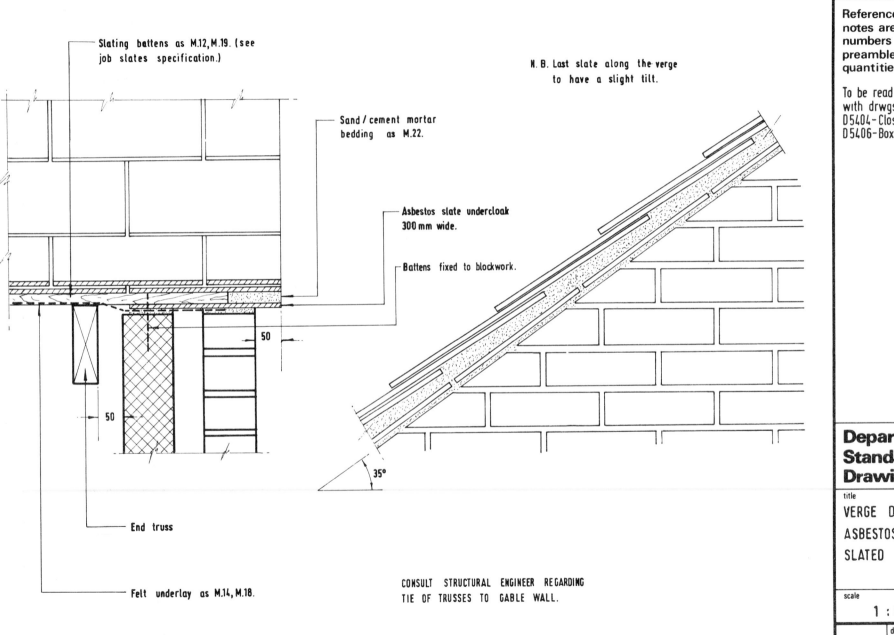

Slating battens as M.12, M.19. (see job slates specification.)

Sand / cement mortar bedding as M.22.

N.B. Last slate along the verge to have a slight tilt.

Asbestos slate undercloak 300 mm wide.

Battens fixed to blockwork.

50

50

35°

End truss

Felt underlay as M.14, M.18.

CONSULT STRUCTURAL ENGINEER REGARDING
TIE OF TRUSSES TO GABLE WALL.

GLC ILEA

Department of Architecture
and Civic Design
County Hall SE1 7PB
Architect Sir Roger Walters
KBE ARIBA FI Struct/E

References following notes are clause numbers from G.L.C. preambles to bills of quantities

To be read in conjunction with drwgs. [47]
D5404-Close eaves or
D5406-Box eaves.

Departmental Standard Drawing

title
VERGE DETAIL FOR ASBESTOS CEMENT SLATED ROOFS.

scale
1 : 5.

GP   drawing no   D.5423   rev

9LE010-010

8 - | bldgtype | spaceuse

47 | element

176 | feature

N | material

O.12 | key

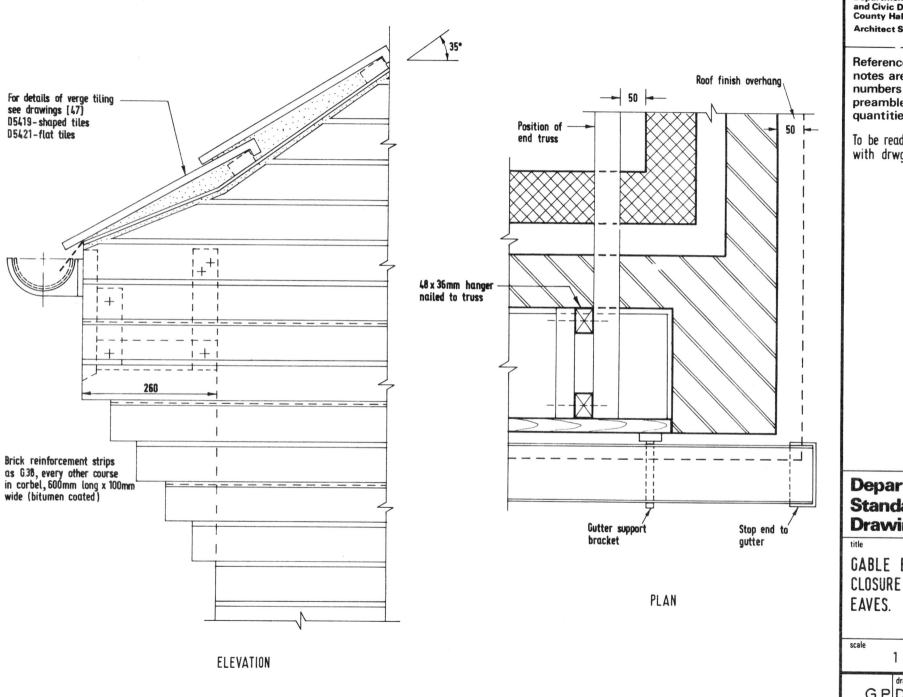

For details of verge tiling
see drawings [47]
D5419 - shaped tiles
D5421 - flat tiles

35°

260

Brick reinforcement strips
as G.38, every other course
in corbel, 600mm long x 100mm
wide (bitumen coated)

ELEVATION

Roof finish overhang

50

Position of
end truss

50

48 x 36mm hanger
nailed to truss

Gutter support
bracket

Stop end to
gutter

PLAN

GLC ILEA

**Department of Architecture
and Civic Design
County Hall SE1 7PB**

Architect Sir Roger Walters
KBE ARIBA FI Struct/E.

References following
notes are clause
numbers from G.L.C.
preambles to bills of
quantities

To be read in conjunction
with drwg. [47] D5402.

9/E010 - 00

bldgtype | 8

**Departmental
Standard
Drawing**

space use

element | 47

title

GABLE END CORBEL
CLOSURE FOR BOX
EAVES.

feature

material

key

scale

1 : 5

	drawing no	rev
G P	D.5418	A

Mono-pitched

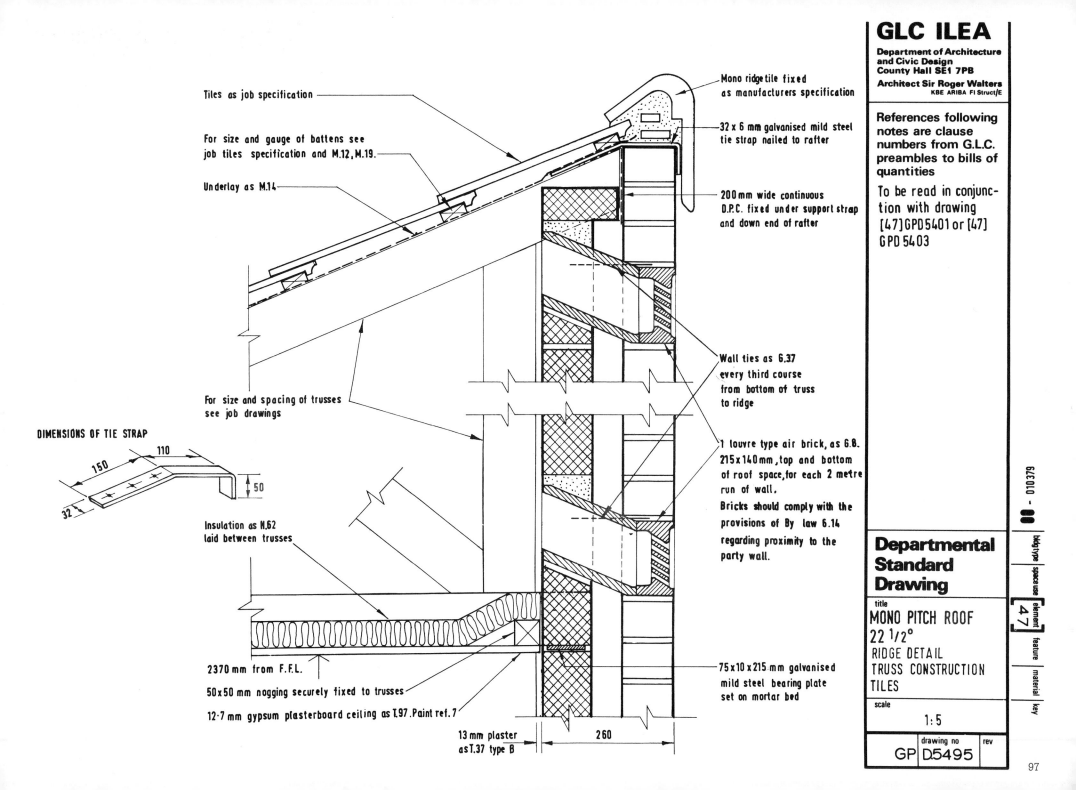

Tiles as job specification

Mono ridge tile fixed
as manufacturers specification

For size and gauge of battens see
job tiles specification and M.12, M.19.

32 x 6 mm galvanised mild steel
tie strap nailed to rafter

Underlay as M.14

200 mm wide continuous
D.P.C. fixed under support strap
and down end of rafter

For size and spacing of trusses
see job drawings

Wall ties as 6.37
every third course
from bottom of truss
to ridge

DIMENSIONS OF TIE STRAP

150
110
50
32

1 louvre type air brick, as 6.8.
215 x 140 mm, top and bottom
of roof space, for each 2 metre
run of wall.
Bricks should comply with the
provisions of By law 6.14
regarding proximity to the
party wall.

Insulation as N.62
laid between trusses

2370 mm from F.F.L.

50 x 50 mm nogging securely fixed to trusses

12·7 mm gypsum plasterboard ceiling as T.97. Paint ref. 7

75 x 10 x 215 mm galvanised
mild steel bearing plate
set on mortar bed

13 mm plaster
as T.37 type B

260

GLC ILEA

**Department of Architecture
and Civic Design
County Hall SE1 7PB
Architect Sir Roger Walters**
KBE ARIBA FI Struct/E

**References following
notes are clause
numbers from G.L.C.
preambles to bills of
quantities**

To be read in conjunc-
tion with drawing
[47] GPD 5401 or [47]
GPD 5403

00 - 010 376

bldg type | space use | element | feature | material | key

47

Departmental
Standard
Drawing

title
MONO PITCH ROOF
22 1/2°
RIDGE DETAIL
TRUSS CONSTRUCTION
TILES

scale
1:5

drawing no | rev
GP D5495

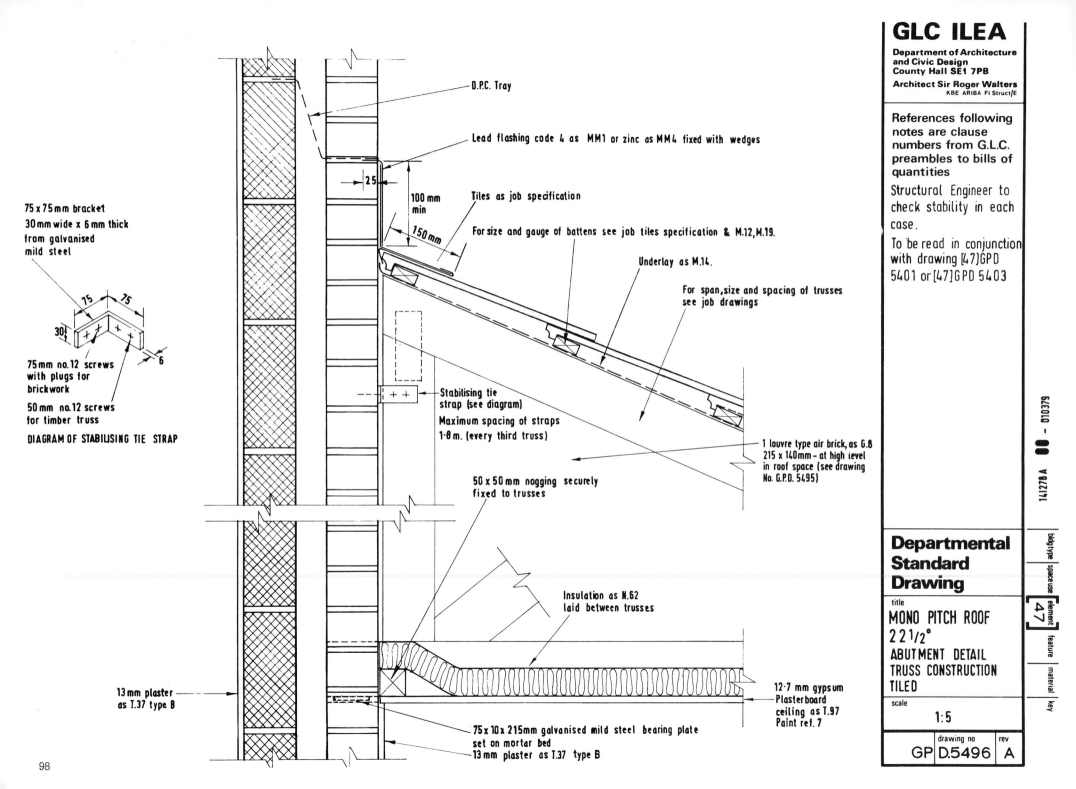

75 x 75mm bracket
30mm wide x 6mm thick from galvanised mild steel

75
75
30
6

75mm no.12 screws with plugs for brickwork

50mm no.12 screws for timber truss

DIAGRAM OF STABILISING TIE STRAP

D.P.C. Tray

Lead flashing code 4 as MM1 or zinc as MM4 fixed with wedges

25

100 mm min

150 mm

Tiles as job specification

For size and gauge of battens see job tiles specification & M.12, M.19.

Underlay as M.14.

For span, size and spacing of trusses see job drawings

Stabilising tie strap (see diagram)
Maximum spacing of straps 1·8 m. (every third truss)

1 louvre type air brick, as G.8 215 x 140mm – at high level in roof space (see drawing No. G.P.D. 5495)

50 x 50 mm nogging securely fixed to trusses

Insulation as N.62 laid between trusses

13 mm plaster as T.37 type B

12·7 mm gypsum Plasterboard ceiling as T.97 Paint ref. 7

75 x 10 x 215mm galvanised mild steel bearing plate set on mortar bed
13 mm plaster as T.37 type B

98

GLC ILEA
Department of Architecture and Civic Design
County Hall SE1 7PB
Architect Sir Roger Walters
KBE ARIBA FI Struct/E

References following notes are clause numbers from G.L.C. preambles to bills of quantities

Structural Engineer to check stability in each case.

To be read in conjunction with drawing [47]GPD 5401 or [47]GPD 5403

0379 - 010379

14127BA 00

bldgtype | spaceuse

Departmental Standard Drawing

element
47

title
MONO PITCH ROOF 2 2 1/2°
ABUTMENT DETAIL
TRUSS CONSTRUCTION
TILED

feature

material

key

scale
1:5

drawing no
GP D.5496

rev
A

Mansard

Type A1
Type B1

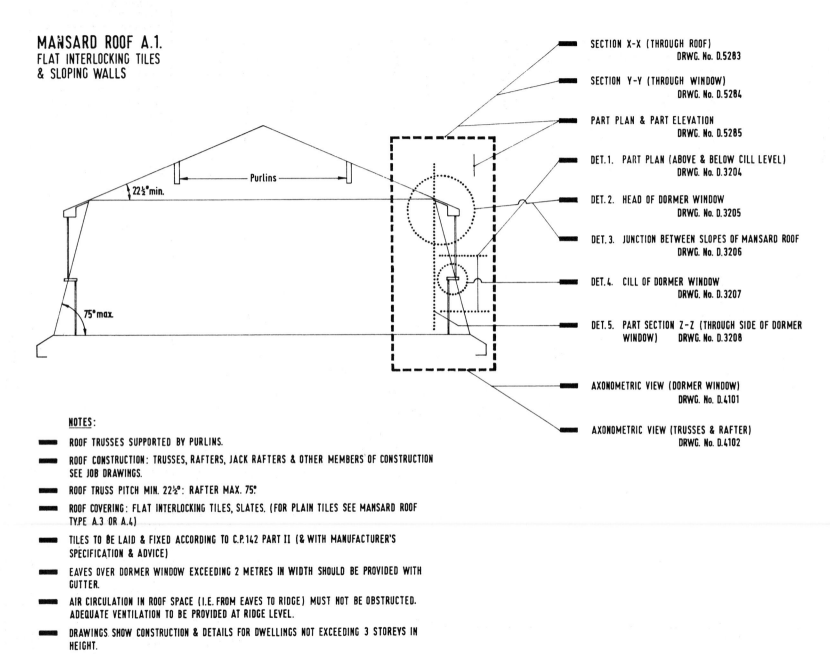

MANSARD ROOF A.1.
FLAT INTERLOCKING TILES & SLOPING WALLS

Purlins

22½° min.

75° max.

SECTION X-X (THROUGH ROOF)
DRWG. No. D.5283

SECTION Y-Y (THROUGH WINDOW)
DRWG. No. D.5284

PART PLAN & PART ELEVATION
DRWG. No. D.5285

DET.1. PART PLAN (ABOVE & BELOW CILL LEVEL)
DRWG. No. D.3204

DET.2. HEAD OF DORMER WINDOW
DRWG. No. D.3205

DET.3. JUNCTION BETWEEN SLOPES OF MANSARD ROOF
DRWG. No. D.3206

DET.4. CILL OF DORMER WINDOW
DRWG. No. D.3207

DET.5. PART SECTION Z-Z (THROUGH SIDE OF DORMER WINDOW)   DRWG. No. D.3208

AXONOMETRIC VIEW (DORMER WINDOW)
DRWG. No. D.4101

AXONOMETRIC VIEW (TRUSSES & RAFTER)
DRWG. No. D.4102

NOTES:

- ROOF TRUSSES SUPPORTED BY PURLINS.
- ROOF CONSTRUCTION: TRUSSES, RAFTERS, JACK RAFTERS & OTHER MEMBERS OF CONSTRUCTION SEE JOB DRAWINGS.
- ROOF TRUSS PITCH MIN. 22½°: RAFTER MAX. 75°.
- ROOF COVERING: FLAT INTERLOCKING TILES, SLATES. (FOR PLAIN TILES SEE MANSARD ROOF TYPE A.3 OR A.4)
- TILES TO BE LAID & FIXED ACCORDING TO C.P.142 PART II (& WITH MANUFACTURER'S SPECIFICATION & ADVICE)
- EAVES OVER DORMER WINDOW EXCEEDING 2 METRES IN WIDTH SHOULD BE PROVIDED WITH GUTTER.
- AIR CIRCULATION IN ROOF SPACE (I.E. FROM EAVES TO RIDGE) MUST NOT BE OBSTRUCTED. ADEQUATE VENTILATION TO BE PROVIDED AT RIDGE LEVEL.
- DRAWINGS SHOW CONSTRUCTION & DETAILS FOR DWELLINGS NOT EXCEEDING 3 STOREYS IN HEIGHT.

GLC ILEA
Department of Architecture and Civic Design
County Hall SE1 7PB
Architect F B Pooley C B E.

References following notes are clause numbers from G.L.C. preambles to bills of quantities

GPD - 12039

bldgtyp1   space use   element   feature   material   key

21

Departmental Standard Drawing

title

MANSARD ROOF -
TYPE A.1
DIAGRAM OF DETAILS

scale

	drawing no	rev
G P	D.2021	

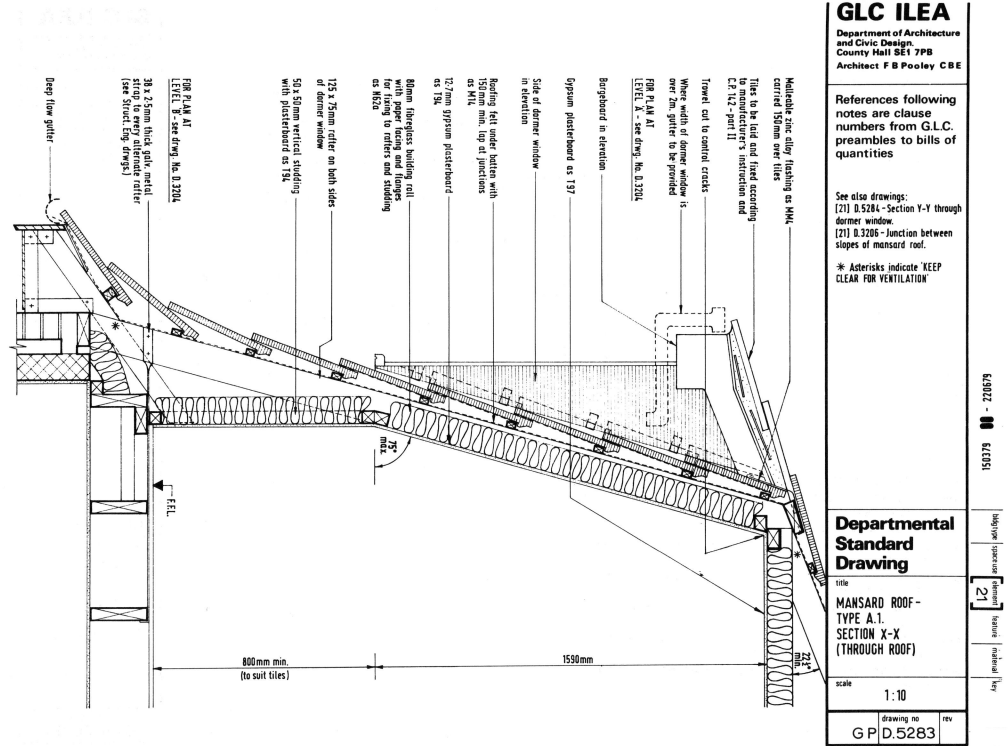

GLC ILEA

Department of Architecture
and Civic Design.
County Hall SE1 7PB
Architect F B Pooley C B E

References following
notes are clause
numbers from G.L.C.
preambles to bills of
quantities

See also drawings:
[21] D.5284 - Section Y-Y through
dormer window.
[21] D.3206 - Junction between
slopes of mansard roof.

✳ Asterisks indicate 'KEEP
CLEAR FOR VENTILATION'

**Departmental
Standard
Drawing**

bldg type | space use | element [21] | feature | material | key

title

MANSARD ROOF -
TYPE A.1.
SECTION X-X
(THROUGH ROOF)

scale

1:10

drawing no

G P D.5283

rev

150629 - 00 150629 150379

Labels (clockwise from top):

- Deep flow gutter
- FOR PLAN AT LEVEL 'B' - see drwg. No. D.3204
- 38 x 2·5mm thick galv. metal strap to every alternate rafter (see Struct. Eng drwgs.)
- 50 x 50mm vertical studding with plasterboard as T94
- 125 x 75mm rafter on both sides of dormer window
- 80mm fibreglass building roll with paper facing and flanges for fixing to rafters and studding as N62a
- 12·7mm gypsum plasterboard as T94
- Roofing felt under batten with 150mm min. lap at junctions as M14
- Side of dormer window in elevation
- Gypsum plasterboard as T97
- Bargeboard in elevation
- FOR PLAN AT LEVEL 'A' - see drwg. No. D.3204
- Trowel cut to control cracks
- Where width of dormer window is over 2m. gutter to be provided
- Tiles to be laid and fixed according to manufacturer's instruction and C.P. 142-part II
- Malleable zinc alloy flashing as MM4 carried 150mm over tiles

Dimensions:
- F.F.L.
- 75° max.
- 22½° min.
- 800mm min. (to suit tiles)
- 1590mm

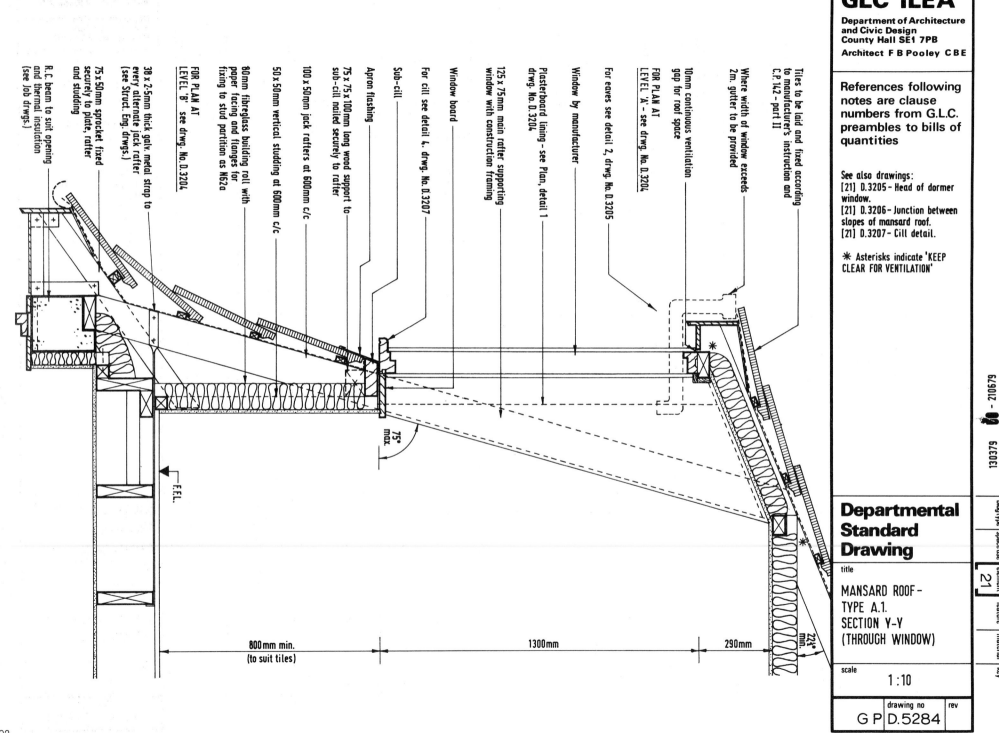

R.C. beam to suit opening and thermal insulation (see Job drwgs.)

75 x 50mm sprocket fixed securely to plate, rafter and studding

38 x 2·5mm thick galv. metal strap to every alternate jack rafter (see Struct. Eng. drwgs.)

80mm fibreglass building roll with paper facing and flanges for fixing to stud partition as NS2a

50 x 50mm vertical studding at 600mm c/c

100 x 50mm jack rafters at 600mm c/c

75 x 75 x 100mm long wood support to sub-cill nailed securely to rafter

Apron flashing

Sub-cill

Window board

125 x 75mm main rafter supporting window with construction framing

Plasterboard lining - see Plan, detail 1 drwg. No. D.3204

Window by manufacturer

10mm continuous ventilation gap for roof space

Tiles to be laid and fixed according to manufacturer's instruction and C.P. 142 - part II

Where width of window exceeds 2m, gutter to be provided

FOR PLAN AT LEVEL 'A' - see drwg. No. D.3204

For eaves see detail 2, drwg. No. D.3205

For cill see detail 4, drwg. No. D.3207

FOR PLAN AT LEVEL 'B' see drwg. No. D.3204

F.F.L.

75° max.

22½° min.

800mm min. (to suit tiles)

1300mm

290mm

GLC ILEA

Department of Architecture and Civic Design
County Hall SE1 7PB
Architect F B Pooley C B E

References following notes are clause numbers from G.L.C. preambles to bills of quantities

See also drawings:
[21] D.3205 - Head of dormer window.
[21] D.3206 - Junction between slopes of mansard roof.
[21] D.3207 - Cill detail.

* Asterisks indicate 'KEEP CLEAR FOR VENTILATION'

13069 - 21069

13069

bldg type | space use | element [21] | feature | material | key

Departmental Standard Drawing

title
MANSARD ROOF - TYPE A.1. SECTION Y-Y (THROUGH WINDOW)

scale
1:10

G P | drawing no D.5284 | rev

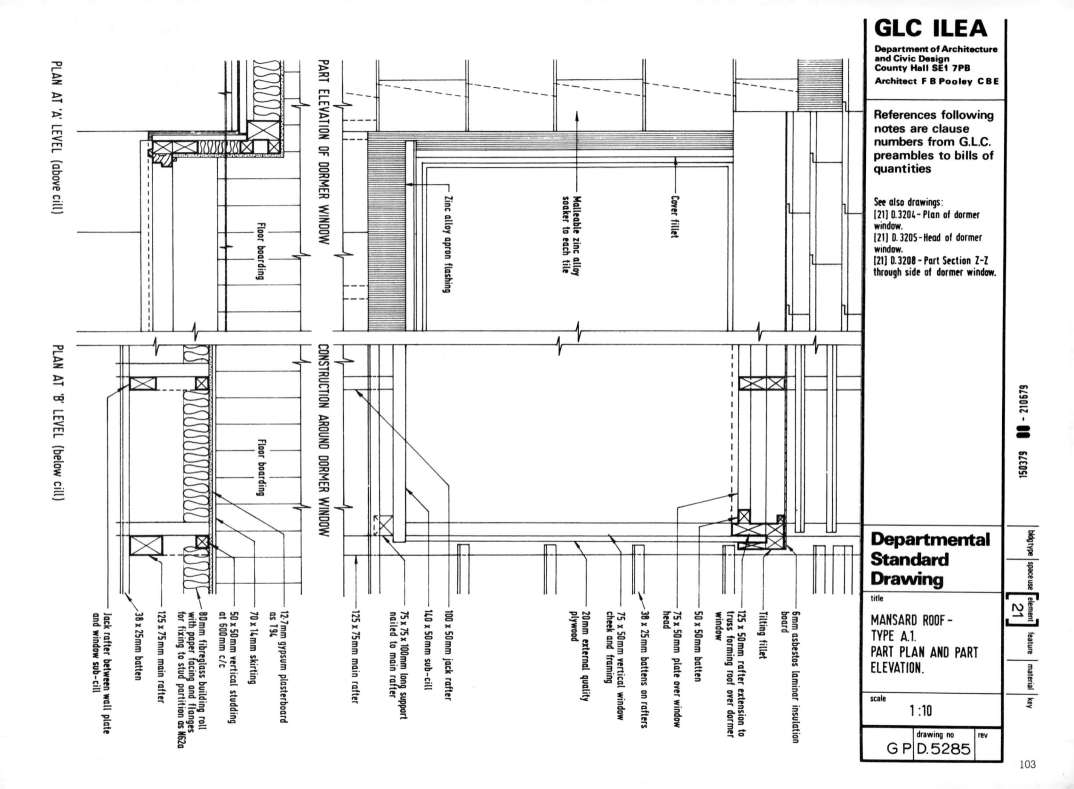

PLAN AT 'A' LEVEL (above cill)

PLAN AT 'B' LEVEL (below cill)

PART ELEVATION OF DORMER WINDOW

CONSTRUCTION AROUND DORMER WINDOW

Floor boarding

Floor boarding

Zinc alloy apron flashing

Malleable zinc alloy soaker to each tile

Cover fillet

Jack rafter between wall plate and window sub-cill

38 x 25mm batten

125 x 75mm main rafter

80mm fibreglass building roll with paper facing and flanges for fixing to stud partition as N62a

50 x 50mm vertical studding at 600mm c/c

70 x 14mm skirting

12·7mm gypsum plasterboard as T94

125 x 75mm main rafter

75 x 75 x 100mm long support nailed to main rafter

140 x 50mm sub-cill

100 x 50mm jack rafter

20mm external quality plywood

75 x 50mm vertical window cheek and framing

38 x 25mm battens on rafters

75 x 50mm plate over window head

50 x 50mm batten

125 x 50mm rafter extension to truss forming roof over dormer window

Tilting fillet

6mm asbestos laminar insulation board

GLC ILEA

Department of Architecture and Civic Design
County Hall SE1 7PB
Architect F B Pooley C B E

References following notes are clause numbers from G.L.C. preambles to bills of quantities

See also drawings:
[21] D.3204 - Plan of dormer window.
[21] D.3205 - Head of dormer window.
[21] D.3208 - Part Section Z-Z through side of dormer window.

150329 - **00** - 210629

Departmental Standard Drawing

bldgtype	space use		
	element	feature	material	key
	21			

title

MANSARD ROOF - TYPE A.1. PART PLAN AND PART ELEVATION.

scale

1:10

	drawing no	rev
G P	D.5285	

103

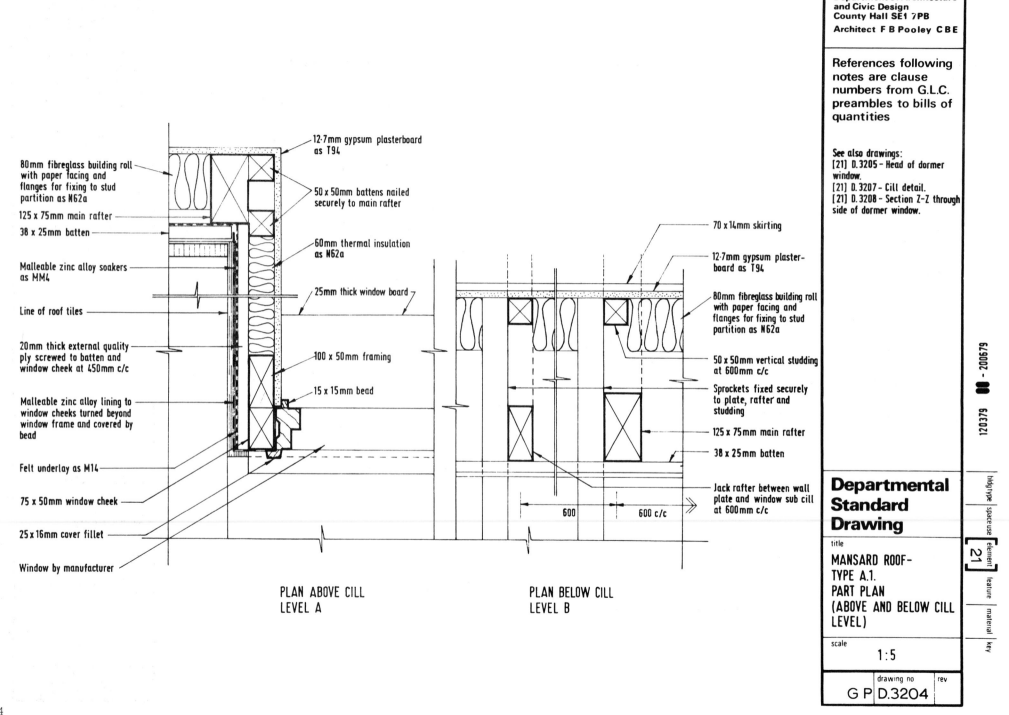

80mm fibreglass building roll with paper facing and flanges for fixing to stud partition as N62a

125 x 75mm main rafter

38 x 25mm batten

Malleable zinc alloy soakers as MM4

Line of roof tiles

20mm thick external quality ply screwed to batten and window cheek at 450mm c/c

Malleable zinc alloy lining to window cheeks turned beyond window frame and covered by bead

Felt underlay as M14

75 x 50mm window cheek

25 x 16mm cover fillet

Window by manufacturer

12·7mm gypsum plasterboard as T94

50 x 50mm battens nailed securely to main rafter

60mm thermal insulation as N62a

25mm thick window board

100 x 50mm framing

15 x 15mm bead

70 x 14mm skirting

12·7mm gypsum plasterboard as T94

80mm fibreglass building roll with paper facing and flanges for fixing to stud partition as N62a

50 x 50mm vertical studding at 600mm c/c

Sprockets fixed securely to plate, rafter and studding

125 x 75mm main rafter

38 x 25mm batten

Jack rafter between wall plate and window sub cill at 600mm c/c

600   600 c/c

PLAN ABOVE CILL
LEVEL A

PLAN BELOW CILL
LEVEL B

GLC ILEA

**Department of Architecture and Civic Design
County Hall SE1 7PB
Architect F B Pooley CBE**

References following notes are clause numbers from G.L.C. preambles to bills of quantities

See also drawings:
[21] D.3205 - Head of dormer window.
[21] D.3207 - Cill detail.
[21] D.3208 - Section Z-Z through side of dormer window.

120379 - 00 - 200379

Departmental Standard Drawing

bldg type | space use | element 21 | feature | material | key

title

MANSARD ROOF-
TYPE A.1.
PART PLAN
(ABOVE AND BELOW CILL LEVEL)

scale

1:5

drawing no | rev

G P D.3204

104

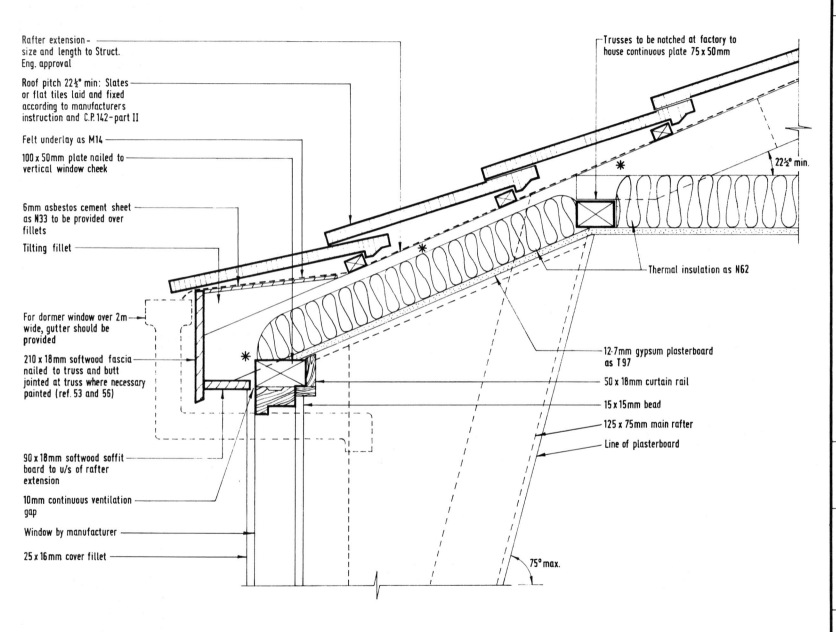

Rafter extension -
size and length to Struct.
Eng. approval

Roof pitch 22½° min: Slates
or flat tiles laid and fixed
according to manufacturers
instruction and C.P.142-part II

Felt underlay as M14

100 x 50mm plate nailed to
vertical window cheek

6mm asbestos cement sheet
as N33 to be provided over
fillets

Tilting fillet

For dormer window over 2m
wide, gutter should be
provided

210 x 18mm softwood fascia
nailed to truss and butt
jointed at truss where necessary
painted (ref. 53 and 56)

90 x 18mm softwood soffit
board to u/s of rafter
extension

10mm continuous ventilation
gap

Window by manufacturer

25 x 16mm cover fillet

Trusses to be notched at factory to
house continuous plate 75 x 50mm

22½° min.

Thermal insulation as N62

12·7mm gypsum plasterboard
as T97

50 x 18mm curtain rail

15 x 15mm bead

125 x 75mm main rafter

Line of plasterboard

75° max.

GLC ILEA

**Department of Architecture
and Civic Design
County Hall SE1 7PB**

Architect Sir Roger Walters
KBE ARIBA FI Struct/E.

**References following
notes are clause
numbers from G.L.C.
preambles to bills of
quantities**

Roof construction as N1, N3,
N5, N8 and N14

For details of trusses. rafters.
spans and sizes see manufacturer's and job drawings.

✳ Asterisks indicate 'KEEP
CLEAR FOR VENTILATION'

See also drawing:
[21] D.5283-Section Y-Y

6/9010Z-ZŁ 00 6/ZE0S1

**Departmental
Standard
Drawing**

title

MANSARD ROOF-
TYPE A.1.
HEAD OF DORMER WINDOW

bldgtype	space use	element
		[21]
		feature
		material
		key

scale

1 : 5

drawing no	rev
G P D.3205	

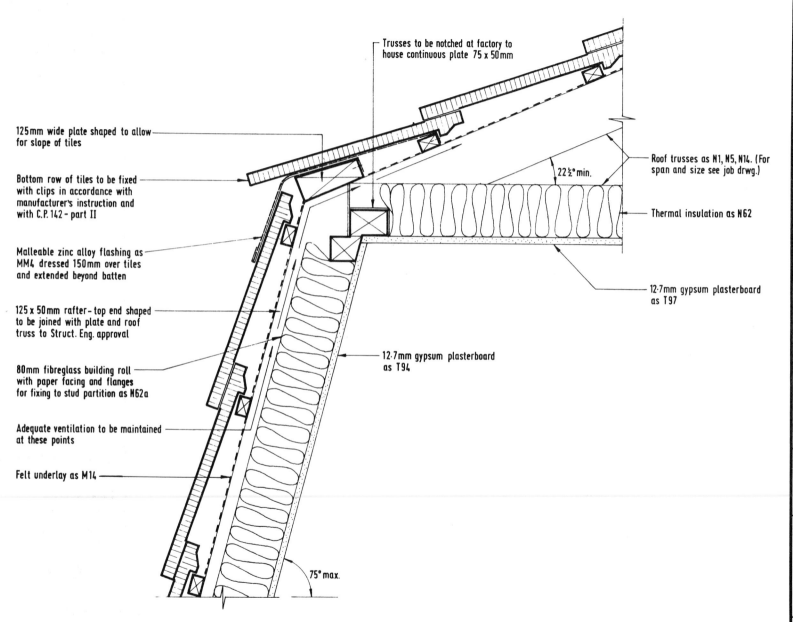

Trusses to be notched at factory to house continuous plate 75 x 50mm

125mm wide plate shaped to allow for slope of tiles

Bottom row of tiles to be fixed with clips in accordance with manufacturer's instruction and with C.P. 142 - part II

Malleable zinc alloy flashing as MM4 dressed 150mm over tiles and extended beyond batten

125 x 50mm rafter-top end shaped to be joined with plate and roof truss to Struct. Eng. approval

80mm fibreglass building roll with paper facing and flanges for fixing to stud partition as N62a

Adequate ventilation to be maintained at these points

Felt underlay as M14

22½° min.

Roof trusses as N1, N5, N14. (For span and size see job drwg.)

Thermal insulation as N62

12·7mm gypsum plasterboard as T97

12·7mm gypsum plasterboard as T94

75° max.

GLC ILEA

Department of Architecture and Civic Design County Hall SE1 7PB

Architect Sir Roger Walters
KBE ARIBA FI Struct/E.

References following notes are clause numbers from G.L.C. preambles to bills of quantities

See also drawings:
[21] D.5283 - Section X-X.
[21] D.5284 - Section Y-Y.
[21] D.3205 - Head of dormer window.

6/019/6 - 210129

160279

Departmental Standard Drawing

bldg type | space use | element | feature | material | key

21

title

MANSARD ROOF - TYPE A.1. JUNCTION BETWEEN SLOPES OF MANSARD ROOF

scale

1:5

drawing no | rev

G P | D.3206

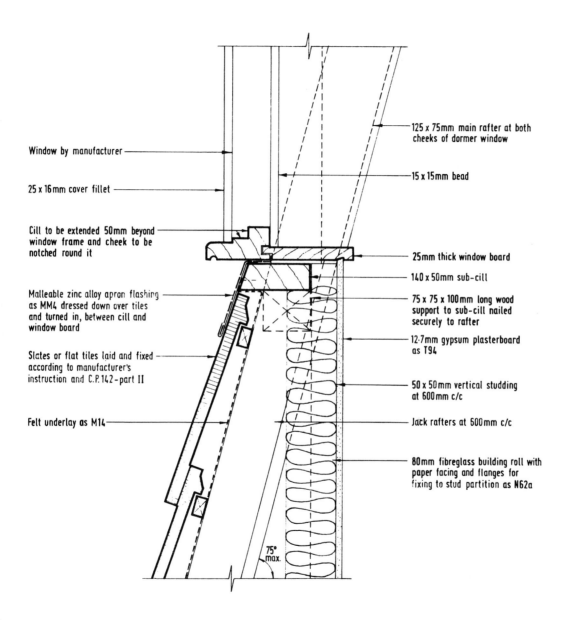

Window by manufacturer

25 x 16 mm cover fillet

Cill to be extended 50 mm beyond window frame and cheek to be notched round it

Malleable zinc alloy apron flashing as MM4 dressed down over tiles and turned in, between cill and window board

Slates or flat tiles laid and fixed according to manufacturer's instruction and C.P.142-part II

Felt underlay as M14

125 x 75 mm main rafter at both cheeks of dormer window

15 x 15 mm bead

25 mm thick window board

140 x 50 mm sub-cill

75 x 75 x 100 mm long wood support to sub-cill nailed securely to rafter

12·7 mm gypsum plasterboard as T94

50 x 50 mm vertical studding at 600 mm c/c

Jack rafters at 600 mm c/c

80 mm fibreglass building roll with paper facing and flanges for fixing to stud partition as N62a

75° max.

GLC ILEA

Department of Architecture and Civic Design County Hall SE1 7PB

Architect Sir Roger Walters
KBE ARIBA FI Struct/E.

References following notes are clause numbers from G.L.C. preambles to bills of quantities

See also drawing:
[21] D.3205 - Head of dormer window.

150679 - 00 - 150679

Departmental Standard Drawing

bldgtype | spaceuse | element | feature | material | key

[21]

title

MANSARD ROOF - TYPE A.1. CILL OF DORMER WINDOW

scale

1:5

	drawing no	rev
G P	D.3207	

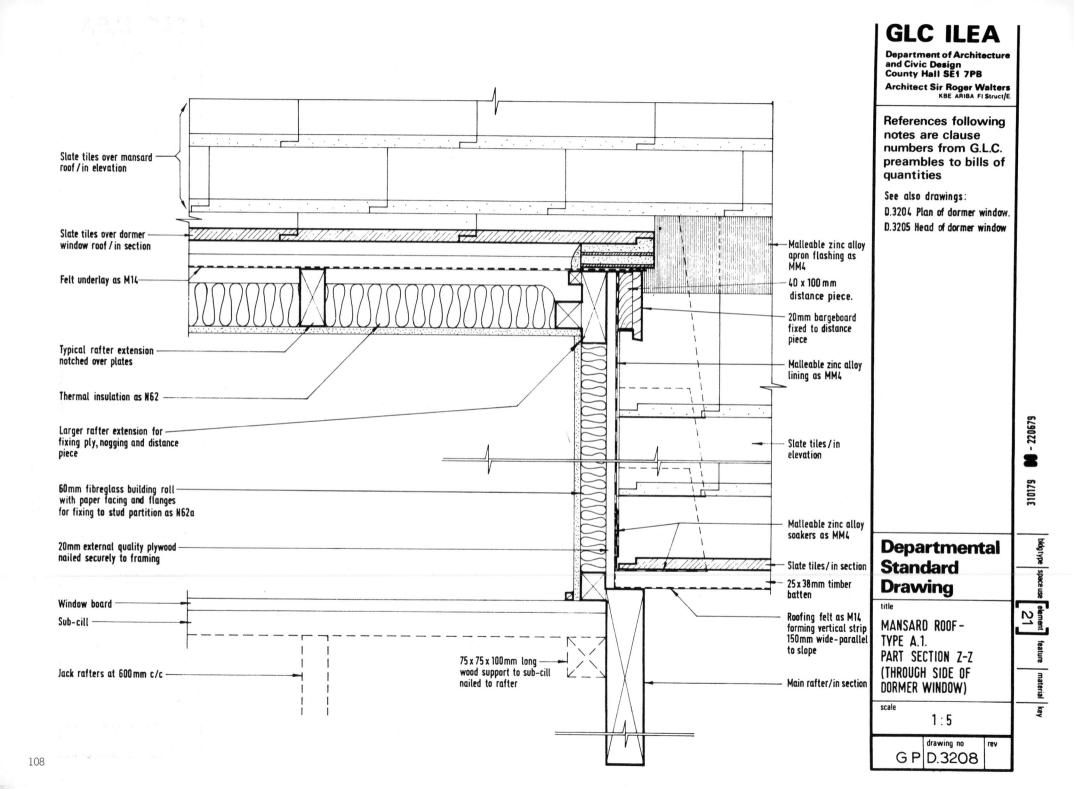

Slate tiles over mansard roof / in elevation

Slate tiles over dormer window roof / in section

Felt underlay as M14

Typical rafter extension notched over plates

Thermal insulation as N62

Larger rafter extension for fixing ply, nogging and distance piece

60mm fibreglass building roll with paper facing and flanges for fixing to stud partition as N62a

20mm external quality plywood nailed securely to framing

Window board

Sub-cill

Jack rafters at 600mm c/c

75 x 75 x 100mm long wood support to sub-cill nailed to rafter

Malleable zinc alloy apron flashing as MM4

40 x 100mm distance piece.

20mm bargeboard fixed to distance piece

Malleable zinc alloy lining as MM4

Slate tiles / in elevation

Malleable zinc alloy soakers as MM4

Slate tiles / in section

25 x 38mm timber batten

Roofing felt as M14 forming vertical strip 150mm wide-parallel to slope

Main rafter / in section

GLC ILEA

Department of Architecture and Civic Design
County Hall SE1 7PB

Architect Sir Roger Walters
KBE ARIBA FI Struct/E.

References following notes are clause numbers from G.L.C. preambles to bills of quantities

See also drawings:
D.3204 Plan of dormer window.
D.3205 Head of dormer window

930622 - 00 310119

bldg type | space use | element | feature | material | key
21

Departmental Standard Drawing

title

MANSARD ROOF-
TYPE A.1.
PART SECTION Z-Z
(THROUGH SIDE OF
DORMER WINDOW)

scale

1:5

drawing no	rev
G P D.3208	

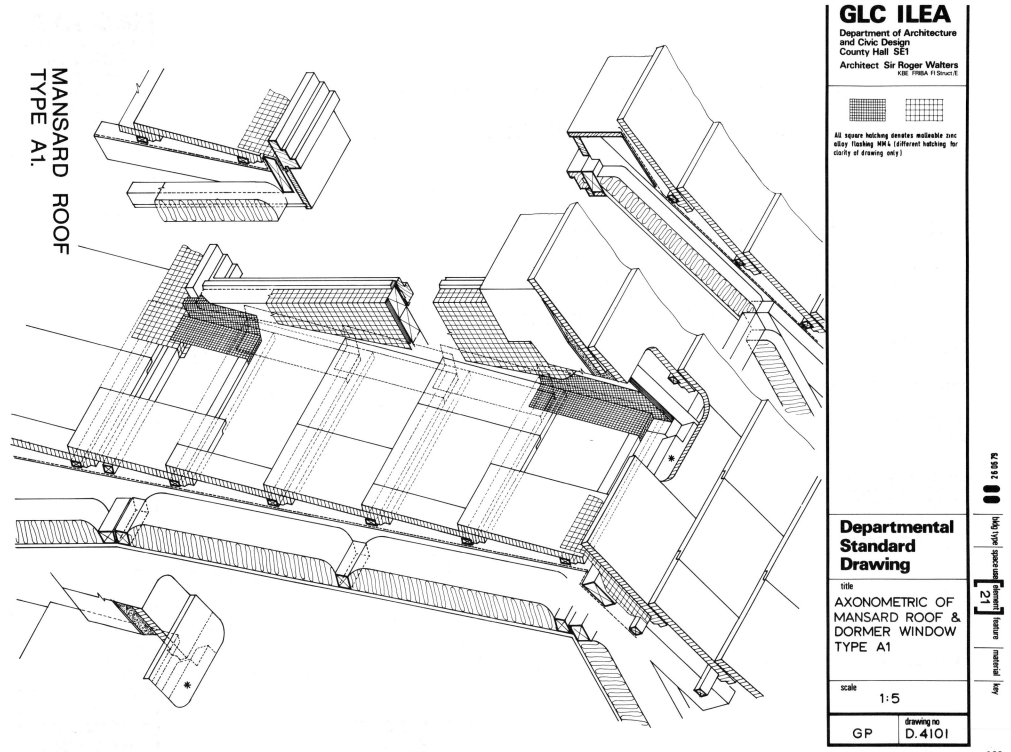

MANSARD ROOF
TYPE A1.

GLC ILEA
Department of Architecture
and Civic Design
County Hall SE1

Architect Sir Roger Walters
KBE FRIBA FI Struct/E

All square hatching denotes malleable zinc alloy flashing MM4 (different hatching for clarity of drawing only)

26 06 79

Departmental Standard Drawing

title

AXONOMETRIC OF MANSARD ROOF & DORMER WINDOW TYPE A1

bldg type | space use | element [21] | feature | material | key

scale

1:5

GP | drawing no D.4101

109

MANSARD ROOF - TYPE. B.1.
FLAT INTERLOCKING TILES
INTERNAL VERTICAL PARTITION.

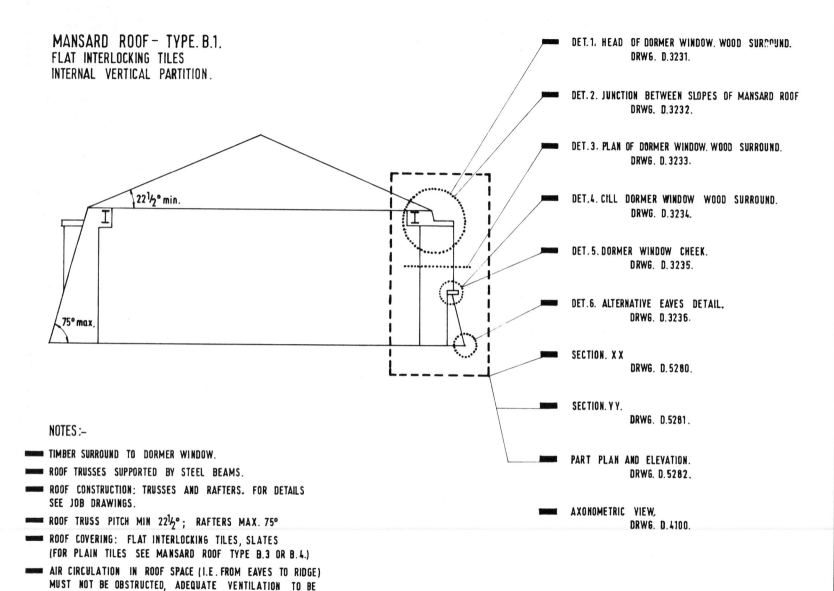

22½° min.

75° max.

NOTES:-

■ TIMBER SURROUND TO DORMER WINDOW.

■ ROOF TRUSSES SUPPORTED BY STEEL BEAMS.

■ ROOF CONSTRUCTION: TRUSSES AND RAFTERS. FOR DETAILS
SEE JOB DRAWINGS.

■ ROOF TRUSS PITCH MIN 22½°; RAFTERS MAX. 75°

■ ROOF COVERING: FLAT INTERLOCKING TILES, SLATES
(FOR PLAIN TILES SEE MANSARD ROOF TYPE B.3 OR B.4.)

■ AIR CIRCULATION IN ROOF SPACE (I.E. FROM EAVES TO RIDGE)
MUST NOT BE OBSTRUCTED, ADEQUATE VENTILATION TO BE
PROVIDED AT RIDGE LEVEL.

■ DRAWINGS SHOW CONSTRUCTION AND DETAILS FOR DWELLINGS
NOT EXCEEDING THREE STOREYS IN HEIGHT.

■ DET.1. HEAD OF DORMER WINDOW. WOOD SURROUND.
DRWG. D.3231.

■ DET.2. JUNCTION BETWEEN SLOPES OF MANSARD ROOF
DRWG. D.3232.

■ DET.3. PLAN OF DORMER WINDOW. WOOD SURROUND.
DRWG. D.3233.

■ DET.4. CILL DORMER WINDOW WOOD SURROUND.
DRWG. D.3234.

■ DET.5. DORMER WINDOW CHEEK.
DRWG. D.3235.

■ DET.6. ALTERNATIVE EAVES DETAIL.
DRWG. D.3236.

■ SECTION. XX
DRWG. D.5280.

■ SECTION. YY.
DRWG. D.5281.

■ PART PLAN AND ELEVATION.
DRWG. D.5282.

■ AXONOMETRIC VIEW.
DRWG. D.4100.

GLC ILEA

Department of Architecture
and Civic Design
County Hall SE1 7PB
Architect F B Pooley C B E

References following
notes are clause
numbers from G.L.C.
preambles to bills of
quantities

30010 - 679

30010 - 00

30010 - 679

bldgtype

space use

Departmental
Standard
Drawing

element

21

title

MANSARD ROOF
TYPE B.1.
DIAGRAM OF DETAILS.

feature

material

key

scale

	drawing no	rev
GP	D.2031	

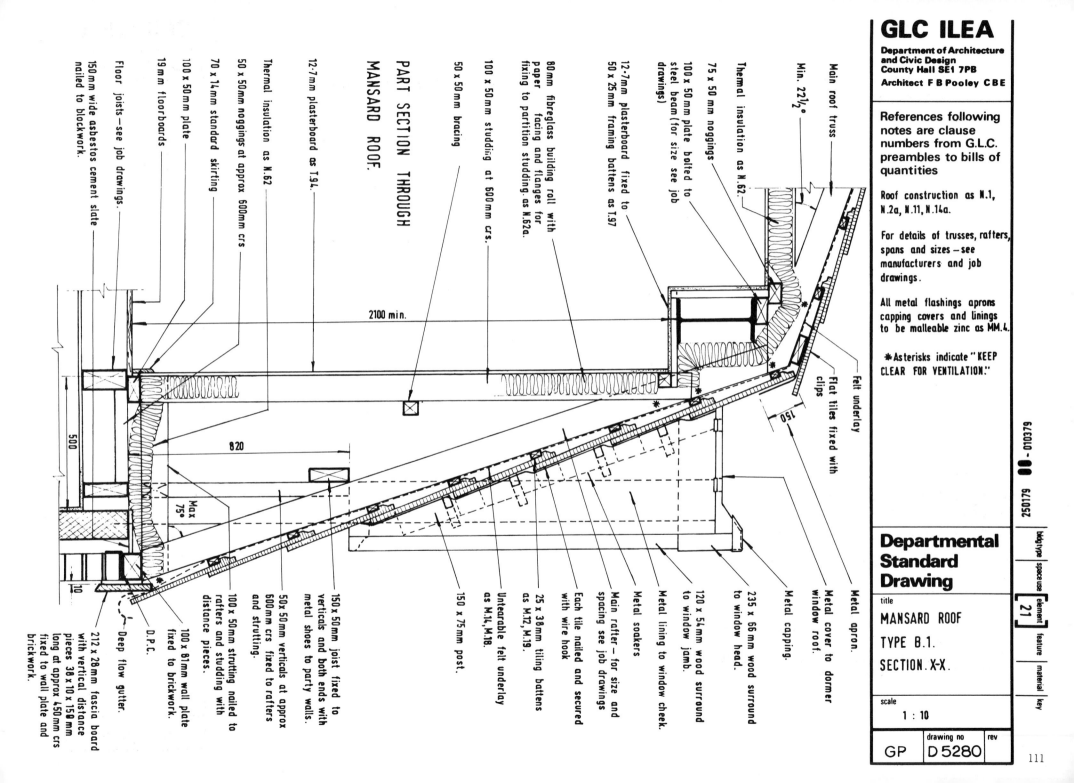

GLC ILEA

Department of Architecture
and Civic Design
County Hall SE1 7PB
Architect F B Pooley C BE

References following
notes are clause
numbers from G.L.C.
preambles to bills of
quantities

Roof construction as N.1,
N.2a, N.11, N.14a.

For details of trusses, rafters,
spans and sizes — see
manufacturers and job
drawings.

All metal flashings aprons
capping covers and linings
to be malleable zinc as MM.4.

＊Asterisks indicate "KEEP
CLEAR FOR VENTILATION."

**Departmental
Standard
Drawing**

bldgtype | spaceuse | element | feature | material | key

[21]

250179 - 00 - 010379

title

MANSARD ROOF
TYPE B.1.
SECTION. X-X.

scale

1 : 10

GP | drawing no D 5280 | rev

111

PART SECTION THROUGH
MANSARD ROOF.

Main roof truss

Min. 22½°

Thermal insulation as N.62.

75 x 50 mm noggings

100 x 50 mm plate bolted to
steel beam (for size see job
drawings)

12·7mm plasterboard fixed to
50 x 25mm framing battens as T.97

80mm fibreglass building roll with
paper facing and flanges for
fixing to partition studding as N.62a.

100 x 50 mm studding at 600mm crs.

50 x 50mm bracing

Thermal insulation as N.62.

12·7mm plasterboard as T.94.

50 x 50mm noggings at approx 600mm crs

70 x 14mm standard skirting

100 x 50mm plate

19mm floorboards

Floor joists—see job drawings.

150mm wide asbestos cement slate
nailed to blockwork.

2100 min.

500

820

Max 75°

10

Metal apron.

Metal cover to dormer
window roof.

Flat tiles fixed with
clips

Felt underlay

Metal capping.

150

235 x 66 mm wood surround
to window head.

120 x 54mm wood surround
to window jamb.

Metal lining to window cheek.

Metal soakers

Main rafter — for size and
spacing see job drawings

Each tile nailed and secured
with wire hook

25 x 38mm tiling battens
as M.17, M.19.

Untearable felt underlay
as M.14, M.18.

150 x 75mm post.

150 x 50mm joist fixed to
verticals and both ends with
metal shoes to party walls.

50 x 50mm verticals at approx
600mm crs fixed to rafters
and strutting.

100 x 50mm strutting nailed to
rafters and studding with
distance pieces.

100 x 81mm wall plate
fixed to brickwork.

D.P.C.

Deep flow gutter.

212 x 28mm fascia board
with vertical distance
pieces 38 x 10 x 150mm
long at approx 450mm crs
fixed to wall plate and
brickwork.

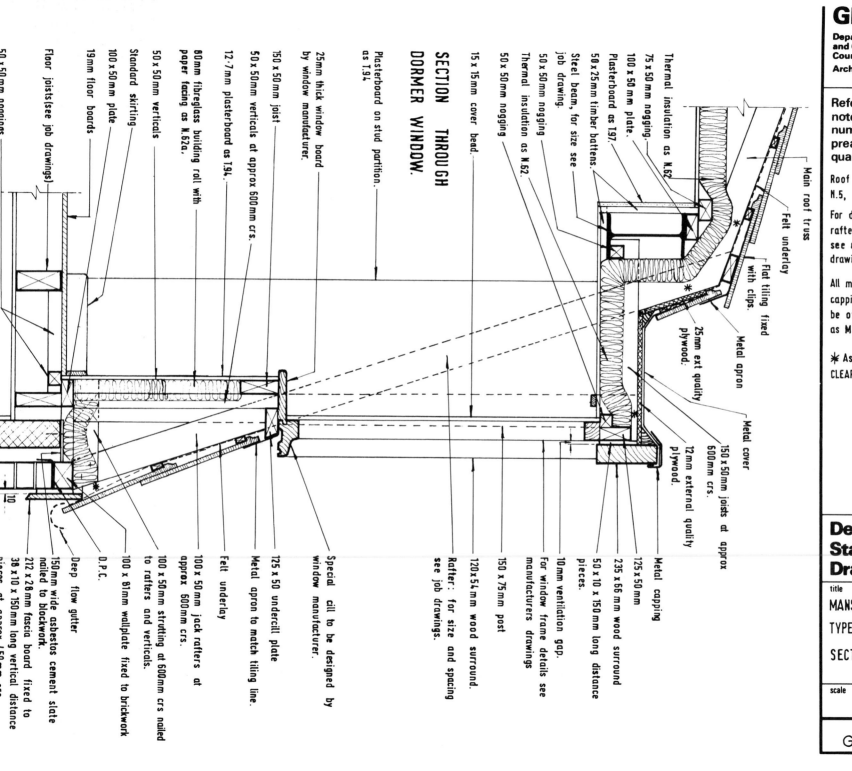

SECTION THROUGH DORMER WINDOW.

Labels (top group):
- Thermal insulation as N.62
- 75 x 50mm nogging.
- 100 x 50 mm plate.
- Plasterboard as T.97.
- 50 x 25mm timber battens.
- Steel beam, for size see job drawing.
- 50 x 50mm nogging
- Thermal insulation as N.62.
- 50 x 50mm nogging
- 50 x 50mm nogging
- 15 x 15mm cover bead.
- Plasterboard on stud partition.
- 25mm thick window board by window manufacturer.
- 150 x 50mm joist
- 50 x 50mm verticals at approx 600mm crs.
- 12·7mm plasterboard as T.94.
- 80mm fibreglass building roll with paper facing as N.62a.
- 50 x 50mm verticals
- 100 x 50mm plate
- Standard skirting
- 19mm floor boards
- Floor joists (see job drawings)
- 50 x 50mm noggings

Labels (right group):
- Main roof truss
- Felt underlay
- Flat tiling fixed with clips.
- Metal apron
- 25mm ext quality plywood.
- Metal cover
- 150 x 50mm joists at approx 600mm crs.
- 12mm external quality plywood.

Labels (bottom group):
- Deep flow gutter
- 150mm wide asbestos cement slate nailed to blockwork.
- 212 x 28mm fascia board fixed to 38 x 10 x 150mm long vertical distance pieces at approx 450mm crs
- D.P.C.
- 100 x 81mm wallplate fixed to brickwork
- 100 x 50mm strutting at 600mm crs nailed to rafters and verticals.
- 100 x 50mm jack rafters at approx 600mm crs.
- Felt underlay
- Metal apron to match tiling line.
- 125 x 50 undercill plate
- Special cill to be designed by window manufacturer.
- Rafter: for size and spacing see job drawings.
- 120x54mm wood surround.
- 150 x 75mm post
- For window frame details see manufacturers drawings
- 10mm ventilation gap.
- 50 x 10 x 150 mm long distance pieces.
- 235 x 66 mm wood surround
- 125 x 50mm
- Metal capping

GLC ILEA

Department of Architecture and Civic Design
County Hall SE1 7PB
Architect Sir Roger Walters
KBE ARIBA FI Struct/E

References following notes are clause numbers from G.L.C. preambles to bills of quantities

Roof construction as N.J; N.5, N.8, N.14.

For details of trusses, rafters, spans and sizes see manufacturers and job drawings.

All metal flashings, aprons, capping, covers, linings to be of malleable zinc alloy as MM.4.

✳ Asterisks indicate "KEEP CLEAR FOR VENTILATION."

bldg type | space use | element | feature | material | key
[21]

Departmental Standard Drawing

title
MANSARD ROOF
TYPE B.1.
SECTION. Y-Y.

scale
1 : 10

drawing no	rev
GP	D.5281	

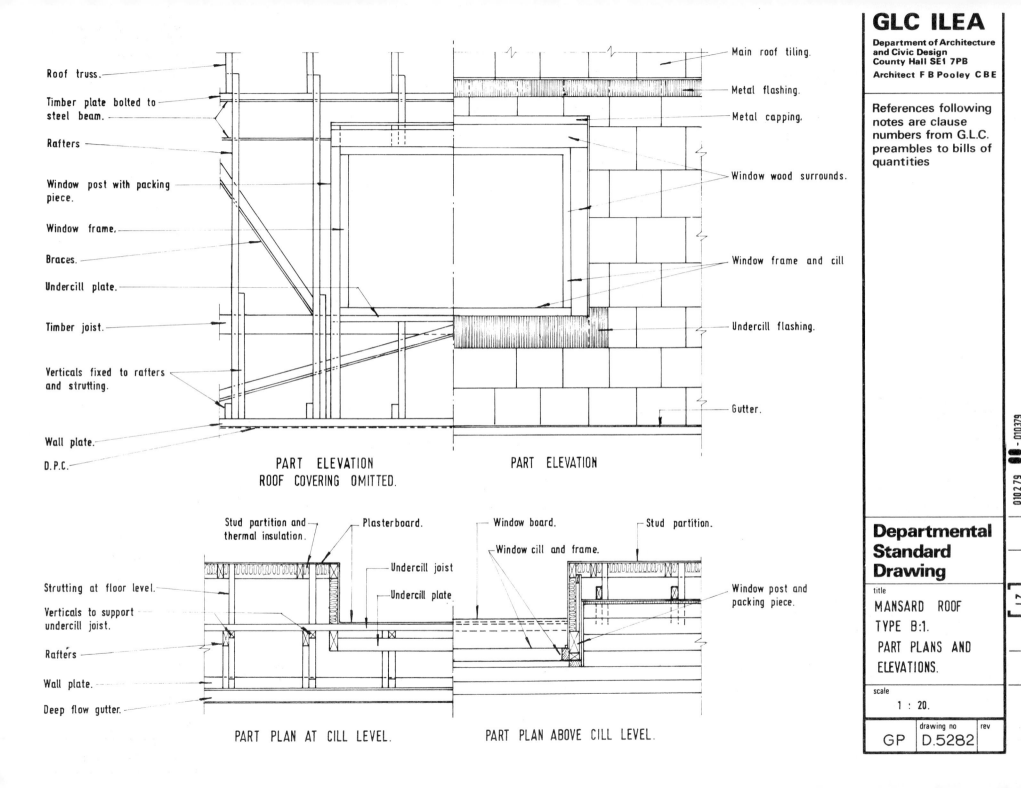

Roof truss.

Timber plate bolted to steel beam.

Rafters

Window post with packing piece.

Window frame.

Braces.

Undercill plate.

Timber joist.

Verticals fixed to rafters and strutting.

Wall plate.

D.P.C.

PART ELEVATION
ROOF COVERING OMITTED.

Main roof tiling.

Metal flashing.

Metal capping.

Window wood surrounds.

Window frame and cill

Undercill flashing.

Gutter.

PART ELEVATION

Stud partition and thermal insulation.

Plasterboard.

Undercill joist

Undercill plate

Strutting at floor level.

Verticals to support undercill joist.

Rafters

Wall plate.

Deep flow gutter.

PART PLAN AT CILL LEVEL.

Window board.

Stud partition.

Window cill and frame.

Window post and packing piece.

PART PLAN ABOVE CILL LEVEL.

GLC ILEA

Department of Architecture and Civic Design
County Hall SE1 7PB
Architect F B Pooley C B E

References following notes are clause numbers from G.L.C. preambles to bills of quantities

010 2 79   010 2 79

Departmental Standard Drawing

title
MANSARD ROOF
TYPE B:1.
PART PLANS AND
ELEVATIONS.

scale
1 : 20.

bldg type | space use | element 21 | feature | material | key

| GP | drawing no D.5282 | rev |

113

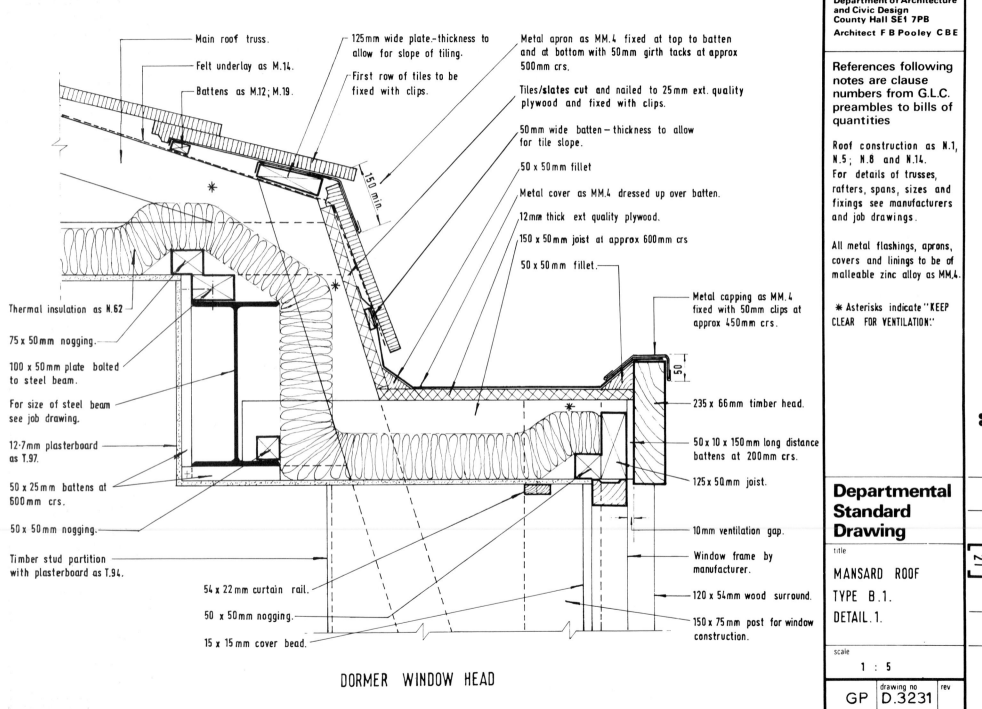

- Main roof truss.
- Felt underlay as M.14.
- Battens as M.12; M.19.
- 125mm wide plate.-thickness to allow for slope of tiling.
- First row of tiles to be fixed with clips.
- Metal apron as MM.4 fixed at top to batten and at bottom with 50mm girth tacks at approx 500mm crs.
- Tiles/**slates cut** and nailed to 25mm ext. quality plywood and fixed with clips.
- 50mm wide batten – thickness to allow for tile slope.
- 50 x 50mm fillet
- Metal cover as MM.4 dressed up over batten.
- 12mm thick ext quality plywood.
- 150 x 50mm joist at approx 600mm crs
- 50 x 50mm fillet.
- 150 min.
- Thermal insulation as N.62
- 75 x 50mm nogging.
- 100 x 50mm plate bolted to steel beam.
- For size of steel beam see job drawing.
- 12·7mm plasterboard as T.97.
- 50 x 25mm battens at 600mm crs.
- 50 x 50mm nogging.
- Timber stud partition with plasterboard as T.94.
- 54 x 22mm curtain rail.
- 50 x 50mm nogging.
- 15 x 15mm cover bead.
- Metal capping as MM.4 fixed with 50mm clips at approx 450mm crs.
- 50
- 235 x 66mm timber head.
- 50 x 10 x 150mm long distance battens at 200mm crs.
- 125 x 50mm joist.
- 10mm ventilation gap.
- Window frame by manufacturer.
- 120 x 54mm wood surround.
- 150 x 75mm post for window construction.

DORMER WINDOW HEAD

GLC ILEA
Department of Architecture and Civic Design
County Hall SE1 7PB
Architect F B Pooley C B E

References following notes are clause numbers from G.L.C. preambles to bills of quantities

Roof construction as N.1, N.5; N.8 and N.14.
For details of trusses, rafters, spans, sizes and fixings see manufacturers and job drawings.

All metal flashings, aprons, covers and linings to be of malleable zinc alloy as MM.4.

* Asterisks indicate "KEEP CLEAR FOR VENTILATION:"

Departmental Standard Drawing

title

MANSARD ROOF
TYPE B.1.
DETAIL.1.

scale

1 : 5

GP | D.3231 | rev

bldgtype | spaceuse | element [21] | feature | material | key

63270 - 00 - 010270

114

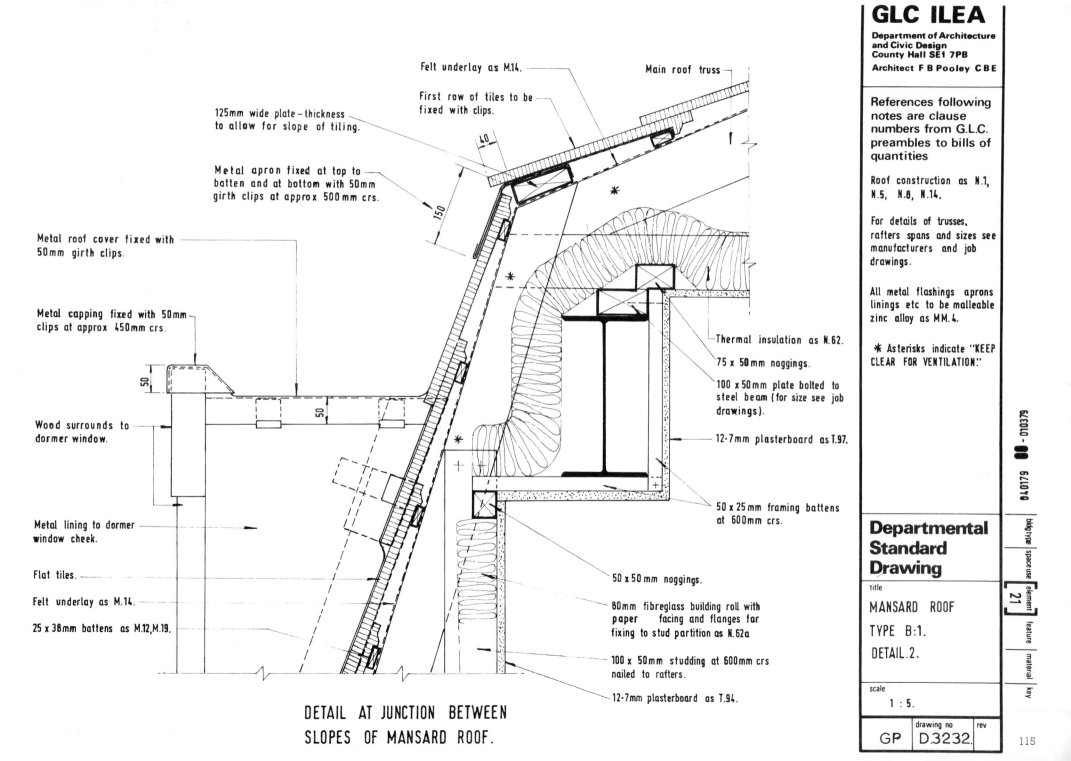

Felt underlay as M.14.

First row of tiles to be fixed with clips.

Main roof truss

125mm wide plate – thickness to allow for slope of tiling.

Metal apron fixed at top to batten and at bottom with 50mm girth clips at approx 500mm crs.

40

150

Metal roof cover fixed with 50mm girth clips.

Metal capping fixed with 50mm clips at approx 450mm crs.

50

50

Wood surrounds to dormer window.

Metal lining to dormer window cheek.

Flat tiles.

Felt underlay as M.14.

25 x 38mm battens as M.12, M.19.

Thermal insulation as N.62.

75 x 50mm noggings.

100 x 50mm plate bolted to steel beam (for size see job drawings).

12·7mm plasterboard as T.97.

50 x 25mm framing battens at 600mm crs.

50 x 50 mm noggings.

80mm fibreglass building roll with paper facing and flanges for fixing to stud partition as N.62a

100 x 50mm studding at 600mm crs nailed to rafters.

12·7mm plasterboard as T.94.

DETAIL AT JUNCTION BETWEEN
SLOPES OF MANSARD ROOF.

GLC ILEA

Department of Architecture and Civic Design
County Hall SE1 7PB
Architect F B Pooley C B E

References following notes are clause numbers from G.L.C. preambles to bills of quantities

Roof construction as N.1, N.5, N.8, N.14.

For details of trusses, rafters spans and sizes see manufacturers and job drawings.

All metal flashings aprons linings etc to be malleable zinc alloy as MM.4.

✳ Asterisks indicate "KEEP CLEAR FOR VENTILATION."

Departmental Standard Drawing

title
MANSARD ROOF
TYPE B:1.
DETAIL.2.

scale
1 : 5.

GP | drawing no D.3232. | rev

bldgtype | space use | element 21 | feature | material | key

00-0102E | 040179

115

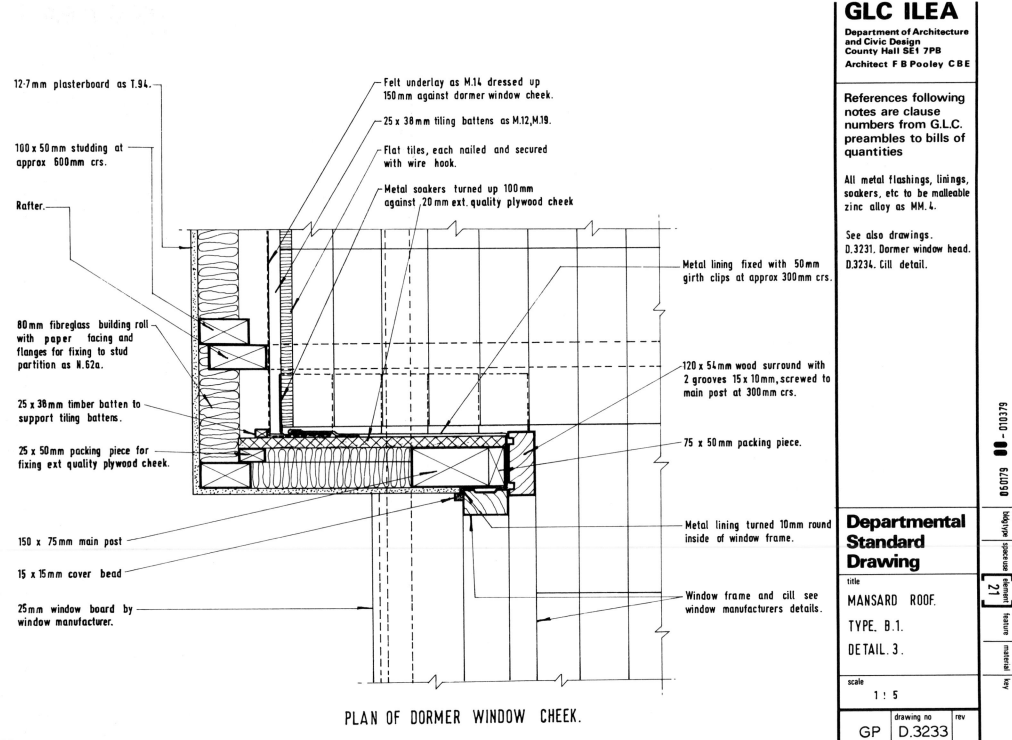

12·7mm plasterboard as T.94.

100 x 50mm studding at approx 600mm crs.

Rafter.

80mm fibreglass building roll with paper facing and flanges for fixing to stud partition as N.62a.

25 x 38mm timber batten to support tiling battens.

25 x 50mm packing piece for fixing ext quality plywood cheek.

150 x 75mm main post.

15 x 15mm cover bead.

25mm window board by window manufacturer.

Felt underlay as M.14 dressed up 150mm against dormer window cheek.

25 x 38mm tiling battens as M.12, M.19.

Flat tiles, each nailed and secured with wire hook.

Metal soakers turned up 100mm against 20mm ext. quality plywood cheek

Metal lining fixed with 50mm girth clips at approx 300mm crs.

120 x 54mm wood surround with 2 grooves 15 x 10mm, screwed to main post at 300mm crs.

75 x 50mm packing piece.

Metal lining turned 10mm round inside of window frame.

Window frame and cill see window manufacturers details.

PLAN OF DORMER WINDOW CHEEK.

116

GLC ILEA

Department of Architecture and Civic Design
County Hall SE1 7PB
Architect F B Pooley C B E

References following notes are clause numbers from G.L.C. preambles to bills of quantities

All metal flashings, linings, soakers, etc to be malleable zinc alloy as MM.4.

See also drawings.
D.3231. Dormer window head.
D.3234. Cill detail.

010.0379 · 00 · 06.0379

bldgtype | spaceuse | element | feature | material | key

[21]

Departmental Standard Drawing

title
MANSARD ROOF.
TYPE. B.1.
DETAIL. 3.

scale
1 : 5

drawing no	rev
GP D.3233	

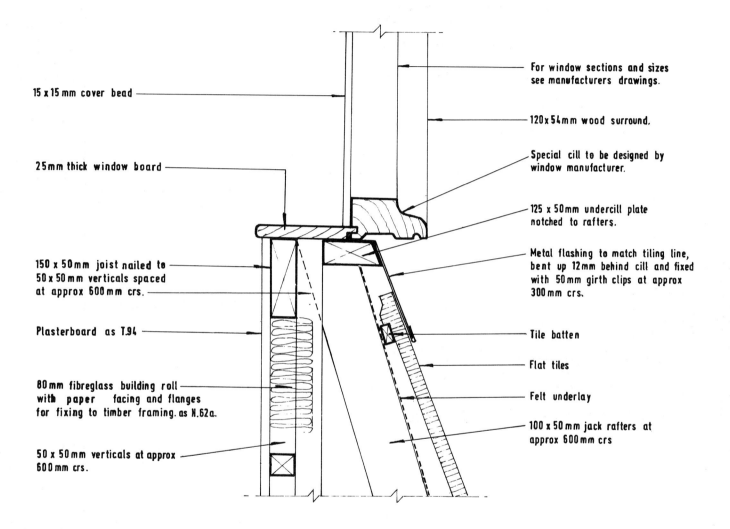

15 x 15 mm cover bead

25mm thick window board

150 x 50mm joist nailed to
50 x 50mm verticals spaced
at approx 600mm crs.

Plasterboard as T.94

80mm fibreglass building roll
with paper facing and flanges
for fixing to timber framing. as N.62a.

50 x 50mm verticals at approx
600mm crs.

For window sections and sizes
see manufacturers drawings.

120 x 54mm wood surround.

Special cill to be designed by
window manufacturer.

125 x 50mm undercill plate
notched to rafters.

Metal flashing to match tiling line,
bent up 12mm behind cill and fixed
with 50mm girth clips at approx
300mm crs.

Tile batten

Flat tiles

Felt underlay

100 x 50mm jack rafters at
approx 600mm crs

DORMER WINDOW CILL

GLC ILEA

**Department of Architecture
and Civic Design
County Hall SE1 7PB
Architect F B Pooley C B E**

References following
notes are clause
numbers from G.L.C.
preambles to bills of
quantities

All metal flashings, aprons,
soakers, covers, linings and
clips to be malleable zinc
alloy as MM.4.

100179 - 00 - 010379

bldg type	space use	element	feature	material	key
		21			

Departmental Standard Drawing

title

MANSARD ROOF

TYPE B.1.

DETAIL. 4.

scale

1 : 5

	drawing no	rev
GP	D.3234	

117

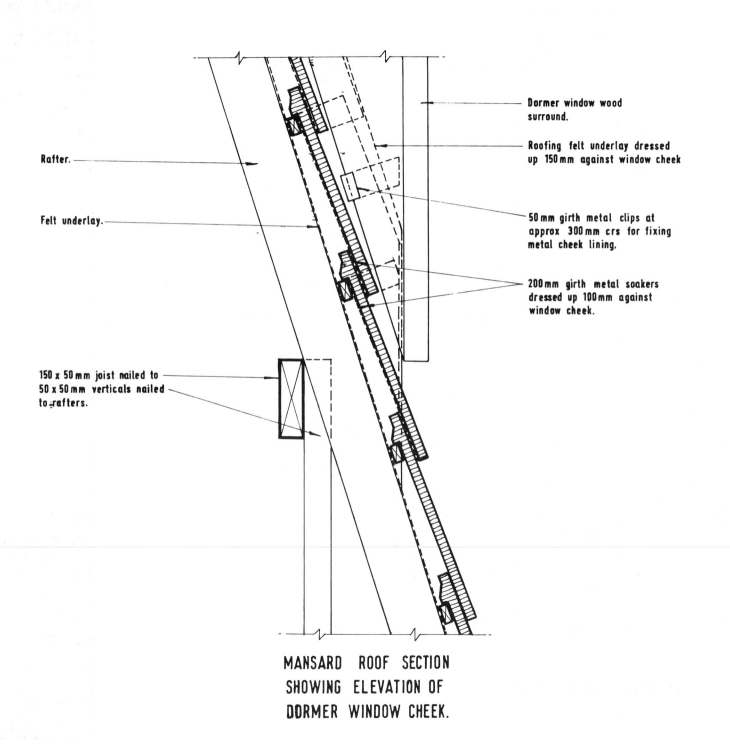

Rafter.

Felt underlay.

150 x 50 mm joist nailed to
50 x 50 mm verticals nailed
to rafters.

Dormer window wood
surround.

Roofing felt underlay dressed
up 150 mm against window cheek

50 mm girth metal clips at
approx 300 mm crs for fixing
metal cheek lining.

200 mm girth metal soakers
dressed up 100 mm against
window cheek.

MANSARD ROOF SECTION
SHOWING ELEVATION OF
DORMER WINDOW CHEEK.

GLC ILEA

**Department of Architecture
and Civic Design
County Hall SE1 7PB
Architect F B Pooley C B E**

References following
notes are clause
numbers from G.L.C.
preambles to bills of
quantities

All metal flashings aprons
soakers covers linings and
clips to be malleable zinc
alloy as M.M.4.

120179

Departmental Standard Drawing

title

MANSARD ROOF
TYPE B.1.
DETAIL. 5.

bldg type | space use | element | feature | material | key

21

scale

1 : 5

GP | drawing no D3235 | rev

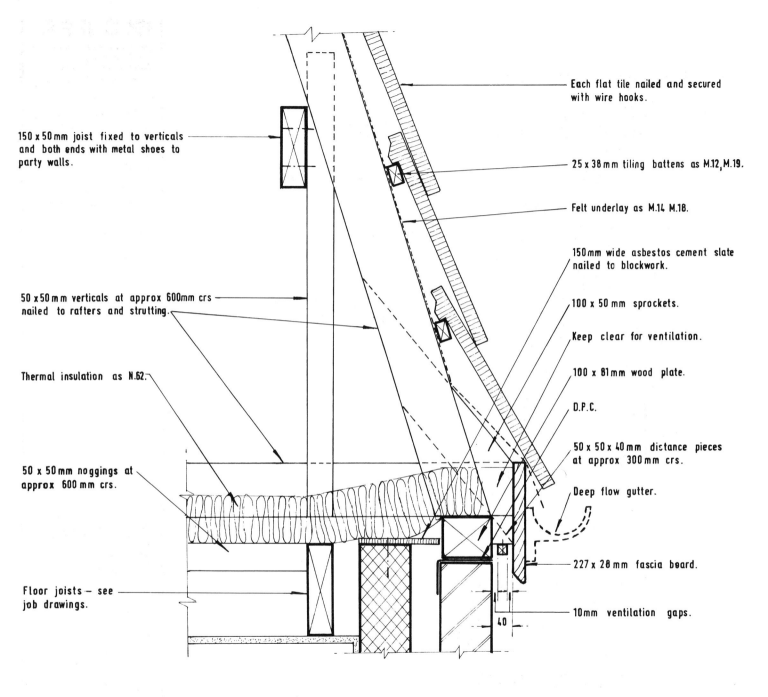

Each flat tile nailed and secured with wire hooks.

150 x 50mm joist fixed to verticals and both ends with metal shoes to party walls.

25 x 38mm tiling battens as M.12, M.19.

Felt underlay as M.14 M.18.

150mm wide asbestos cement slate nailed to blockwork.

50 x 50mm verticals at approx 600mm crs nailed to rafters and strutting.

100 x 50mm sprockets.

Keep clear for ventilation.

100 x 81mm wood plate.

Thermal insulation as N.62.

D.P.C.

50 x 50 x 40mm distance pieces at approx 300mm crs.

50 x 50mm noggings at approx 600mm crs.

Deep flow gutter.

227 x 28mm fascia board.

Floor joists — see job drawings.

10mm ventilation gaps.

40

ALTERNATIVE EAVES DETAIL.

GLC ILEA

Department of Architecture and Civic Design
County Hall SE1 7PB

Architect F B Pooley C B E

References following notes are clause numbers from G.L.C. preambles to bills of quantities

2001/79 00 - 0103/79

Departmental Standard Drawing

title
MANSARD ROOF
TYPE B.1.
DETAIL.6.

bldg type | space use | element 21 | feature | material | key

scale
1 : 5

GP | drawing no D.3236 | rev

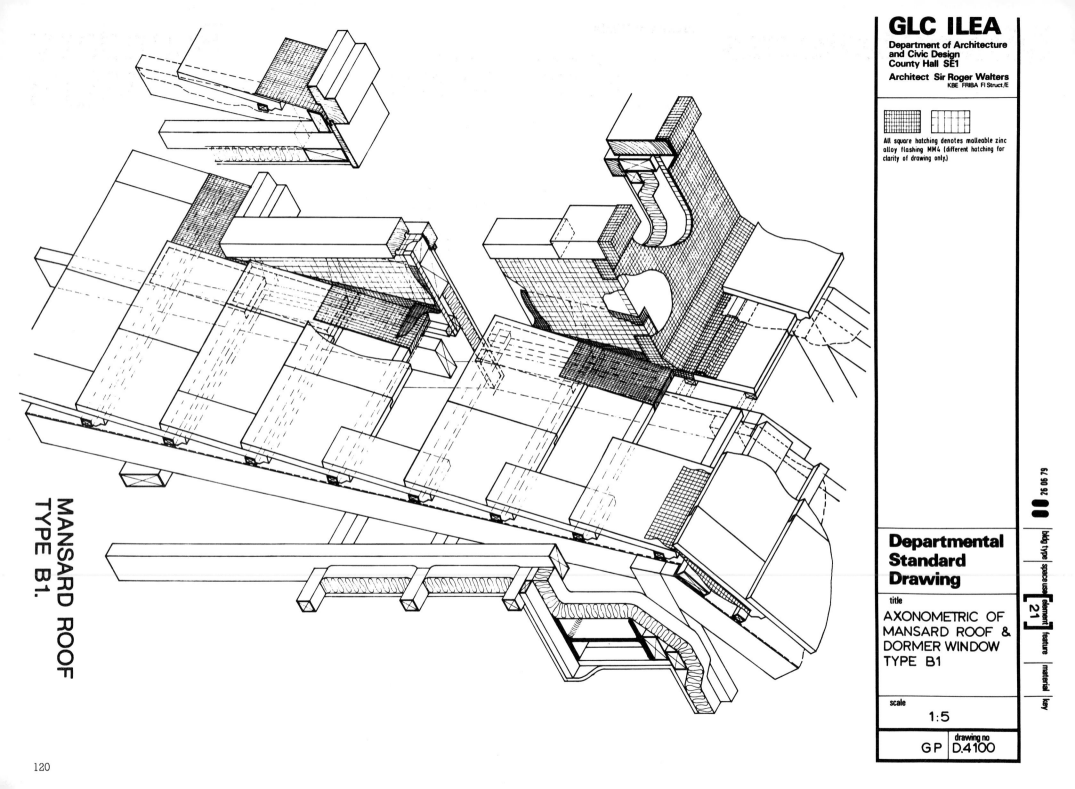

MANSARD ROOF
TYPE B1.

Department of Architecture and Civic Design
County Hall SE1

Architect Sir Roger Walters
KBE FRIBA FI Struct/E

All square hatching denotes malleable zinc alloy flashing MM4 (different hatching for clarity of drawing only.)

79 50 92

88

bldg type | space use | element | feature | material | key

21

Departmental Standard Drawing

title
AXONOMETRIC OF MANSARD ROOF & DORMER WINDOW TYPE B1

scale
1:5

GP | drawing no D.4100

Miscellaneous

Boundary Walls

The main principle in the design of boundary
walls is to keep the foundation as high as possible
consistent with the ground bearing conditions. The
position and type of dpc's should be noted and
the mortar mix should be chosen with care.

Dust Bin Stores

Various combinations of bin stores are shown.
Those related to porches are intended to be used
in conjunction with the GLC Preferred Dwelling
Plans (previously published by The Architectural
Press, ISBN : 0 85139 252 0). Where outside works
permit, it is preferable to have free standing
bin stores away from entrance doors.

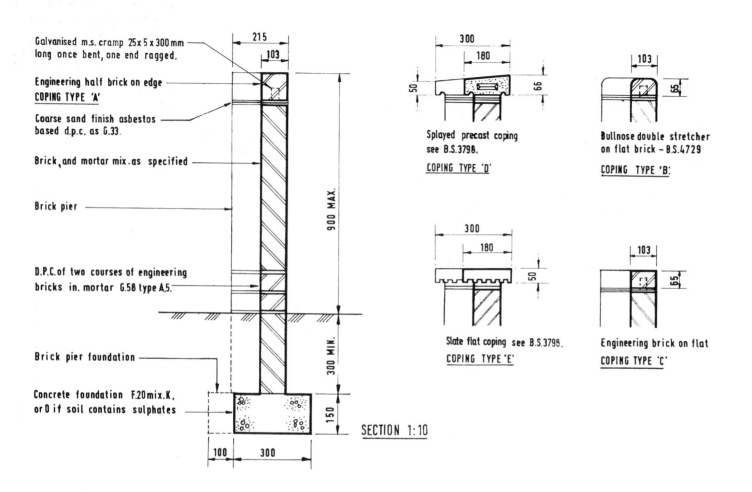

Galvanised m.s. cramp 25 x 5 x 300 mm long once bent, one end ragged.

Engineering half brick on edge
COPING TYPE 'A'

Coarse sand finish asbestos based d.p.c. as G.33.

Brick, and mortar mix as specified

Brick pier

D.P.C. of two courses of engineering bricks in. mortar G.58 type A.5.

Brick pier foundation

Concrete foundation F.20 mix. K. or D if soil contains sulphates

215
103
900 MAX.
300 MIN.
150
100   300

SECTION 1:10

Splayed precast coping see B.S.3798.
COPING TYPE 'D'
300
180
50
99

Bullnose double stretcher on flat brick – B.S.4729
COPING TYPE 'B'
103
65

Slate flat coping see B.S.3798.
COPING TYPE 'E'
300
180
50

Engineering brick on flat
COPING TYPE 'C'
103
65

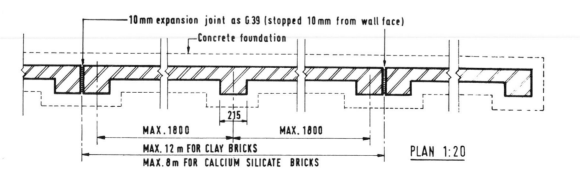

10 mm expansion joint as G.39 (stopped 10 mm from wall face)

Concrete foundation

215
MAX. 1800   MAX. 1800
MAX. 12 m FOR CLAY BRICKS
MAX. 8m FOR CALCIUM SILICATE BRICKS

PLAN 1:20

GLC ILEA

Department of Architecture and Civic Design
County Hall SE1
Architect Sir Roger Walters
KBE FRIBA FI Struct/E

References following notes are clause numbers from G.L.C. preambles to bills of quantities

This drawing is to be read in conjunction with job drawings.

A. 13037.9   8/0310-00

Departmental Standard Drawing

title
FREE STANDING BRICK WALL
MAXIMUM 900 mm HIGH

bldg type | space use
element 20
feature 202
material Fg2
key A1

scale
1:10 and 1:20

GP   drawing no D.5156 B

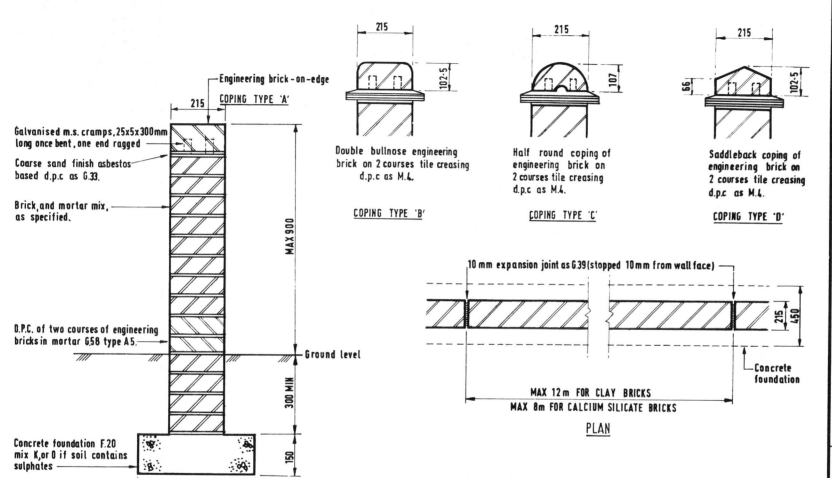

- Engineering brick-on-edge

COPING TYPE 'A'

215

Galvanised m.s. cramps, 25×5×300mm long once bent, one end ragged

Coarse sand finish asbestos based d.p.c as G.33.

Brick, and mortar mix, as specified.

MAX 900

D.P.C. of two courses of engineering bricks in mortar G.58 type A5.

Ground level

300 MIN

Concrete foundation F.20 mix K, or O if soil contains sulphates

150

450

SECTION

215

102·5

Double bullnose engineering brick on 2 courses tile creasing d.p.c as M.4.

COPING TYPE 'B'

215

107

Half round coping of engineering brick on 2 courses tile creasing d.p.c as M.4.

COPING TYPE 'C'

215

66   102·5

Saddleback coping of engineering brick on 2 courses tile creasing d.p.c as M.4.

COPING TYPE 'D'

10 mm expansion joint as G.39 (stopped 10mm from wall face)

215   450

Concrete foundation

MAX 12m FOR CLAY BRICKS
MAX 8m FOR CALCIUM SILICATE BRICKS

PLAN

GLC ILEA

**Department of Architecture and Civic Design
County Hall SE1**

Architect Sir Roger Walters
KBE FRIBA FI Struct/E

References following notes are clause numbers from GLC. preambles to bills of quantities

This drawing is to be read in conjunction with job drawings

A.120379 - 00 - 010379

Departmental Standard Drawing

title
FREE STANDING BRICK WALL
MAXIMUM 900mm HIGH

bldg type	space use	element	feature	material	key
		20	202	Fg2	A2

scale
1:10 and 1:20

GP   drawing no D.5157 B

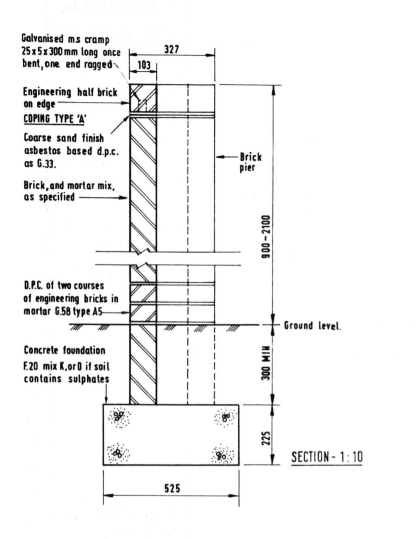

Galvanised m.s cramp 25 x 5 x 300mm long once bent, one end ragged

327

103

Engineering half brick on edge
COPING TYPE 'A'

Coarse sand finish asbestos based d.p.c. as G.33.

Brick, and mortar mix, as specified

Brick pier

900 - 2100

D.P.C. of two courses of engineering bricks in mortar G.58 type A5

Ground level.

Concrete foundation F.20 mix K, or 0 if soil contains sulphates

300 MIN

225

SECTION - 1:10

525

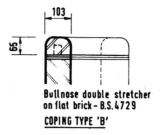

103

65

Bullnose double stretcher on flat brick - B.S.4729
COPING TYPE 'B'

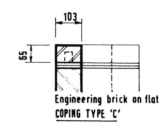

103

65

Engineering brick on flat
COPING TYPE 'C'

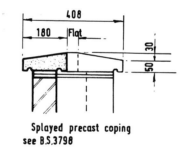

408

180   Flat

30

50

Splayed precast coping see B.S.3798

COPING TYPE 'D'

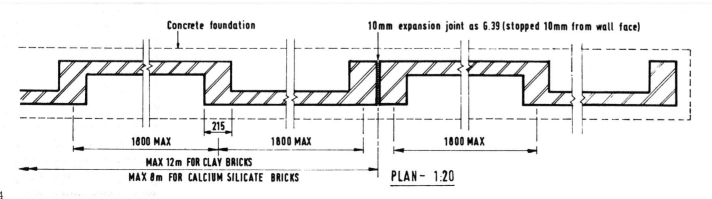

Concrete foundation

10mm expansion joint as G.39 (stopped 10mm from wall face)

215

1800 MAX   1800 MAX   1800 MAX

MAX 12m FOR CLAY BRICKS
MAX 8m FOR CALCIUM SILICATE BRICKS

PLAN - 1:20

124

GLC ILEA

Department of Architecture and Civic Design
County Hall SE1
Architect Sir Roger Walters
KBE FRIBA FI Struct/E

References following notes are clause numbers from GLC. preambles to bills of quantities.

This drawing is to be read in conjunction with job drawings.

Boundary walls over 1800 mm high to be approved by District Surveyor in the Inner London Area.

Y. 13039   Y. 13039 - 010 - 00   01010370

Departmental Standard Drawing

bldg type	space use	element	feature	material	key
		20	202	Fg2	B1

title
FREE STANDING BRICK WALL
900 - 2100 mm HIGH

scale
1:10 and 1:20

GP   drawing no   D.5158   B

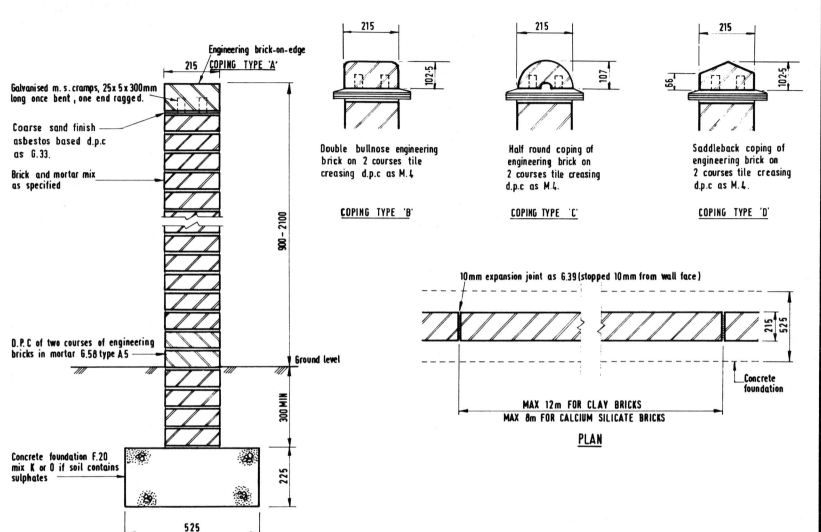

COPING TYPE 'A'

Engineering brick-on-edge

215

Galvanised m.s. cramps, 25x5x300mm long once bent, one end ragged.

Coarse sand finish asbestos based d.p.c as G.33.

Brick and mortar mix as specified

900 – 2100

D.P.C of two courses of engineering bricks in mortar 6.58 type A5

Ground level

300 MIN

Concrete foundation F.20 mix K or 0 if soil contains sulphates

225

525

SECTION

215

102·5

Double bullnose engineering brick on 2 courses tile creasing d.p.c as M.4

COPING TYPE 'B'

215

107

Half round coping of engineering brick on 2 courses tile creasing d.p.c as M.4.

COPING TYPE 'C'

215

102·5

99

Saddleback coping of engineering brick on 2 courses tile creasing d.p.c as M.4.

COPING TYPE 'D'

10mm expansion joint as 6.39 (stopped 10mm from wall face)

215

525

Concrete foundation

MAX 12m FOR CLAY BRICKS
MAX 8m FOR CALCIUM SILICATE BRICKS

PLAN

GLC ILEA

**Department of Architecture and Civic Design
County Hall SE1
Architect Sir Roger Walters**
KBE FRIBA FI Struct/E

References following notes are clause numbers from G.L.C. preambles to bills of quantities.

This drawing is to be read in conjunction with job drawings.

Boundary walls over 1800mm high to be approved by District Surveyor in the Inner London Area.

A.120379   A.120379 - 00

Departmental Standard Drawing

bldg type | space use [20] | element 202 | feature Fg2 | material key B2

title

FREE STANDING BRICK WALL.
900 – 2100mm HIGH

scale

1:10 and 1:20

GP | drawing no D.5159 B

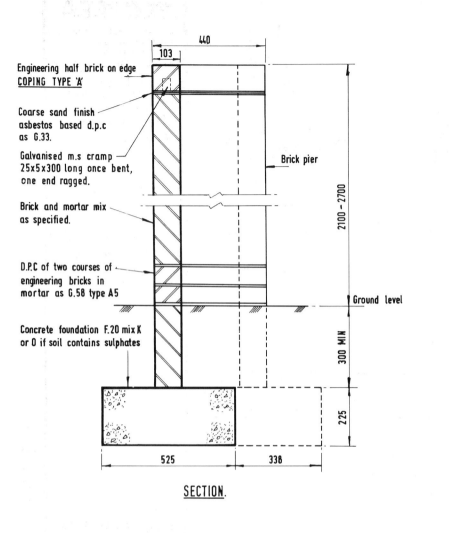

Engineering half brick on edge
COPING TYPE 'A'

Coarse sand finish
asbestos based d.p.c
as G.33.

Galvanised m.s cramp
25×5×300 long once bent,
one end ragged.

Brick pier

Brick and mortar mix
as specified.

D.P.C of two courses of
engineering bricks in
mortar as G.58 type A5

Ground level

Concrete foundation F.20 mix K
or O if soil contains sulphates

440
103
2100 – 2700
300 MIN
225
525
338

SECTION.

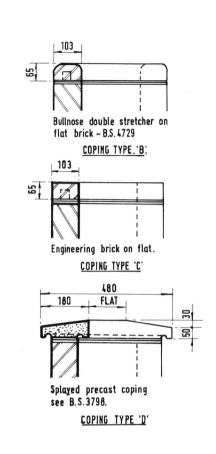

103
65
Bullnose double stretcher on
flat brick – B.S. 4729
COPING TYPE 'B'.

103
65
Engineering brick on flat.
COPING TYPE 'C'

480
180 FLAT
30
50
Splayed precast coping
see B.S. 3798.
COPING TYPE 'D'

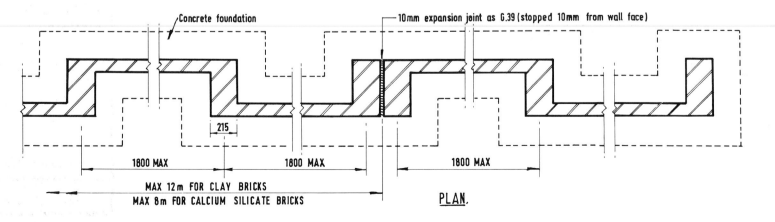

Concrete foundation

10mm expansion joint as G.39 (stopped 10mm from wall face)

215

1800 MAX   1800 MAX   1800 MAX

MAX 12 m FOR CLAY BRICKS
MAX 8 m FOR CALCIUM SILICATE BRICKS

PLAN.

GLC ILEA

**Department of Architecture
and Civic Design
County Hall SE1 7PB
Architect F B Pooley C B E**

References following
notes are clause
numbers from G.L.C.
preambles to bills of
quantities

This drawing is to be read
in conjunction with job
drawings.

Boundary walls over
1800mm high to be approved
by District Surveyor in
the Inner London Area.

010379 - B 00   A.140379

bldg type | space use

**Departmental
Standard
Drawing**

element 20

title
FREE STANDING BRICK
WALL.
2100 – 2700 mm HIGH.

feature | material | key

scale
1:10, 1:20

GP | drawing no D.5160 | rev B

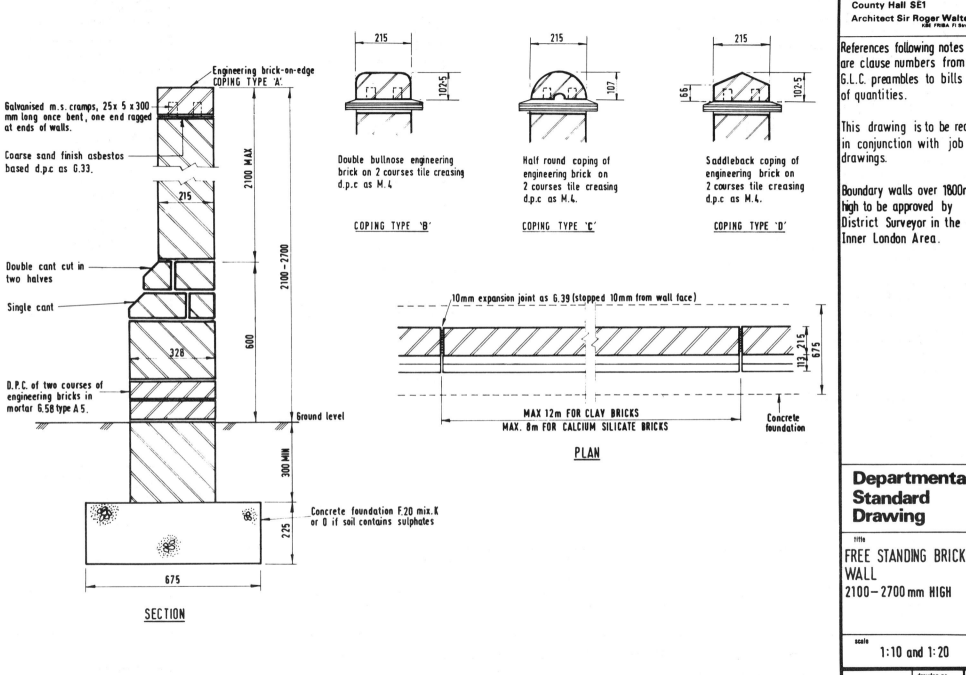

Engineering brick-on-edge COPING TYPE 'A'.

Galvanised m.s. cramps, 25 x 5 x 300 mm long once bent, one end ragged at ends of walls.

Coarse sand finish asbestos based d.p.c as G.33.

Double cant cut in two halves

Single cant

D.P.C. of two courses of engineering bricks in mortar G.58 type A5.

2100 MAX

215

2100 – 2700

600

328

300 MIN

Ground level

225

675

Concrete foundation F.20 mix. K or 0 if soil contains sulphates

SECTION

215

102·5

Double bullnose engineering brick on 2 courses tile creasing d.p.c as M.4

COPING TYPE 'B'

215

107

Half round coping of engineering brick on 2 courses tile creasing d.p.c as M.4.

COPING TYPE 'C'

215

66

102·5

Saddleback coping of engineering brick on 2 courses tile creasing d.p.c as M.4.

COPING TYPE 'D'

10mm expansion joint as G.39 (stopped 10mm from wall face)

113   215

675

MAX 12m FOR CLAY BRICKS
MAX. 8m FOR CALCIUM SILICATE BRICKS

Concrete foundation

PLAN

GLC ILEA

Department of Architecture and Civic Design
County Hall SE1
Architect Sir Roger Walters
KBE FRIBA FI Struct/E

References following notes are clause numbers from G.L.C. preambles to bills of quantities.

This drawing is to be read in conjunction with job drawings.

Boundary walls over 1800mm high to be approved by District Surveyor in the Inner London Area.

A. 1·0·379 — 01·0010/9

Departmental Standard Drawing

bldg type	
space use	20
element	202
feature	Fg2
material	C2
key	

title
FREE STANDING BRICK WALL
2100 – 2700 mm HIGH

scale
1:10 and 1:20

GP   drawing no   D 5161 B

Dust Bin Stores

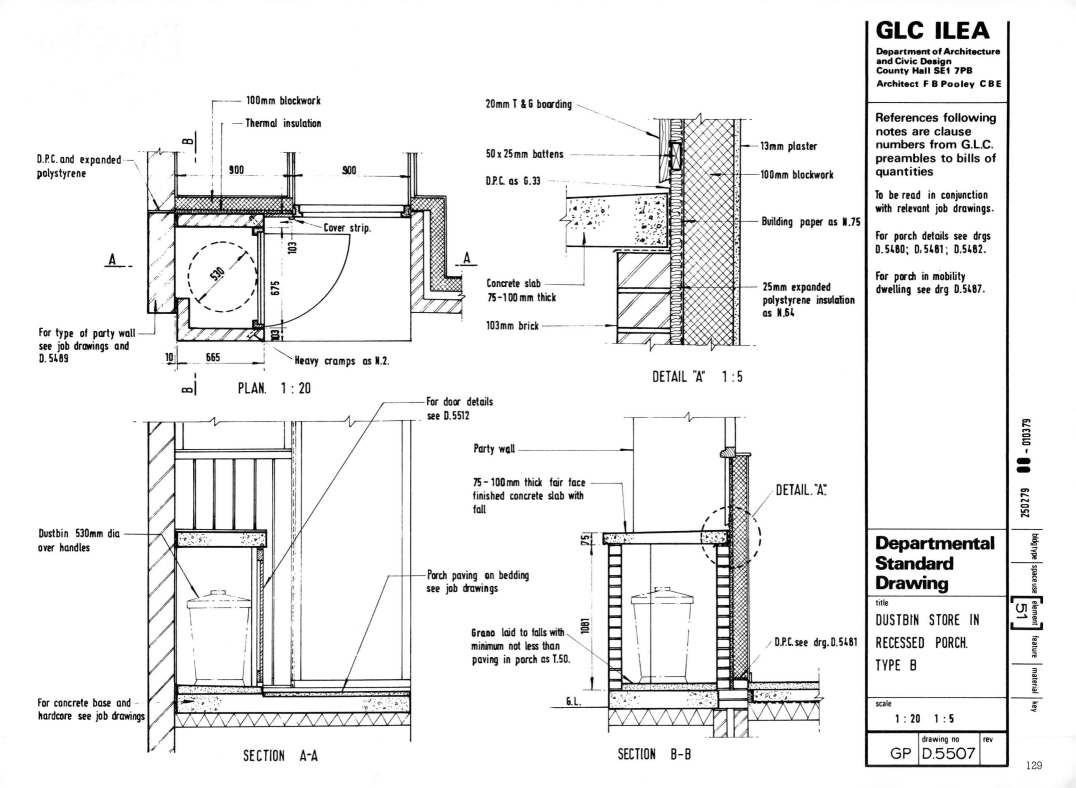

PLAN. 1:20

- 100mm blockwork
- Thermal insulation
- D.P.C. and expanded polystyrene
- For type of party wall see job drawings and D.5489
- Cover strip.
- Heavy cramps as N.2.

900 900
530
675
103
103
10 665

A — A
B

DETAIL "A" 1:5

- 20mm T & G boarding
- 50 x 25mm battens
- D.P.C. as G.33
- Concrete slab 75-100 mm thick
- 103mm brick
- 13mm plaster
- 100mm blockwork
- Building paper as N.75
- 25mm expanded polystyrene insulation as N.64

SECTION A-A

- For door details see D.5512
- Dustbin 530mm dia over handles
- Porch paving on bedding see job drawings
- For concrete base and hardcore see job drawings

SECTION B-B

- Party wall
- 75 - 100mm thick fair face finished concrete slab with fall
- Grano laid to falls with minimum not less than paving in porch as T.50.
- DETAIL "A".
- D.P.C. see drg. D.5481
- G.L.

75
1081

GLC ILEA

Department of Architecture and Civic Design
County Hall SE1 7PB
Architect F B Pooley CBE

References following notes are clause numbers from G.L.C. preambles to bills of quantities

To be read in conjunction with relevant job drawings.

For porch details see drgs D.5480; D.5481; D.5482.

For porch in mobility dwelling see drg D.5487.

Departmental Standard Drawing

title
DUSTBIN STORE IN RECESSED PORCH. TYPE B

scale
1:20   1:5

bldg type | space use | element | feature | material | key

51

drawing no   rev
GP | D.5507

010379 - 00 052279

129

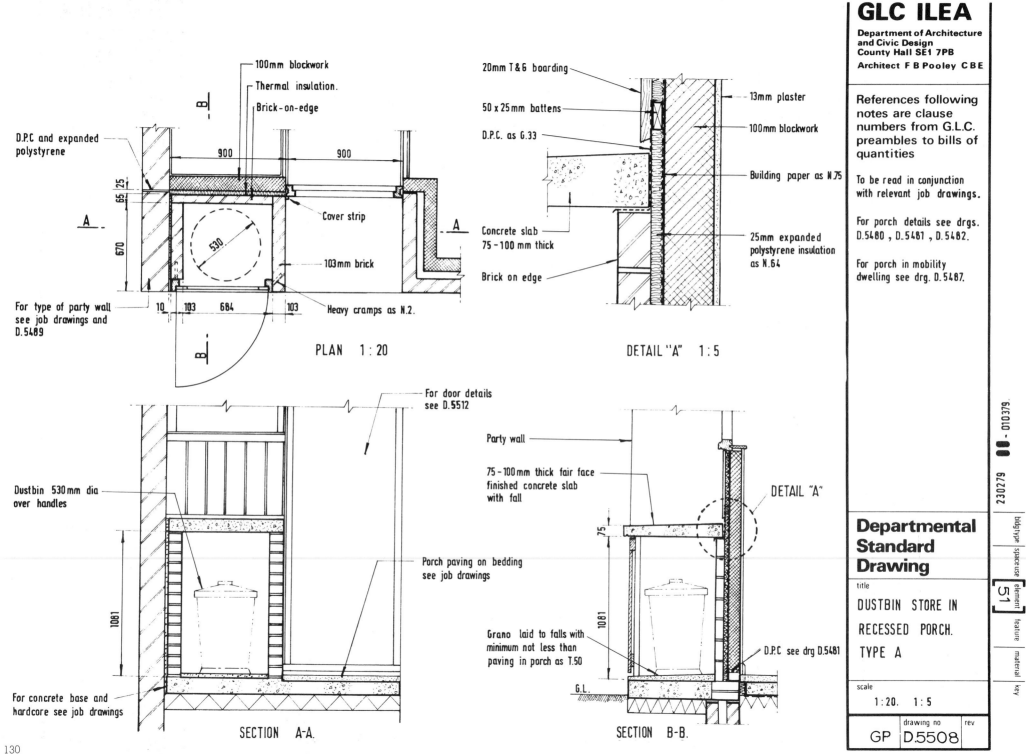

PLAN 1:20

- 100mm blockwork
- Thermal insulation.
- Brick-on-edge
- D.P.C and expanded polystyrene
- Cover strip
- 103mm brick
- For type of party wall see job drawings and D.5489
- Heavy cramps as N.2.

900   900

25
65
670

530

10   103   684   103

DETAIL "A" 1:5

- 20mm T&G boarding
- 50 x 25mm battens
- D.P.C. as G.33
- Concrete slab 75 - 100 mm thick
- Brick on edge
- 13mm plaster
- 100mm blockwork
- Building paper as N.75
- 25mm expanded polystyrene insulation as N.64

SECTION A-A.

- For door details see D.5512
- Dustbin 530mm dia over handles
- Porch paving on bedding see job drawings
- For concrete base and hardcore see job drawings

1081

SECTION B-B.

- Party wall
- 75 - 100mm thick fair face finished concrete slab with fall
- Grano laid to falls with minimum not less than paving in porch as T.50
- DETAIL "A"
- D.P.C see drg D.5481

75

1081

G.L.

GLC ILEA

**Department of Architecture and Civic Design
County Hall SE1 7PB
Architect F B Pooley CBE**

References following notes are clause numbers from G.L.C. preambles to bills of quantities

To be read in conjunction with relevant job drawings.

For porch details see drgs. D.5480, D.5481, D.5482.

For porch in mobility dwelling see drg. D.5487.

230279 **00** - 010379.

bldgtype | spaceuse | element | feature | material | key

Departmental Standard Drawing

title

DUSTBIN STORE IN RECESSED PORCH. TYPE A

51

scale

1:20. 1:5

GP D.5508 rev

130

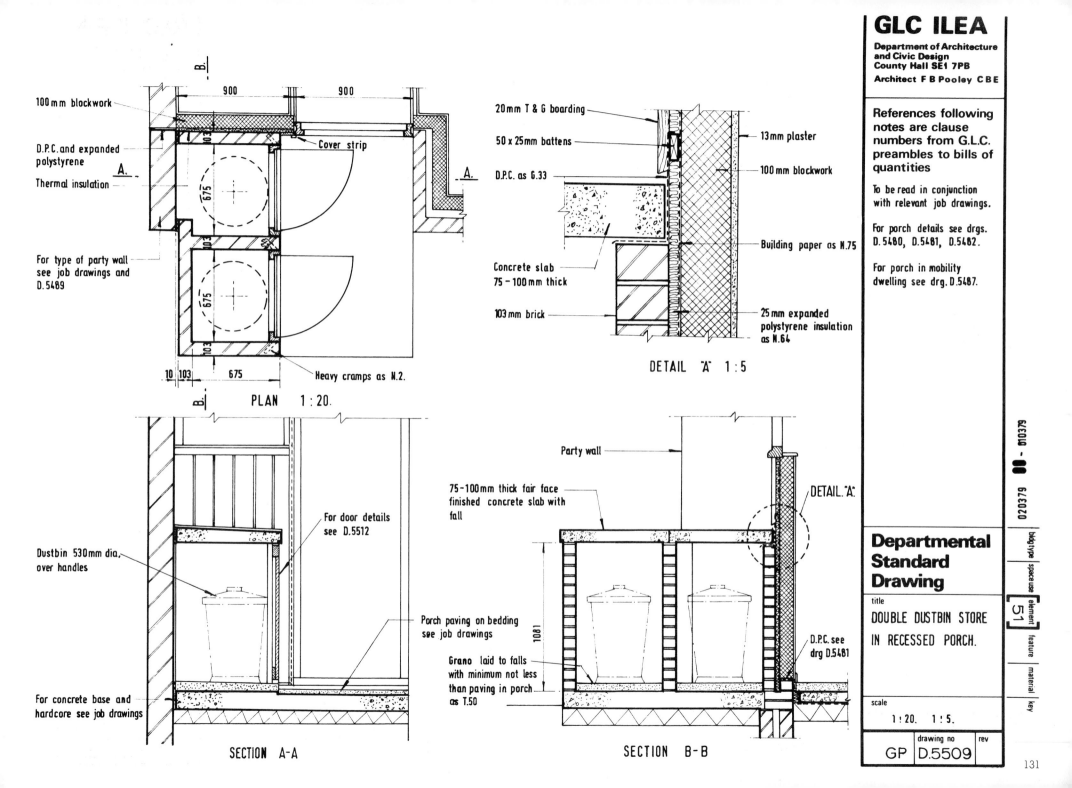

100 mm blockwork

D.P.C. and expanded polystyrene

Thermal insulation

900   900

Cover strip

675

B.

A.   A.

675

For type of party wall see job drawings and D.5489

10 103   675   103

Heavy cramps as N.2.

B.

PLAN   1:20.

For door details see D.5512

Dustbin 530mm dia, over handles

For concrete base and hardcore see job drawings

Porch paving on bedding see job drawings

SECTION A-A

20mm T & G boarding

50 x 25mm battens

D.P.C. as G.33

Concrete slab 75 - 100mm thick

103 mm brick

13mm plaster

100 mm blockwork

Building paper as N.75

25mm expanded polystyrene insulation as N.64

DETAIL "A" 1:5

Party wall

75-100mm thick fair face finished concrete slab with fall

1081

DETAIL "A"

D.P.C. see drg D.5481

Grano laid to falls with minimum not less than paving in porch as T.50

SECTION B-B

GLC ILEA

Department of Architecture and Civic Design
County Hall SE1 7PB
Architect F B Pooley CBE

References following notes are clause numbers from G.L.C. preambles to bills of quantities

To be read in conjunction with relevant job drawings.

For porch details see drgs. D.5480, D.5481, D.5482.

For porch in mobility dwelling see drg. D.5487.

020379 - 010379

00   020379   bldg type | space use

51   element

feature | material | key

Departmental Standard Drawing

title
DOUBLE DUSTBIN STORE IN RECESSED PORCH.

scale
1:20.   1:5.

GP   drawing no   rev
D.5509

131

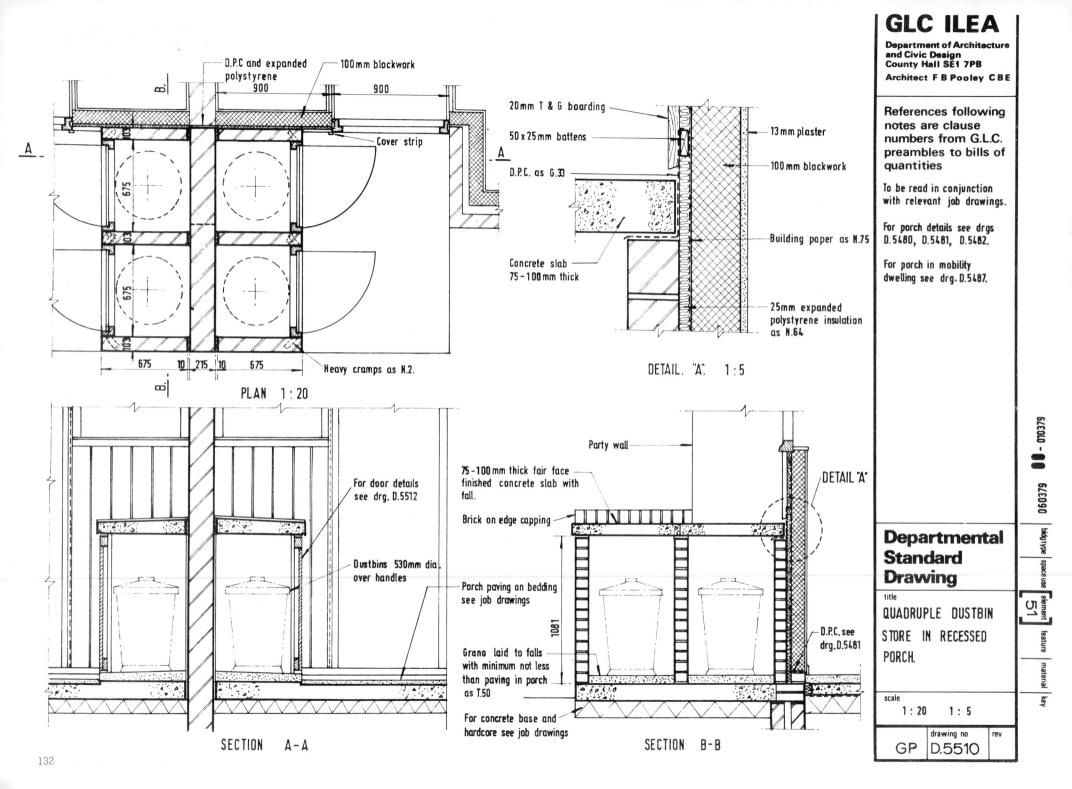

PLAN 1:20

- D.P.C and expanded polystyrene
- 100mm blockwork
- 900 / 900
- Cover strip
- 675 / 675
- 675 / 10 / 215 / 10 / 675
- Heavy cramps as N.2.
- A — A
- B. / B.

DETAIL "A". 1:5

- 20mm T & G boarding
- 50 x 25mm battens
- D.P.C. as G.33
- Concrete slab 75-100mm thick
- 13mm plaster
- 100mm blockwork
- Building paper as N.75
- 25mm expanded polystyrene insulation as N.64

SECTION A-A

- For door details see drg. D.5512
- Dustbins 530mm dia. over handles
- Porch paving on bedding see job drawings

SECTION B-B

- Party wall
- 75-100mm thick fair face finished concrete slab with fall.
- Brick on edge capping
- DETAIL "A"
- 1081
- Grano laid to falls with minimum not less than paving in porch as T.50
- For concrete base and hardcore see job drawings
- D.P.C. see drg. D.5481

GLC ILEA

Department of Architecture and Civic Design
County Hall SE1 7PB
Architect F B Pooley CBE

References following notes are clause numbers from G.L.C. preambles to bills of quantities

To be read in conjunction with relevant job drawings.

For porch details see drgs D.5480, D.5481, D.5482.

For porch in mobility dwelling see drg. D.5487.

Departmental Standard Drawing

title
QUADRUPLE DUSTBIN STORE IN RECESSED PORCH.

scale
1:20   1:5

GP   drawing no D.5510   rev

bldgtype space use element 51 feature material key

00 - 010379   060379

132

GLC ILEA

Department of Architecture and Civic Design
County Hall SE1 7PB
Architect F B Pooley C B E

References following notes are clause numbers from G.L.C. preambles to bills of quantities

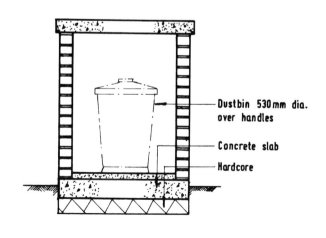

PLAN.

SECTION B-B

- Dustbin 530mm dia. over handles
- Concrete slab
- Hardcore

NOTES.

For level of concrete foundation slab and paving around see job drawings.

For door construction and building-in details see drg D.5512.

For door handing see job drawings.

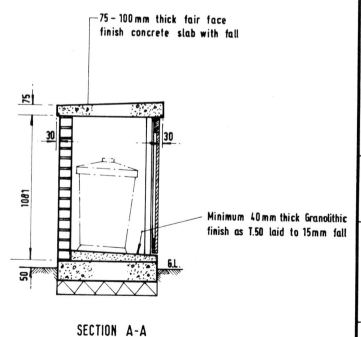

- 75 - 100mm thick fair face finish concrete slab with fall

- Minimum 40mm thick Granolithic finish as T.50 laid to 15mm fall

SECTION A-A

Departmental Standard Drawing

title

FREESTANDING SINGLE DUSTBIN STORE.

scale 1 : 20

GP | drawing no D.5511 | rev

010379 - 00 07079 | bldg type | space use | 51 | element | feature | material | key

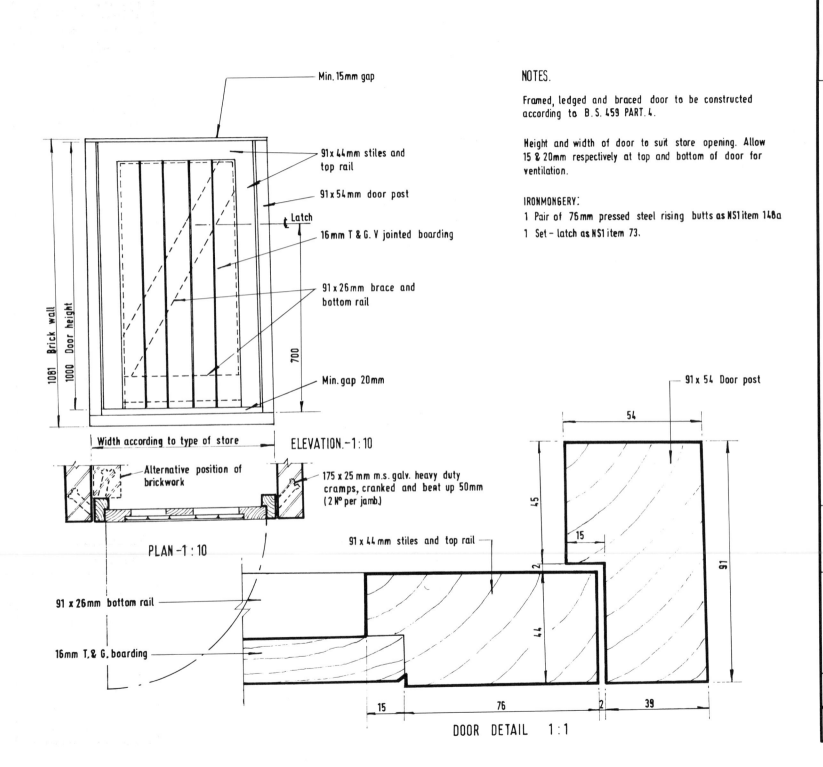

Min. 15mm gap

91 x 44mm stiles and
top rail

91 x 54mm door post

Latch

16mm T & G. V jointed boarding

91 x 26mm brace and
bottom rail

Min. gap 20mm

1081 Brick wall

1000 Door height

700

Width according to type of store

ELEVATION.-1:10

Alternative position of
brickwork

175 x 25 mm m.s. galv. heavy duty
cramps, cranked and bent up 50mm
(2 N° per jamb.)

PLAN -1 : 10

91 x 44mm stiles and top rail

91 x 26mm bottom rail

16mm T.& G. boarding

15   76   2   39

91 x 54 Door post

54

45

15

2

44

91

DOOR DETAIL   1:1

NOTES.

Framed, ledged and braced door to be constructed
according to B.S. 459 PART.4.

Height and width of door to suit store opening. Allow
15 & 20mm respectively at top and bottom of door for
ventilation.

IRONMONGERY:

1 Pair of 76mm pressed steel rising butts as NS1 item 148a

1 Set – latch as NS1 item 73.

GLC ILEA

Department of Architecture
and Civic Design
County Hall SE1 7PB

Architect F B Pooley C B E

References following
notes are clause
numbers from G.L.C.
preambles to bills of
quantities

00 - 01037B

260279

bldg type | space use

element   51

feature | material | key

**Departmental
Standard
Drawing**

title

FRAMED, LEDGED AND
BRACED DOOR FOR
DUSTBIN STORE.

scale

1 : 10.   1 : 1

GP   drawing no D.5512   rev

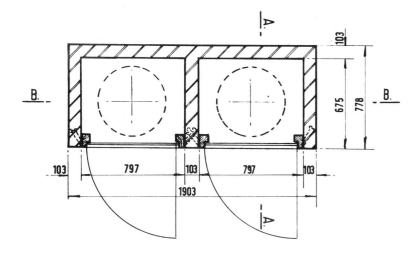

PLAN

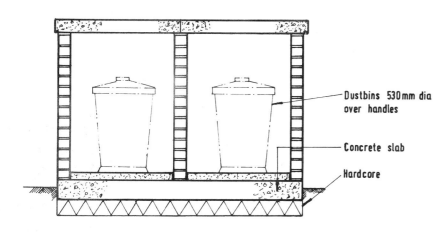

SECTION B-B

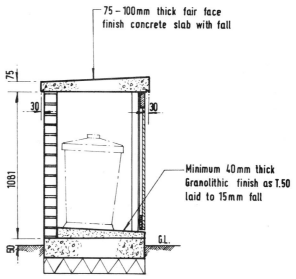

SECTION A-A

Dustbins 530mm dia over handles

Concrete slab

Hardcore

75 - 100mm thick fair face finish concrete slab with fall

Minimum 40mm thick Granolithic finish as T.50 laid to 15mm fall

NOTES.

For level of concrete foundation slab and paving around see job drawings.

For door construction and building-in details see drg. D.5512.

For door handing see job drawings.

GLC ILEA

Department of Architecture and Civic Design
County Hall SE1 7PB
Architect F B Pooley C B E

References following notes are clause numbers from G.L.C. preambles to bills of quantities

670010 - 88   670379   bldgtype | space use

Departmental Standard Drawing

element   51

title

FREESTANDING DOUBLE DUSTBIN STORE.

feature | material | key

scale

1 : 20

GP   drawing no   D.5513   rev

135

Cost Information

Prepared by the GLC Quantity Surveyor

1 Purpose

1.1 Object This Cost Information was produced for the use of job architects in the GLC Department of Architecture and Civic Design to assist them in the selection of Good Practice Details for use in particular schemes and to give them an indication of the cost effects where there is an alternative choice of treatment. It was not intended to provide him with a ready reckoner for 'do-it-yourself' cost planning. Because of the limitations outlined below (Part 3) it will give him only a rough indication of the likely additional or reduced cost of a scheme resulting from each decision, but it is a guide to their importance in relative cost terms. *It must be emphasized that none of the cost data which follows is by any means a substitute for the job QS as a source of cost information on any individual scheme or dwelling type. In particular, the information is likely to be completely misleading once a project is in contract, or if alterations to existing buildings are involved.*

2 Basis of Costing

2.1 PDP 5155 The cost of each detail needs to be related to representative quantities and assessed on that basis so that account is taken of its significance to the overall cost of the scheme. Since the Good Practice Details are intended for use on housing schemes, the obvious choice of a quantitative basis for costing them is the superstructure of a typical medium frontage two-storey house, and the one which has been selected is the PDP House Type 5155. A copy of the type plan is attached at Appendix A.

2.2 Block Costs Many of the Good Practice Details relate to verges, flank walls, and other conditions which do not apply to each individual house. Furthermore, the cost of flank walls is a significant factor in the cost of a scheme as a whole. Accordingly, the basis of all the costing has been extended to cover the superstructure of a straight block of 6 PDP 5155 Houses, so that it can apply to all Good Practice Details.

2.3 Superstructure The Good Practice Details deal almost exclusively with the shell elements (including party walls) of the superstructure of 2-storey housing, the internal elements being covered by the PDP documentation. Since foundation and external works costs vary widely from scheme to scheme the broad cost advice on schemes has been expressed in relation to the superstructure cost only, unless it clearly deals with the other parts of the scheme. *The Basis of Costing for the Good Practice Details is therefore the cost of the Superstructure of a straight block of 6 PDP Type 5155 Houses (with no steps or staggers).* This cost includes the internal elements as well as those covered by Good Practice Details.

2.4 Specification The specification which applies to the Basis of Costing is given in outline in Appendix B. It represents the minimum standard currently acceptable, so that all alternatives are seen as an increase over it, as demanded by the form of presentation of the cost data which is detailed in Part 4.

2.5 Details Many Good Practice Details have been used in the Basic Costing and are listed as 'Basic Details' in Appendix C. They have been selected as the cheapest alternatives in the current range of Good Practice Details.

3 Limitations on Reliability

3.1 Actual scheme It is unlikely that any actual scheme will consist entirely of the particular block or blocks of houses selected as the Basis of Costing. It follows that any cost advice given on such a basis must be taken only as being indicative, the extent depending on the degree of similarity between the actual scheme and the basis.

3.2 Type When the dwelling under review is different from the PDP 5155, involving a different frontage or a different length of party wall, it is evident that the influence of those elements on the total cost will also be different. Even when the frontage is the same, the different layout will affect the overall cost, so that the proportion of that cost allocated to the front and back walls is close but not identical to the basis. The differences are more pronounced, of course, when applied to flats rather than houses.

3.3 Length of block If the number of dwellings in a block varies from the basis, it is evident that the influence of the cost of flank walls and verges also changes.

3.4 Specification Most schemes will have a specification which differs in some way from the one outlined in Appendix B. In one or two simple cases of changed materials (such as a different basic cost of facing bricks, or asbestos cement slates in lieu of concrete interlocking tiles) there is cost information in the following pages to show the effect of this. However, it would be impossible to cover every alternative or combination. Any change in specification is likely to affect the overall cost, so that a costing system which relates to the overall cost (as this one does) will be less accurate the more the specification changes.

3.5 Details Similarly, changing the selection of details applicable to the scheme affects the overall price. The cost information which follows is intended to deal with this problem, within the range of the Good Practice Details, provided that the general rule can be borne in mind that *the cost data is cumulative (ie, compounding) rather than acting as simple addition* (see para. 4.3) with few exceptions.

3.6 Price changes However accurate any cost advice is at the time of preparation, there are factors which render it less so with the passage of time. For the present purposes these can be identified as:

a Changes in general pricing levels due to increases in building costs and fluctuations in market conditions.

b Differential price movements between trades,

particular materials or operations for the same reasons as *(a)* but where the average movements in pricing levels are not truly representative.

c Constructional changes due to amended policy or regulations or to non-availability of materials.

3.7 Cost Index When publishing standard cost data, the changes in general pricing levels can often be simply dealt with by using a Cost Index system rather than stating actual costs. This system has been adopted for the cost advice on Good Practice Details, though it takes the form of percentages rather than index numbers (see Part 4).

3.8 Differential movements The differential price movements *(3.6(b))* can only be dealt with by recalculating and amending the cost data. These movements are monitored in the GLC Quantity Surveying Division for a number of purposes and the need for revising the cost advice on Good Practice Details will be kept under review. However, it is likely to be some time before these movements will be significant enough to warrant changing such broad cost information.

3.9 Constructional changes Changes in construction will need to be covered by new or revised Good Practice Details, and these will be accompanied by the appropriate cost advice.

4 Presentation of Cost Information

4.1 Requirements Two requirements have been identified for the presentation of the general cost information on Good Practice Details.

a A cost index system to take account of fluctuating price levels (para 3.7).

b A means of establishing the relative importance in selecting a detail or a set of details to the cost of a scheme as a whole (para 2.1).

4.2 Calculation These needs can both be satisfied (within the limitations described in Part 3) by pricing the effect of each selection on the basic block of houses—Basis of Costing, see Part 2—and expressing the result as a percentage of the total superstructure cost. In other words, the Basis of Costing (which is the superstructure cost of a block of houses employing the cheapest selection of details and materials) represents an index of 100, and a different selection of details or materials ; a cost which is expressed as a percentage increase on that index. The fact that no percentages are negative, so that all the cost data represents an addition helps to simplify its presentation and use.

4.3 *Percentages* A temporary disadvantage of this method of presenting the data is that the percentages may, in the first instance, appear to be of less significance than they actually are. In time, this situation should improve as users grow accustomed to the data. In the meantime, in order to keep the percentages in perspective it is essential to remember that they normally act by compounding on each other (eg, $100 + 10\% + 10\% = 121$ not 120). Also the DOE yardsticks are quite stringent cost limits and fairly small increases in standards of specification and detailing can result in an excess above basic yardstick.

4.4 *Presentation* The specification has been arranged under 'Cost Feature' headings (The 'Cost Feature' system is a set of elements specially defined for use by the GLC Quantity Surveying Division in the preparation of Bills of Quantities and Cost Data for GLC housing work).

Appendix A

Dual aspect house
4.800m frontage

This two-storey five person house can be planned in terraces with front door entry from north, east or west. The front door may be recessed to form a covered porch with a dustbin store if required.

The ground floor entrance hall serves the dining-kitchen, living room and WC. The staircase lies across the middle of the plan. The two ground floor rooms are connected by a door, with the option of building in storage at a later date. A broom cupboard is provided under the stair. Where the dwelling is located at the end of a terrace, an additional window to the dining-kitchen can be provided in the gable wall. The back garden is accessible from the living room. An external store of 2.000m² is required to conform to mandatory standards.

Upstairs there are two double bedrooms and one single bedroom, with bulkhead storage in one of the larger bedrooms. A bathroom is provided with combined WC. The central heating boiler adjoins the linen cupboard and is accessible from the landing.

When planning the layout, the proximity of the public footpath to the front porch and kitchen window will be subject to the positioning of the dustbin store. The length of the back garden will be determined by the privacy distance required when dual-aspect dwellings back on to each other.

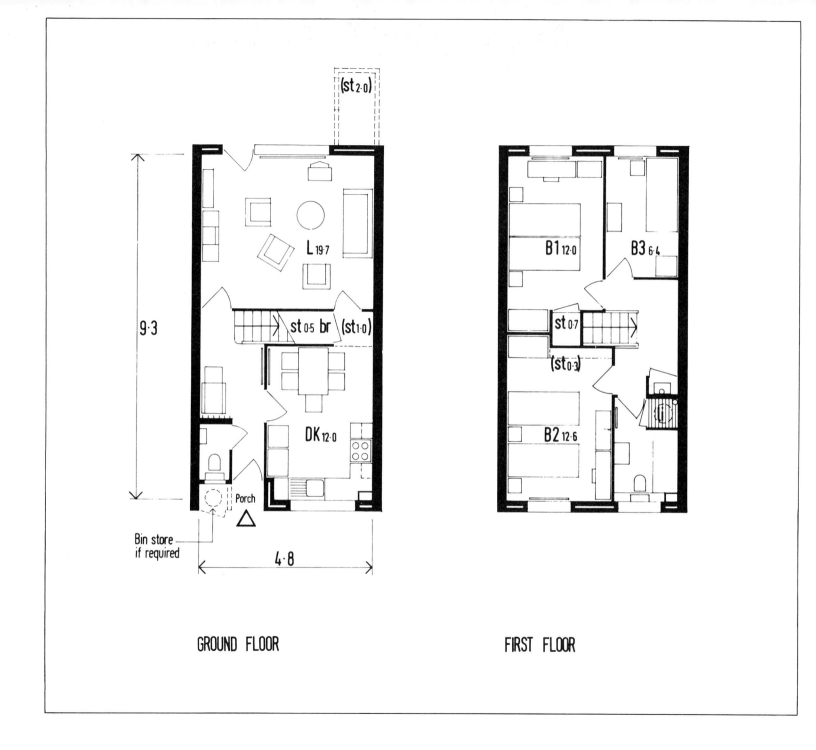

GROUND FLOOR

(st 2·0)

L 19·7

st 0·5 br (st 1·0)

DK 12·0

Porch

Bin store
if required

9·3

4·8

FIRST FLOOR

B1 12·0   B3 6·4

st 0·7

(st 0·3)

B2 12·6

PDP 5155
Dual aspect
2 storey house
4.800m frontage

5 person north entry type

Space (m²)		Mandatory	±%
Net	85·6	85·0	+0·7
Storage			
Int	2·5	4·5	
Ext	2·0		

Scale

0   1   2   3   4

Appendix B

Specification notes for basis of costing 'Good Practice Details' (Straight block of six PDP 5155 houses)

Note:
The specification notes which follow are sub-divided under 'Cost Feature' headings (see paragraph 4.4 of Cost Information). Cost Features in which Good Practice Details have been used in the costing have the suffix 'GPD'.

External Walls (GPD)

Cavity wall comprising half brick outer skin in sand faced fletton facing bricks, in cement lime mortar (1:1:6) mix C, pointed with bucket handle joint as the work proceeds, block inner skin comprising 100mm aerated concrete blocks in cement lime mortar (1:1:6) mix C with 47mm cavity with galvanised mild steel ties 200mm long at 900mm centres horizontally and 450mm centres vertically. Damp-proof courses to be 0.46mm minimum polythene as BS 743 paragraph 6, bedded in mortar.

Windows (GPD)

To be softwood side hung casement windows to the current GLC specification complete with easy clean hinges and 'permavents'.

Living Room   2025 × 1300mm with 2 No. side hung casements and 2 No. horizontally hung vents.

Dining Kitchen   1800 × 1070mm with 2 No. side hung casements and 2 No. horizontally hung vents.

Ground Floor WC   450 × 690mm with 1 No. side hung casement and 1 No. horizontally hung vent.

Bedrooms Nos 1 & 2   1570 × 1070mm with 1 No. side hung casement and 1 No. horizontally hung vent.

Bedroom No 3 and Bathroom   1120 × 1070mm with 1 No. side hung casement and 1 No. horizontally hung vent.

External Doors (GPD)

815 × 2000mm × 44mm softwood doors with two glazed panels.

Party Walls (GPD)

One brick wall in flettons (20.5 N per square mm) in mortar mix C.

Internal Walls

50mm, 63mm & 75mm Gyproc self finished partition. Small area of studwork.

Internal Doors

Door sets 2343mm high on ground floor.
2370mm high on 1st floor.
Ply or glazed panels over doors as appropriate.

Flush Doors

Door Type	Location
726 × 2040 × 44mm ½ hr firecheck hardboard faced flush door	Boiler Cupboard
626 × 2040 × 40mm thick hardboard faced flush door	WC
726 × 2040 × 40mm thick hardboard faced flush door	Store, Bathroom, Linen Cupboard, Bedroom
826 × 2040 × 40mm thick hardboard faced flush door	Dining/Kitchen, Living Room, Broom Cupboard

Timber Suspended Floors

Joists   50 × 225mm sw joists at 400mm centres.

Noggins   50 × 50 sw noggins to support edges of ceiling lining. 100 × 50 sw noggins to support partitions.

Joist Hangers   Saddle type built into brickwork—size to suit joists.

Boarding   19mm sw t & g floor boarding.

Timber Stairs

Traditional construction including balustrading—
staircase in one straight flight 900mm wide,
2.600m in total rise, 2.700m total going.

Roof Structure (GPD)

Impregnated softwood gang-nail trusses to $22\frac{1}{2}°$
pitch at 600mm centres (9 No. to each house) on
impregnated 100×500mm softwood plates.
50mm Insulation laid between trusses. Includes
impregnated softwood tilting fillet, 50×50mm
noggin, 219×28mm wrot softwood fascia painted
and 6mm asbestos cement tilting sheet all as
Drawing GP D5401.

$2.7m^2$ of 21mm chipboard as BS 2604 part 2 as
gang boarding.

Roof Finishes (GPD)

430×380mm Redland 'Stonewold' concrete
interlocking tiles as BS 473, 550 : Part 2 group B,
laid to 75mm laps. Tiles for undercloak to be
asbestos cement slates to BS 690 : Part 7. Battens
25×50mm as CP 142 Part 2, paragraph 3-8, table 3
pressure impregnated. Underlay reinforced
bitumen felt to BS 747 : Part 2 type 1F. Ridge tiles
120° angle type bedded and pointed in cement
mortar (1 :3).

Rainwater Installation (GPD)

102mm half-round plastic gutter, fittings and
accessories. Include allowance of 76mm plastic
rainwater down pipe with wire balloon and joint
to drain per dwelling.

Internal Wall Finish

13mm thick plaster ref B and 2 coats emulsion
paint to brick walls.
13mm thick plaster ref G and 2 coats emulsion
paint to blockwork.
2 coats emulsion paint on Gyproc partitions.
Tile splashback to bath, basin, sink.

Floor Finish

Ground Floor   47mm cement and sand screed with
3mm thermoplastic tiles & 14mm × 68mm sw skirting.

1st Floor   14mm × 68mm sw skirting to timber
suspended floors.

External Porches   Quarry tile paving.

Ceiling Finish

12.7mm plasterboard with plastic compound finish.

Refuse Disposal

Standard dustbin.

Cold Water Installation

Copper tube and fittings, AC Cistern with cover,
insulation and polythene overflow pipe.

Hot Water Installation

Copper tube and fittings with copper indirect
cylinder complete with insulating jacket.
Thermostatic valve and fittings.

Basic Heating Installation

Individual gas-fired boiler, indirect copper
cylinder, copper pipes and fittings, pressed steel
radiators to accord with wall space and heat
emission requirements.

Bedroom Heating

Pressed steel radiators served by basic heating
installation.

Gas Services

Gas carcassing charge included.

Basic Electrical Installation

Installation to PM minimum standard including
allowance for Electricity Board's charges.

Extra Power Points

Allowance for extra power points (current GLC policy).

TV Conduit and Aerial Installation

Allowance for TV conduit.

Fluorescent Lighting

Kitchen fluorescent fitting.

Kitchen Fittings

Cupboard Units   3 WMA K2 range pre-finished kitchen units by approved manufacturer (Parker Morris standards).

Sanitary Fittings

Direct purchase.

Soil and Waste Installation

a   UPVC soil and vent pipe.

b   MUPVC waste pipe to bath and basin.

c   Copper waste pipe to sink only.

d   Plastic overflow to cold water storage tank.

Ducts

Full height 2 sided duct casing comprising sw framing with 9mm ply lining primed and painted with 2 coats oil paint.

Sundry Fittings

Linen cupboard shelving. Hat and coat hooks and rail.

Appendix C

Good Practice Details used for basis of costing

Walls

GPD 2015	Dimensional co-ordination
*GPD 5239A	Tiled pitched roof and party wall London Building Byelaws
GPD 5459	Cavity and party wall junction
*GPD 5472	Tiled pitched roof $22\frac{1}{2}°$ party wall at close eaves
GPD 5476	Setting out of concrete block for party wall at eaves

Windows

GPD 5450	Brick size openings for preferred windows
GPD 5432	Window lintels at eaves (Dorman Long combined type)
GPD 5451	Wood window—built in

Roof

GPD 5401	Close eaves for pitched roof $22\frac{1}{2}°$ tiled
*GPD 5412	Close eaves stopped end at gable
*GPD 5422	Verge detail for tiled roofs (interlocking flat tile)
GPD 5425	Ridge tiles

Note:
Drawings above marked * have not been included in the foregoing collection of details.

Appendix D

overleaf

| | Range of Options Available | | | Drawing Numbers of Applicable Detail | | | | | | | Cost Effect |
Pitch	Finish	Eaves	Party Wall Junction	Eaves	End of Eaves	Verge	Ridge	Vent Pipe	Party Wall Junction	Eaves/Pitch Junction	(over basis)
				GPD	GPD	GPD	GPD	GPD	GPD	GPD	%
			Basic Drawings used	5401	5412	5422	5425	5430	5239	5472	0.0
22½°	Interlocking concrete tiling	Close	Flush	5401	5412	5422	5425	5430	5239	5472	0.0
			Oversailed	5403	5412	5422	5425	5430	5237	5474	0.3
		Fixed-up	Flush	5403	5410	5422	5425	5430	5239	5464	0.4
			Oversailed	5403	5410	5422	5425	5430	5237	5466	0.7
	Asbestos-cement slating	Close	Flush	5405	5412	5424	5425	5431	5239	5473	1.2
			Oversailed	5405	5412	5424	5425	5431	5237	5475	1.5
		Fixed-up	Flush	5407	5410	5424	5425	5431	5239	5465	1.6
			Oversailed	5407	5410	5424	5425	5431	5237	5467	1.9
35°	Interlocking concrete tiling	Close	Flush	5400	5412	5488	5425	5430	5239	5468	1.6
			Oversailed	5400	5412	5488	5425	5430	5237	5470	1.9
		Boxed (with box ends)	Flush	5402	5408	5488	5425	5430	5239	5460	2.2
			Oversailed	5402	5408	5488	5425	5430	5237	5462	2.5
		Boxed (with corbel ends)	Flush	5402	5418	5488	5425	5330	5239	5460	2.2
			Oversailed	5402	5418	5488	5425	5430	5237	5462	2.5
	Asbestos-cement slating	Close	Flush	5404	5412	5423	5425	5431	5239	5469	2.9
			Oversailed	5404	5412	5423	5425	5431	5237	5471	3.2
		Boxed (with box ends)	Flush	5406	5439	5423	5425	5431	5239	5461	3.4
			Oversailed	5406	5439	5423	5425	5431	5237	5463	3.7
		Boxed (with corbel ends)	Flush	5406	5442	5423	5425	5431	5239	5461	3.4
			Oversailed	5406	5442	5423	5425	5431	5237	5463	3.7

Notes:

1 This table has been included as indicative of the cost information now being prepared within the GLC Department of Architecture and Civic Design. Several of the drawings quoted above and in the

Notes on the next page have not been included in the selection for this book for reasons of duplication of typical details.

2 For Specification Notes of options see next page.

Specification Notes applicable to alternative Good Practice Details

A   35° Pitch in lieu of 22½°

Roof Structure   All as Basis, but trusses to 35° pitch and fascia 244 × 28mm as Drawing GPD 5400.

B   Asbestos cement slates in lieu of "Stonewold" interlocking tiles

Roof Structure   All as Basis, but with fascia 194 × 28mm and without softwood tilting fillet or asbestos cement tilting sheet, all as Drawing GPD 5405.

Roof Finishes   610mm × 305mm × 4mm Grey asbestos cement slates as BS 690—Part 4 (except for dimensions), laid to 100mm laps. Battens 25 × 50mm as CP 142 Part 2, paragraph 3-8, table 3 pressure impregnated. Each slate centre nailed with two copper nails and fixed with one copper disc rivet. Underlay and ridge tiles all as Basis.

C   Eaves details as listed in lieu of Close eaves

1   FIXED UP EAVES

Roof Structure   All as Basis but with extended trusses and 9mm asbestos cement sheet soffite board, painted as Drawing GPD 5403.

2   BOXED EAVES WITH BOXED ENDS

Roof Structure   All as Basis but amended as Drawing GPD 5402:—

a   trusses to 35° pitch and extended to form overhang.

b   fascia 244 × 28mm (tiles) or 194 × 28mm (slates).

c   9mm asbestos cement sheet soffite board, painted, on 36 × 48mm softwood eaves hangers.

d   9mm asbestos cement sheet boxed ends to eaves as Drawing GPD 5408.

3   BOXED EAVES WITH CORBELLED ENDS

Roof Structure   All as Alternative 2 but with sand faced fletton facing brick corbelled ends to eaves as Drawing GPD 5410.

D   Oversailed party wall at junction with roof in lieu of flush party wall

Party Walls   All as Basis but with single course of 100mm aerated concrete blocks laid flat (440mm wide) on top of wall including additional width of mineral wood infill, all as Drawing GPD5237A.

Credits

Produced in the Department of Architecture and Civic Design, Greater London Council.

Architect to the Council
Sir Roger Walters, succeeded by F B Pooley, CBE

Housing Architect   Gordon Wigglesworth

Quantity Surveyor   H S Page

Text and Drawings produced in Technical Policy Division.

Divisional Architect   Malcolme Gordon

Technical Information Group
Roger Cass
J Max-Jarzabek
Z F Janik
D R Thomas
S A Higgs
A A J Izzi
G Noak

Drawing Selection Panel
R Apsey
R Garton
F Hand
M Hohmann
K Lyall
K Nicholson
Ms J Price
G Stewart

Graphics and Book Design   John Beake

Editorial Control by David Atwell, Departmental Information Officer, to whom any enquiries regarding the contents of this book should be addressed.